CW00863424

Mysterious Ways

JOHN LINDECK

authorHOUSE®

AuthorHouse™ UK Ltd.
500 Avebury Boulevard
Central Milton Keynes, MK9 2BE
www.authorhouse.co.uk
Phone: 08001974150

First published by AuthorHouse 4/29/2009

ISBN: 978-1-4389-5108-9 (sc)

Printed in the United States of America
Bloomington, Indiana

This book is printed on acid-free paper.

Acknowledgments

Many people have assisted me by reading and commenting on this book or parts of it. Among those who come to mind are Barbara Bateman, Angela and Ian Beer, the late Penny Brookman, John Jackson, the late David James, John Mash, Nansi Parker, David Price, David Streater, John Taylor, Mike Vockins, John Woodger and Rob Hemmings from the Malvern Writers Circle. David Gegg, through his bible studies, has been a constant source of new thoughts. Alan Pratt read the whole text to pick up all the grammatical errors. Darin Jewell from the Inspira Group Agency has always been a great source of support.

The greatest help has, of course, been my family. Diane has put up with me shutting myself away and with my bad temper when things wouldn't go as I wanted and my children Jeremy, Judy and Jackie have all gone out of their way to help me. I am deeply grateful.

Introduction

Christianity is about change. People encounter Jesus and their lives and personalities are altered, sometimes temporarily, sometimes for ever. In the New Testament we read about a number of individuals who met Jesus. Most came to hear the stories Jesus told and to see the wonderful things he did. Some hoped to have their physical or mental needs met. For a very few it was, literally, a matter of life or death. None would ever forget Jesus or his teaching.

What we read about these meetings is a snapshot of a particular moment. We have no idea what happened before and we are left to guess what happened after. In reading the gospels, it is clear that the writers did not meet many of the characters about whom they wrote apart from the occasion when these people met Jesus. They can not therefore describe the feelings of those involved. Rather they have recorded what they have been told second hand because this helps to create the picture they want.

These stories are told as illustrations of Jesus' ministry or in terms of what the disciples learned from the events described. The effect on the main character involved is largely ignored. You only have to look at the woman taken in adultery as an example. Would she have been left alive but homeless, without money or clothes or any means of support? I don't think so. Jesus was and still is extremely protective of the welfare of anyone he meets.

This book is an attempt to see what happened to some of the men and women Jesus met. Some had happy futures, others not. Some are major characters and some are bit players. In a way the latter are more fun because there is greater scope for imagination. It is clear that the writers of the gospels never met many of those about whom they wrote. They are putting down what they have been told because it helps in creating the picture they want. They can not therefore describe the feelings of those involved. What I found astonishing, particularly with the characters involved in the crucifixion, was that they were all true to themselves. Each one had a strong and valid reason for behaving in the way they did. I found this greatly reassuring.

In the mid 20th century when I was young, the church's concentration was on conversion. Once people had been converted, they were considered to be all right; their eternal future was assured. As a result of not nurturing these new converts, many of them gave up their faith. Today, thankfully, there is more focus on the continuing spiritual journey of the convert and how he can be helped. Perhaps we have now gone too far in looking at the changes in people's lives rather than the cause of the change.

Two facts become clear from these studies. The first is that Jesus was human. He got hurt, he grew tired, he was let down, he loved and was loved. We have no idea what happened in the fifteen or so years when Jesus lived as a grown up in his local community in Nazareth. Did he have girl friends? Did he take a leading role in the synagogue? We don't know the answer to these or many other questions but if he didn't go through the same joys and problems as the rest of us, he wasn't fully human and the whole gospel is meaningless. It is only because he was like us yet without blemish that his sacrifice of himself was acceptable.

Secondly a new perspective on the gospel emerges. Things which might otherwise be missed are thrown into high profile. Maybe this will help readers to see and understand the story more clearly. What is obvious is that the people alive in New Testament times were not that different from us in their reaction to what was happening around them. You will certainly recognize likenesses to people you know today in many of them.

The rules used in writing this book are simple. Whatever was included in the Bible about a person has to be accepted as fact. All the references are included in the section at the end named 'Sources'. I could not allow myself to alter or omit what a character did or said just because it did not fit in with a story line. These facts have been used as a series of pegs on which to hang fictional story lines. All 'Direct Speech' quotations are based on the NIV. They have been paraphrased into modern English but every effort has been made to ensure that the meaning has not been changed. Where the same story is told in more than one gospel, there are often substantial differences in the accounts. For example the versions of the story of the centurion in Galilee in the gospels of Matthew and Luke vary widely. In such cases one account has been chosen as the primary source. However this has not always been possible as extracts from different accounts allow a fuller account of a story. One is often left wondering how the writers became aware of these stories.

These are my imaginings gathered as I have tried to understand Jesus. I hope they are not yours. You should have your own ideas and thoughts about what Jesus was like.

Enjoy your read!

Contents

Sources...373

Birth

Mary

After the death of Jesus, Mary went to live with John the Apostle (as Jesus had proposed when he was on the Cross). It was in Jerusalem some years after the death and resurrection of Jesus that Luke interviewed Mary to gather information for his gospel. John was also there. Mary by then was an old lady but still in full possession of her faculties. She was small and slight with grey hair and the softest brown eyes you will ever see. Luke was fortunate to meet Mary and John before they fled to Ephesus because of the increasing persecution of the Christians in Jerusalem following the execution of James, John's brother, by Herod.

Luke:- Thank you for agreeing to see me. If you don't mind, I would like to go right through your life starting from the beginning. Otherwise we are going to get muddled and leave something important out. Is that all right?

Mary:- Yes that's fine. I just hope my memory is up to it.

Luke:- So where were you born?

Mary:- I was born in Nazareth. Mum's name was Ann and Dad's James. He was a carpenter. I had no brothers and only one sister, Salome. I know how disappointed Mum and Dad were not to have a son. She and I mostly got on well together. From an early age, I loved to help Mum but my happiest times were when Dad came in from the shop after work. He was never too tired to play and talk with us. We had a lot of fun when we were all able to be together.

Luke:- When did you first meet Joseph?

Mary:- Dad usually took on an apprentice who helped him with the simpler jobs. In return Dad taught him his trade. All the apprentices I remember were nice fellows but Joseph stood out. He first came when I was about eleven years old. He was originally from Bethlehem but had moved to Galilee with his parents as a child when life in Judea was more than usually rowdy. He was kind to all of us. He became very much a member of the family and I never realised he was particularly interested in me. He was firm and gentle and he never lost his temper with me. He had a lovely funny mouth and twinkling eyes and was the most attractive man I ever saw. Every time his hands touched my skin a shudder went up my spine . He was gentle but firm with me and treated me as an equal. Even at my age I knew how unusual that was. However it was a great surprise that, when I was about thirteen, he asked Dad if he and I could become betrothed. Dad asked me if this was what I wanted and, after thinking about it, I said yes. I found out later how rare it was for a young girl to be given any say in choosing who she was going to wed. It was agreed that we could be married when I was fifteen.

Luke:- Did anything unusual happen in the next year?

Mary:- Yes as you very well know. Joseph and I were betrothed which meant that we had formally given each other our word that, when I was old enough, we would get married. The arrangement was legally binding but, until the actual wedding, I would continue to live at home. One day, soon after my fourteenth birthday, I went to bed early to be by myself and lay dreaming. Life was good and I could see my future laid out before me. It was a future to which I was looking forward with great delight. Suddenly there was another presence with me in the room – a kindly presence. I heard a voice speaking to me in the dark. "Greetings, you who are highly honoured! The Lord is with you". I didn't understand what was going on. Who was this and what did he want? I wasn't frightened but I was mystified. Why me?

The voice spoke again. "Do not be afraid, Mary. God has a special purpose for you. You will become pregnant and give birth to a son, and you must give him the name Jesus. He will be very important and will be called 'The Son of the Most High'. He will succeed to the throne of his ancestor David, and he will reign over Israel forever; his kingdom will never end."

It wasn't the why or the when which I thought about but the how. From the beginning I knew that I would do as I was asked. All I could think of to say was "But I am still a virgin? How can someone who has no husband and is still a virgin have a child?"

He went on "The Holy Spirit will come to you and the power of the Most High will protect you. You must call your son Jesus, the Son of God. What's more, your aunt Elizabeth is going to have a child although normally she would be too old and everyone thinks she is barren. She is already six months pregnant. Nothing is impossible with God." If this was true, how could I not believe him?

I was stunned and couldn't grasp what was happening but managed to say, "I am the Lord's servant. I will do whatever you ask me". And then I was alone in the room. I was in no doubt that my life had changed for ever. It wasn't until later that I understood the risk I was taking. I had heard about a woman stoned for adultery. Strangely I never worried about the Law. I knew that Joseph would always protect me from this. I was however worried about the name Jesus (The same as Joshua and meaning 'The Lord saves'). It was not a name I would have chosen and it made me think of wars and fighting. There was nothing like that in our family. Would my son be a great soldier? I hoped not as the thought of a child of mine hurting or being hurt in battle was horrible. I imagined Jesus as another Solomon, sitting on his throne giving out wisdom and judgment to all who came. My main concern was that it would affect my relationship with Joseph. It could easily be the end of it and I was far from happy about this. It also began to dawn on me how honoured I was. Why had I been chosen to be the mother of God's son?

I didn't sleep much that night and, as I lay there, I felt a strange and pleasant presence within me. Next morning I managed to get Mum by herself and told her what had happened. At first she said I had been dreaming but in the end she became persuaded that I was serious. We discussed what had taken place and she suggested that, since Elizabeth had been mentioned. I should pay her a visit. I knew her from our yearly trips to the Temple but she was a lot older than me and I had had little to do with her. It was not the place I would have chosen to visit under normal circumstances although she was always very kind The thought of her having a child at her age was quite funny. She lived in Judea in the hill country above Jerusalem. By going to see her, I would be able to confirm that at least one part of what I had been told was true. I would not speak of these things to Joseph until I came back. My trip was arranged and two days later I set off. In any event a period away from home seemed sensible.

Luke:- What happened when you got to Elizabeth's?

Mary:- When I arrived, it was almost as if she was expecting me. I took one look at her and saw that she was indeed pregnant. She gave me a wonderful welcome but, as we were still hugging, she almost screamed with pain. I was frightened and asked her what had happened and she said her baby had nearly jumped out of her.

Elizabeth and I went inside to talk. Her husband Zechariah was there but he was unable to speak. A few months earlier he had been honoured by being chosen to burn incense in the Inner Temple in Jerusalem and, when he emerged, he could not say even a single word. Elizabeth explained to me that, while in the Inner Temple, he had seen an angel who told him that Elizabeth would have a baby who must be named John. Because he doubted what he had been told, he had been struck dumb and would remain so until the baby was born. He too made me very welcome.

I told Elizabeth how an angel had also visited me and what he had said. We hugged each other excited by what was happening and I found myself singing:-

> "Oh how I praise and glorify the Lord.
> How glad I am that he is my saviour.
> He chose to honour me, a poor country girl;
> and now people through all ages will call me blessed.
> He, the All powerful One, has chosen me – Holy is his name.
> He is merciful to all those who worship him.
> He has done wonderful things for us
> and he humbles those who are proud and haughty.
> How greatly he has helped his people Israel –
> He has never forgotten the promises he made to Abraham and our forefathers."

Luke:- How did you feel when you realised what was happening to you?

Mary:- Shocked! Why me? I was no different from other girls. I remember being surprised that the Son of God was to be born as a baby at all. For him to be dependent on me for survival was incredible and very frightening. I was totally inexperienced and raising children is a risky business. What if he had an accident or became ill? It was quite a responsibility.

Luke:- When did you go back to Nazareth?

Mary:- Three months later, just before Elizabeth's baby was due. When I got home there was little doubt that I was pregnant. I talked over with Mum how I was to tell Dad and Joseph. Mum agreed to tell Dad and he believed exactly what she told him. He came to see me and told me I would always be welcome in their house. Most fathers would not have taken that attitude. My major concern was how I was going to tell Joseph. I really did love him and the last thing I wanted to do was hurt him but it was obvious that I was pregnant. It must be me who spoke to him. When I plucked up my courage to do so, Joseph was devastated. His first thought was that he would have nothing more to do with me. Because of his respect for my parents and his love for me, he did not want me to be publicly disgraced and he would therefore break off our betrothal quietly. A few days later he came to see me again. He told me that an angel had visited him in a dream and told him that what I was saying was true. "Joseph, son of David, do not be afraid to take Mary home as your wife. The Holy Spirit fathered the child she is carrying. She will give birth to a son and you are to give him the name Jesus because he will save his people from their sins". It must have been difficult for him. He told me that, having thought about what the angel had said, he still loved me and wanted to marry me. I became even more aware of what a wonderful man Joseph was. His understanding was a huge relief, particularly as some of the girls in the village were quite unpleasant about my condition. What Salome thought of all this I have no idea. We never talked about it.

After this we all got together and agreed that Joseph and I should live together to try and prevent gossip. Joseph took me back to where he was staying and we became as man and wife except that we did not have sexual relations. It was because of this arrangement that, when the Romans called for a census, I had to go with Joseph to Bethlehem where he had been born. This meant that I would not be in Nazareth when my baby was due. I expected that the birth of the Son Of God would happen without any problems. However Mum would not be with me when the baby came and I was worried and frightened about this. Mum was extremely upset that she would not be with me. However, thinking about it later, it did save any awkward questions.

Luke:- So you set out for Bethlehem?

Mary:- Yes. Joseph was very sweet and arranged for me to ride on a donkey. Relations between Joseph and me were still a little strained when we set out and having this time alone together was good for us. It must have been hard for him to accept what was happening to me. As we got near Bethlehem, I got more and more uncomfortable and it was obvious that the baby was on its way. I was terrified that it would be born by the roadside. However we arrived safely at the inn only to find that all their rooms were full of other people visiting because of the census. The landlord, seeing the state I was in, agreed that we could bed down in a cave where he kept his animals. It was filthy but we were given clean straw. At least we were sheltered from the cold and damp and could light a fire. Hannah, the innkeeper's wife, came to help me and Jesus was born just after midnight. Hannah was wonderful – so caring and she even lent me her own swaddling bands – she had a little boy aged two.

Luke:- I suppose that you settled down with your baby then?

Mary:- Not quite! I lay down to rest but was almost immediately disturbed by a loud banging outside. A group of shepherds was standing there and they came in and told us why they had come. As they were watching over their sheep in the fields, there was suddenly a brilliant light in the sky and a figure that they could only assume to be an angel appeared. He was dressed in shining white and spoke to them saying, "Don't be afraid. I bring you good news that will bring great joy to everyone. Today in Bethlehem, the town of David, the Saviour, the Promised One, has been born; he is Christ the Lord. Go and see him: You will find him wrapped in swaddling bands and lying in a manger." Suddenly a great crowd of other angels appeared, singing and praising God. Just as quickly they were gone and all was quiet again. The shepherds agreed that they must see this miracle baby. So here they were. They had come straight to the cave we were in because they knew that that was where the manger was. Next day they told others about the night's events and a steady flow of people came to visit us.

I was astonished by what was happening and began to wonder why Jesus had been born. I thought about all that had happened and tried to make sense of it. Jesus was a good baby, quite content to lie on a rug and watch what was going on around him. The only time he made a fuss was when he was hungry and that's fair enough isn't it?

Luke:- Did you have the baby circumcised?

Mary:- Yes when he was eight days old.

Luke:- How long did you stay in Bethlehem?

Mary:- Nearly six weeks. As soon as the people who, like us, had come to Bethlehem for the census had gone, Hannah invited us to move into the inn. We did so and they were so kind to us. We stayed there until the time came to take Jesus to Jerusalem and present him, as our firstborn son, to the priests at the Temple.

Luke:- Did that go off uneventfully?

Mary:- Hardly. We got there on the fortieth day, as laid down in the Law. We couldn't afford to sacrifice a lamb so we planned to offer a pair of doves. As we arrived in the Temple courts, a frail old man approached us. As he came near us, puffing as if he had been on a long run, we could see that his face was shining with joy. Without any hesitation he came straight to us, told us his name was Simeon and started to talk. He had been promised in a dream that he would not die until he had seen the Lord's Christ. Moved by something he didn't understand, he had been led to Jesus. He took the baby into his arms and spoke about his joy that he had been spared to see the one who would be both the Saviour of Israel and a guiding light to all those who were not Jews. He praised God for this and stayed talking for a while. I asked him how he had recognised Jesus as the one he had been told about. He said he had been expecting a great teacher or a mighty warrior and could not believe that the one he had been waiting for was a little baby but, having seen us, he had no doubt that my little son was the one. Jesus would open up deep disagreements among the people of Israel. He would be rejected by many of them and they would suffer greatly for this. However those who accepted him would know the greatest joy. He turned, looked straight at me and said that the child would cause me as much suffering as if a sword had pierced my heart. We could only marvel at what he was saying but I didn't understand and spent much time wondering what it might all mean. Surely, as the mother of the Son of God, nothing could go wrong.

As he moved away, Simeon was talking aloud to himself. As far as I could understand he was saying,

> "Lord, as you promised, now let your servant die in peace
> for I have seen the Saviour you have given to all people.
> He is the light who will reveal God to every nation
> and he will be the glory of your people Israel."

While we were talking to Simeon, a very old woman approached us. She greeted us and told us that her name was Anna. We found out later that she was 84 years old and had been a widow for many years. She lived in the Temple and worshipped night and day, fasting and praying. Coming up to us she gave thanks to God and spoke to all those around us about Jesus and how he would become the Saviour of Israel. By this time quite a crowd had gathered and the Temple Guards were looking a bit worried. I was very surprised that God had already made it known to people who Jesus was. His future was risky enough as it was.

Having done what the Law required, we returned to Bethlehem.

Luke:- What did you think of what had happened?

Mary:- I was bewildered. Of course I knew that Jesus was not like other children but I had no idea of what Simeon and Anna meant. I wanted to forget the circumstances of Jesus' birth but already I knew that this wouldn't possible. Particularly because of Simeon's warning, I feared for the future.

Luke:- How long did you stay in Bethlehem this time?

Mary:- Well we had another surprise shortly after. Three strangers from Persia came to see us. They told us how they had been guided to Bethlehem by a bright star that had led them straight to the inn. It was still overhead. They had come by way of Jerusalem where they had been called to meet King Herod. He had wanted to know all about the dream that had persuaded them to follow the star. They explained how they had come to be in the city and, before they went on their way, he made them promise to come back to Jerusalem and let him know what they had found.

The three men didn't have any clear idea why they were in Bethlehem. Herod had told them that there was a Jewish prophecy that the Jewish king would be born in the town. They had been aware, while they were with Herod, that he was jealous of the baby born to be king and could not bear the thought of anyone taking his kingdom. The men listened to the story of the shepherds and, I think, began to believe that Jesus was to be this king. They then did something amazing; they each produced a present that they had brought with them from Persia and knelt and, with all due reverence, presented gifts of gold and frankincense and myrrh to Jesus. I didn't realise it at the time but each of these gifts had a special significance. It was a very moving experience. The angel had told me that Jesus was the Son of God but I was astonished that so many people were being made aware of it. I had no idea of his future or why God had allowed his son to be born as a human and subject to all the limitations of a normal child.

One of the men was warned in a dream that they should not return to Jerusalem so, after a few days they left by another route. They were such kind men and it was a great privilege to have them with us.

Luke:- Did things settle down then?

Mary:- No. That same evening Joseph too had a dream warning us that, for Jesus' safety, we must escape to Egypt and the next day we started on our way. Fortunately, when we arrived, Joseph's skill as a carpenter enabled him to get work easily. We were told that Herod had sent spies to Egypt to try to find us and we therefore didn't stay in any one place for too long. We ended up quite a long way from the border, just outside Cairo. Two years later Joseph had another dream and was told that Herod was dead and that it was safe to return to Galilee. Even then we were told not to go to Jerusalem, as Archelaeus, who had succeeded his father as king, was not to be trusted. It was a shame as we hoped to visit Hannah and her family on the way. Anyway we went straight back to Nazareth.

Luke:- Did you think your life would become more normal when you got back to Nazareth?

Mary:- I hoped so but I could not forget the circumstances of Jesus' birth and all that had happened since. I knew that there must be a reason for Jesus' birth but I could not see what it was. All I could do was bring him up with as much love and care as I was able and try to keep him from harm. I knew that Joseph would help me with this. When the time came we would have to let him go about his business without complaint. I was mystified by Simeon's words that Jesus would bring me great suffering.

Luke:- I think that is enough for one session. Let's go on again tomorrow.

Elizabeth

*By the time these stories were being collected together, Eliza-
beth had passed on and so I, as her closest and possibly her
only friend, was asked to record my memories of her. Elizabeth was a loner who found it very difficult to express her
feelings and so, on occasions, I have had to assume what she
was thinking but I am sure I knew her well enough to be
able to do this.*

I first knew Elizabeth when we were children. I
wouldn't say that I was her friend because she was not
the kind of girl you became friendly with. Even when
she was young, she was not the sort of person you asked
to join in. She seemed self contained, content in her
own company. She was an only child and perhaps her
shyness was because she spent too much of her time
with adults. Her father was a teacher and it was no
surprise when she married Zechariah, a priest. Theirs
was a strange courtship. He was ten years older than
her and already settled in his position. Somehow you

could not imagine them behaving like a normal married couple. They never showed any sort of affection for each other in public or, on the rare occasions when I was alone with them in their home. I became really friendly with her when she was astonishingly kind to me after I lost my first child while he was still a baby. The children all loved her and she was wonderful with them although she would not let them get away with anything. I found that she was still as shy as a young girl and very lonely. She and her husband didn't seem to talk together much although I was never aware of any rows.

When we got to know each other, she started to confide in me and once the floodgates were opened, they could not be closed again. At the time I am talking about she was around fifty years old although it was difficult to tell as she was one of those women whose appearance never seems to change. She had given up all hope of becoming a mother and compensated by being highly involved in the life of the synagogue. She told me that Zechariah still prayed each day for a son and that she felt humiliated by this. However Elizabeth still had a good relationship with her husband and she was very proud when Zechariah, on his annual tour of duty in Jerusalem, was chosen by lot to be the priest to go into the inner temple and burn incense. This was something which only happened once in a lifetime and then only to the honoured few. Elizabeth went with Zechariah for the great occasion. She told me later that he was so nervous and felt so unworthy that she had real doubts if he would be able to perform his duties. He eventually plucked up courage and went in to the altar. Instead of the usual five minutes in the inner temple, he didn't emerge for over an hour. There was great consternation. Had he had an accident or fainted? The High Priest was about to send someone in to investigate when eventually Zechariah stumbled out.

It was quite clear, as he came out that something was wrong. The High Priest went to talk to him but he was unable to reply. Instead he signed that he wanted pen and paper. He told them that he had had a vision while by the altar but he wouldn't tell them any more than that. It was only later that he explained to Elizabeth what had happened. He had gone in and set about his duties. Before he had started to burn the incense, while he was preparing himself for what he had to do, he had suddenly become conscious of another presence with him. When he looked, he saw a bright shining figure dressed in white and staring at him. He was terrified. The angel spoke. "Do not be frightened Zechariah; your prayers have been heard. Your wife Elizabeth will bear you a son and you are to name him John. He will bring you great joy and gladness; many will rejoice because of his birth, for he will be great in the eyes of the Lord. He must never drink wine or hard liquor. He will be filled with the Holy Spirit, even from before his birth. He will persuade many Jews to seek the Lord, their God. He will be a man with the spirit and power of Elijah, the prophet of old. He will pave the way for the coming of the Lord, preparing the people for his arrival. Fathers will be more aware of the needs of their children and the disobedient will start to think about their need for cleansing. Through him people will be prepared for the coming of the Lord." Elizabeth did not have to remember these words as Zechariah had written them down because he couldn't speak. She even showed me the piece of paper that Zechariah had used.

As you can imagine, Zechariah was astonished and wondered what was happening. He told Gabriel of his doubts. He was old to be a father and Elizabeth was beyond normal child bearing age. The angel replied, "I am Gabriel. I stand in the presence of God and I have been sent to speak to you and to bring you this good news. Because you do not believe what I have said, you will be struck dumb until your son is born. What I have told you will happen in due course". When the High Priest saw that Zechariah could not speak, he excused him from further duty and sent him home.

Not surprisingly Elizabeth was in quite a state when she heard this. At her age she wasn't sure that she wanted to be a mother or to have her comfortable life disturbed. She was much more worried about Zechariah's dumbness. I don't think Elizabeth really believed she would become pregnant but two months later she knew that she was. She had an awful time. She had terrible morning sickness and was really ill. For the first five months of her pregnancy she didn't go out because she was so unwell and because she didn't want people to see her condition. I wondered if she was going to bring her baby to term but Zechariah seemed to take no notice of his wife's problems. He spent his time in study because of course he couldn't teach. I think I was the only person, other than Zechariah, to have seen Elizabeth between when she was sure she was pregnant and when her visitor came.

About six months after she returned from Jerusalem and completely out of the blue, a niece called Mary came to stay. I had never even known she existed until she turned up quite unexpectedly. She was young, about 13 or 14, and it was obvious that she too was pregnant. She was a lovely girl and she was betrothed to a carpenter named Joseph. There was a calmness about her that was very unusual in a girl of her age. She lived in Nazareth in Galilee and it was quite a trek to Judea where we lived. They shut themselves away together and it was not until much later that I heard what had happened. Gabriel had also visited Mary and told her that she was to have a baby. She couldn't believe this, as she was still a virgin. Joseph had apparently accepted the situation because he too had been visited by an angel in a dream. Visits from angels and meaningful dreams seemed common in that family.

When Elizabeth greeted Mary on her arrival, she was immediately aware of the special nature of Mary's child. She even began singing which was most unlike her.

"Blessed are you among all women
and blessed is the child you will bear.
But why am I so highly honoured,
that the Lord's mother should come to me?
When you came and greeted me
my baby leaped for joy within me.
Because you have believed what the Lord said
you have been greatly favoured."

She told me that as she greeted Mary, her baby gave a most violent leap and she thought he was going to jump right out of her womb. Mary stayed almost until Elizabeth's baby was due.

The baby was born after a long and difficult delivery. He was a big boy and, right from the word go, he made his presence felt. As usual all the relatives had gathered and they discussed among themselves what the baby should be called. The consensus was that he be given the same name as his father. When they suggested this to Elizabeth, she just said that the baby would be called John. No argument! It was pointed out that no one in the family had ever been called John but Elizabeth was adamant. Zechariah was asked what he thought and he wrote on a tablet, 'His name is John' as instructed by Gabriel. As soon as he had written this, Zechariah's power of speech was restored. He burst into song praising God which caused quite a sensation. Some of the claims made by Zechariah in his song were outrageous. "You, my child, will be called a prophet of the most high for you are to go before the Lord to prepare his way for him". I think some of the neighbours thought that, during his period of silence, he had gone mad.

There was never anything quiet about John. His arrival caused a great stir in the village as, during her pregnancy, Elizabeth had kept very much to herself. She turned out to be a good mother but she had a difficult task. I have never seen a child with as much energy as John. He never walked when he could run or stood if he could jump. He wasn't just physically active – he learnt to talk before he was two. I suppose the over-riding impression he gave was of boisterousness. He was very close to his mother but grew impatient when she didn't catch on to what he meant as quickly as he thought she should. Zechariah was very proud of him but really did not know how to handle him. You had to be firm or else he would have you running all over the place. Unfortunately Zechariah's health was never good after he came back from Jerusalem and he died when John was about five years old. John brought great happiness to both his parents.

As he grew up, John began to talk about going to live in the desert. Elizabeth told me how hurt she was by this. She felt that she had failed him in some way. I think if Zechariah had still been around, he might have been able to comfort her but as it was, she had no one to talk to and I really wasn't able to help. Eventually John said that he was going to join a group of Essene hermits near the Dead Sea and nothing Elizabeth said could dissuade him. This was the beginning of the end for her. Her reason for living seemed to have gone and within four years, she had passed on. Once he had left home, John never came back to see his mother.

One of the highlights each year was the visit of Mary and her family for the Passover feast. Elizabeth seemed particularly interested in Jesus, almost more than her own son. He was certainly an exceptionally attractive child, both in looks and behaviour, but when he was around everything and everybody else was forgotten.

Jesus was very good to her and made no fuss when she hovered around him hanging on his every word. There was certainly something special about him.

All this took place many years ago. I do not know how Elizabeth would have reacted to what eventually happened to John. To have a son murdered, even by a king, is not something that should happen to any mother. I expect she would have been pleased at the success of his ministry. He preached repentance from sin and baptism as a symbol of a person turning to God. I imagine however that she would have preferred him to become a priest like his father and grandfather.

To me Elizabeth was a sad woman. She never really learnt to relax and be herself. She was happy when John was a child but even then she seemed to know that her happiness would not last. When he left home there was nothing left in her life. This became clear to me when I couldn't even contact John to tell him of his mother's death and the funeral arrangements. Elizabeth turned out to be a good friend though and I miss her. I never really understood what happened to Zechariah at the temple but it changed the lives of both him and his wife in a way that could not be missed.

Later Mary gave me this verse written by Zechariah at the time of John's birth and passed on to her by Ann, the friend who looked after Elizabeth

John Lindeck

The birth of John

The Lord God of Israel is greatly to be praised.
Out of the lineage of his mighty servant, David
he has provided a way of salvation for us
as he promised to us all through his holy prophets

He showed kindness and mercy to our forefathers
and rescued them from the hand of their enemies.
He enabled those who loved him to serve without fear
in holiness and righteousness before him all their days.

He gives us peace from the raids of our adversaries,
and a safe refuge from the hands of those who hate us.
Each day he recalls the everlasting covenant
which he swore before our ancestor, Abraham

You, my son, will be called the prophet of the Most High;
and you will go before the Lord to prepare his way.
You will lead his people on the road to salvation.
They will receive pardon and forgiveness from their sins.

Through your great kindness, O Lord, the sun will rise
and bring its light to all those who dwell in the darkness.
The feet of those who live under the shadow of death
will be directed along the paths of light and peace.

The Innkeeper

She was the most beautiful girl I have ever seen. Not just physically although Hannah had lovely lustrous hair and glorious soft brown eyes. There was something about her, a joy, and a sparkle that could not fail to attract any one who came across her. When I met her at my sister's wedding, she was 16 and I was 21. Father had died when I was 15 and I had to take over the running of the family inn. There is not much time for social life when you are learning to run a hotel on the job. I was painfully shy but eventually I plucked up courage to speak to her and it was every bit as enjoyable as I had anticipated. She was from one of the local farms and her parents gave me permission to visit her although I am not sure they liked the idea of an innkeeper marrying their beloved daughter. Anyway to cut a long story short, we were married a year later.

She took to the role of the Innkeeper's wife as if she had been doing it all her life. She was calm and able to cope with emergencies and she had lots of good ideas about improving the service we offered. That doesn't mean that she did not also have bad ones too but we were able to discuss them and come to amicable decisions – in other words she came round to my point of view. We were in no hurry to start a family but, in due course, she told me that she was expecting a baby and our happiness was complete. Solomon was a wonderful child, full of fun and vitality and a great delight to both of us. Running the business and looking after a child was hard but we shared the work and our little world gave us great joy.

Our son remained an only child for longer than we would have liked but we were not worried. Whatever would be would be. Solomon was coming up to two years old and full of mischief when we heard of the census decreed by the Romans. I suppose it was because tax revenues were dropping off as people escaped the net by moving around. We were the only inn in Bethlehem and we knew we would be busy. We bought in extra supplies and took on one of the girls from the village to help with the serving. Sure enough we rapidly filled up the accommodation we had available.

It was late on the evening of the day before the census when we heard yet another knock on the door. I remember that it was a lovely clear night with little moon but with the stars standing out clearly against the dark sky. It was bitterly cold. Hannah went to see who was there and she found a young couple, a man of around 24 and a girl who looked no more than 13 or 14. He was walking and she was riding a donkey.

They were desperate for help as she was heavily pregnant and looked as if the baby was due any minute. We explained to them that all our accommodation was full. He begged us for any space we could find and Hannah came to ask me if I had any ideas. The only place we had was the cave where we kept the mules that we hired out to needy travellers and the other animals. They could be put out into the fields but the cave would still be filthy. The best we could offer was clean straw. We explained the situation to them and they jumped at the chance to stay there. They came into the bar and ate while I changed the straw and cleaned up as much as I could and lit a fire.

When I came back inside it was clear that the baby was on its way. We helped Mary into the cave and Hannah offered to stay with her while the child was delivered. Fortunately it did not take long and just after midnight, a lovely baby boy arrived. They had obviously decided on a name in advance and called him Jesus. They had brought no baby clothes with them and Hannah went and fetched those we had had for Solomon. She was keeping them for when his brother or sister arrived. She had already become friendly with Mary and she offered to look after the baby so that Mary could get some sleep. The poor girl looked totally exhausted. Hannah told me alter how calm Mary had been during the birth.

I went to sleep in the inn and didn't hear what happened until later. Around three o'clock in the morning there seemed to be music in the air and there appeared at the stable door some of the shepherds who looked after the sheep in the fields round Bethlehem. Hannah recognised them as they often came to the bar for warm drinks on the cold nights. She asked them what they were doing. They had been in the fields when an angel appeared and told them of a baby boy born in a manger at the inn. He was the Promised One. They were all totally mystified. They agreed they must come to the inn to see what was what. They could not believe that, if the child were the Christ, the Promised One, he would be born in a stable. They came, they looked, they cooed and they went.

Next morning, they told their friends what had happened and what they had been told about this child. The local rabbi tried to persuade them to keep quiet but they were too full of the wonder of it all to do so. People were amazed at what they said and everyone discussed what had happened.

The census took place and most of our visitors departed. Mary was still recovering from the birth and, as soon as a room was available, we invited her, Joseph and Jesus to move into the inn. They did so and we became very close to them. Jesus was a wonderful baby. He was quite content to lie and watch the shadows flitting across the sky until he got hungry when he could yell with the best of them. Solomon kept on bringing him things to look at and the baby's face lit up when he appeared. Mary seemed so at peace and already I could see how close their relationship was going to be. She was a delight – happy and cheerful and glorying in her new child. Joseph was a quiet man who seemed to be having difficulty accepting what was happening. Something was worrying him.

Forty days after the birth of a first-born son Mary and Joseph, as was customary took Jesus to be presented at the Temple. They agreed to return to us on their way back to Galilee.

Shortly after their return we had another set of unexpected visitors. It was early evening when the knocking came and I went to see who was there. I found three young strangers who looked as if they had come from the East. They had followed a star that led them to Bethlehem and the inn. They asked to see Mary and the child and presented expensive gifts to Jesus paying homage to him as if he was a king. Hannah told me that she thought Mary was as startled as she was at all that was going on.

After the three had gone, Mary and Joseph discussed with us all that had happened. They seemed to take the strange events in their stride as if they had knowledge that they were not at liberty to share but they were worried about Jesus' safety. That evening Joseph had a dream in which he was told that he must not go back to Nazareth but escape to Egypt straight away as Jesus was in danger. Accordingly next morning they set out for Egypt. Hannah had grown very close to Mary and her child and when the time eventually came for them to go, she was very upset. We all missed them enormously.

After Joseph and Mary and little Jesus had gone, Hannah and I sat down and tried to make sense of all that had occurred. Of course we both knew of the prophecies about the Messiah. We imagined that a great warrior would suddenly appear and drive the Romans out of Judea. Maybe he could even cure the corruption that was rife in the Temple. We could not imagine that the Messiah would come as a little baby and be born in a cave usually occupied by animals. Yet we couldn't forget the Shepherds and the Wise Men and the dream telling Joseph to take his young family to Egypt. There were too many strange happenings for them all to be coincidence. Mary had told us a little of what had happened in Jerusalem and that too had been far from normal. There was no doubt that the little baby was somebody special. But how was he with no influence and no money going to grow up to be a leader. We didn't know much about Herod but the little we did was not nice. He was a cruel, unpleasant man. We had looked forward to seeing the family again when they came up for the Passover each year but we wondered now if this would ever happen.

A peculiar feature of all these events was the importance of dreams. I am a down to earth man, a realist and had never believed dreams to be significant. They did however seem to have played a major part in the happenings I have described. It was as if there was a greater power in control, which was making sure that events conformed to a preset pattern.

It was only a week after the family had left that the soldiers came. There was a sudden banging on the door and, when I answered, three soldiers barged in and asked if there were any boys under three years old in the house. We both realised why they had come. They were looking for Jesus. There was nothing we could do to hide Solomon who was playing in the front room. They said they had been ordered by King Herod to seek out all young boys aged 2 years or under and kill them. Nothing we could do or say would make them change their minds. They must have been well paid for what they were doing as they wouldn't even accept the substantial bribes we offered them. They took Solomon off, kicking and screaming, and we never saw him again. They did not even return his body for burial.

The effect on Hannah was devastating. All her bounce and sparkle went. She lay round listlessly and couldn't take any interest in what was going on around her. It was as if her reason for living had been taken away. We discussed what had occurred endlessly and she could not find it in her to criticise Mary or Joseph who had been as much victims as she was. She could not understand or accept what had happened or how any one could be so evil as Herod or the soldiers who did his bidding. In the end she just faded away. She could not sleep, she would not eat and she got weaker and weaker until she could no longer go on. The idea of having another child was abhorrent to her. No one could replace Solomon and who was to say that the same thing wouldn't be repeated.

I survive. There is nothing else for me to do but the best part of my life is over. I sometimes wonder if it would have been better if Joseph and Mary had never come. I would like to know what happens to Jesus. Was his life worth the death of Solomon and so many other children? It is 10 years since these events and we have heard nothing of Mary or Joseph or Jesus. I was caught up in events which were too big for me and which I couldn't understand. I feel used and I don't know why.

The Three Wise Men

We think of the three magi or kings as being old with long white beards and very wise. The possibility however is that they were not so old and, at the time of their tour to Bethlehem, not even so wise. The rigours of such a trip would mean that only those who were fit and able to endure the hardships and dangers involved in 1ˢᵗ century travel would consider setting out on such a journey.

We have no real idea of where the Magi came from but it is thought they might have lived in Persia. Nor do we know how the three travellers met. They may have been from different communities who met at gatherings of the local great and good.

In any event the three young men did go travelling together and they became lifelong friends. Every year they used to meet to discuss what was happening in their world and of course to reminisce. And naturally they became very old with long white beards and very wise. So they were when Matthew, in the course of doing the research for his book, sought them out and asked about their experiences at the time of their grand tour. And so Matthew described them when he eventually got round to writing what we today know as his gospel. The last time that Caspar, Melchior and Balthassar met was with Matthew 40 years after their trip and, as old men are, they were only too eager to remember. They wondered why this small insignificant Jew was so interested but the pleasure of reminiscence was too strong for them to question him much. We have been lucky to have the notes of their conversation and this is what was said.

Matthew:- I am trying to write a book about this man Jesus who you met when he was a newborn baby. I have been visiting those who met him. Mary, his mother, told me of your journey to Bethlehem and I wanted to hear in your own words what happened. So tell me what you can remember?

Melchior:- I can remember the excitement with which we all set out on our great adventure. This really was going to be a once in a lifetime experience.

Balthassar:- I had never been away from the local area before.

Caspar:- I can remember our fathers insisting that we should each take valuable gifts with us. I know how I resented having to carry the heavy gold round with me.

Melchior:- I never thought we would use our gifts. The last thing I intended was to become involved with high society.

Balthassar:- Do you remember when I fell off my donkey and my dread that the case in which I kept my frankincense would crack and I would have to live with the smell for the rest of the trip?

Melchior:- and we got all the way to Caesarea without having used any of our gifts.

Caspar:- Yes it was only then that unusual things started to happen. We had been warned before we started that there were problems in Jerusalem. The Jews were saying that a great leader was going to appear who would become the King of the Jews. The priests had whipped them up into a frenzy of excitement about this. They hoped that not only would the Romans be expelled but also that King Herod would be forced off his throne in Galilee.

Balthassar:- It was in Caesarea that we first saw that very bright star in the sky. When we had been taught together, we had been told of the importance of Astrology, and, therefore, none of us took the appearance of this star for granted. It must have real significance. I had earlier had a very clear dream that we should follow a star that would appear in the East because it would lead us to see something of extreme importance. And now here was the star, low in the sky and very bright and we began to follow it. If we moved off the path, it stopped until we were back on the right route. It seemed to be waiting for us.

Melchior:- It was as if it had been specially sent to lead us. It was like being on a magical mystery tour and eventually it led us to Jerusalem.

Caspar:- When we got there we were stopped at the gates and searched. The guards seemed to be looking for some particular people and we were the ones.

Balthassar:- I remember worrying about what we had done when the guards said we had to go with them. We were led to Herod's palace.

Melchior:- We were taken straight in to see King Herod leaving all our baggage with the guards. Perhaps this was the time when our gifts might come in useful. But when I looked round and saw the luxury, I knew that they would not be appreciated.

Caspar:- The gold I had been carrying wouldn't even have made half of one of the salvers that were lying around.

Melchior:- Then the questioning started. Why were we here, where had we come from, what were we looking for? He didn't seem able to understand that we were there just for fun.

Balthassar:- His questions concentrated on a special child who was to come. Herod seemed paranoid about him and you could sense his fear.

Melchior:- I thought at first it was fear of the supernatural and it was only later that it dawned on me that he was frightened of a rival king.

Balthassar:- I heard later that Herod had held a meeting of the leading Priests and the teachers of religious law, to find out as much as he could about where the King of the Jews would be born. He and many of the people in Jerusalem were very worried about what was going to happen.

Caspar:- We told him of the star and he got very excited. He wanted to know when we had first noticed it and what we thought it meant. He seemed really interested in it and we promised to let him know where it led us. I was glad to get away from Herod as he seemed obsessive about what we were doing. We promised that we would go home by way of Jerusalem and tell him what we found.

Melchior:- I was very surprised that we got all our baggage back untouched.

Balthassar:- Looking back on it he knew that we were being led the short distance to Bethlehem because that was where the old Jewish prophecies said the baby would be born but we didn't know that at the time.

Melchior:- It was astonishing that he didn't send someone to go with us or follow us but I suppose he thought that would scare us off.

Caspar:- Anyway when we got outside we couldn't get away quickly enough. We were delighted to find that the star was still there to guide us and it led us to the Bethlehem road.

Matthew:- What did you expect to find when you arrived in Bethlehem?

Balthassar:- We had not heard of the prophecy of a great king being born until we saw Herod. I imagined someone from an important family who would grow up to be a great scholar or lead a mighty army.

Caspar:- Herod obviously thought it would be a child but I found this difficult to believe. The person to come was to be a great king, a conqueror and that ruled out a baby. I didn't know what to expect.

Melchior:- If he was to be a child, I thought he would be housed in great splendour with every comfort provided. I could not imagine a suitable place in a village like Bethlehem. That was apparently the place named in the prophecies. Anyway we followed the star.

Balthassar:- When we got near the village we were led to the inn and the star stood still right over it. We went in and asked for lodgings. We were lucky and there was plenty of room. We got talking to the landlord, Nathaniel and his wife and son and they were full of what had happened; of the baby born in a cave where the mules were usually kept and of the visit of the shepherds. The baby, named Jesus, was still there with his parents, Mary and Joseph, because, in accordance with custom, they had wanted to present Jesus their firstborn son at the Temple in Jerusalem when he was forty days old. They had just got back from doing so and were preparing to go home to Nazareth.

Melchior:- I remember going to their room to see the new baby and the effect he had on me. He didn't seem much like a king or a warrior but was a lovely, happy child. It was difficult to see how, with his background, he was going to become a great ruler or lead an army. There didn't seem much for Herod to be afraid of.

Balthassar:- As soon as a room had become available, the landlord had let them use it free of charge. I went to see the cave later and it was as dirty and smelly as I expected.

Caspar:- All new born babies are wonderful but this one had a special glow. He was wrinkled like all young babies but he also had an unusual serenity about him.

Balthassar:- This didn't mean he couldn't cry when he was hungry. There was nothing wrong with his lungs.

Melchior:- The mother Mary was so young. I don't think she was more than thirteen or fourteen but there was a peace about her. She knew what she was doing and was very happy. She was so pleased with her little boy and was already forming a strong bond with him.

Caspar:- The father was very much in the background and he seemed rather wistful. It was almost as if he was wishing that the situation had been slightly different. He didn't appear quite as pleased as a new father should be.

Balthassar:- Perhaps Joseph had heard the prophecies too and was frightened for Jesus' future. Or maybe he had heard rumours of Herod's search for this child.

Caspar:- As soon as I saw the mother and child I was in no doubt that these were the people for whom our presents were intended. Mary took my gold and promised to keep it for the baby. She was so gracious in the way she accepted it and she had a sort of inner glow as if she understood something that nobody else did.

Balthassar:- When I gave my frankincense the baby had such a knowing look about him that I thought he was going to thank me. He seemed aware of everything that was happening.

Melchior:- I too gave the mother my present of myrrh. Later I went into the fields to meet the shepherds. They told me about the angels appearing and the heavenly choir and why they had decided to go and see Jesus. They were convinced that he would grow up to be someone important although they had no idea in what way. They were certain something special had occurred. I wanted to see what happened to the little boy and I asked Nathaniel to keep me informed. He promised he would if he could but the family planned to go back to their home in Nazareth so he might well lose touch.

Caspar:- When we went to sleep on our last night at the inn, we were all ready to go back to Jerusalem as we had promised but I think it was you Melchior who said that you had dreamt that Herod was going to harm the child and that you thought we should go straight home.

Melchior:- That's right. I knew beyond doubt that someone was telling me that this was what we should do. Anyway all of us thought that Herod wished the child no good. So, early in the morning, we set off over the hills on our way home. I still wouldn't have been surprised if we had been followed but we were lucky. I was horrified when I heard from Nathaniel that Herod had ordered that all little boys in Bethlehem less than three years old should be killed and that his son, little Solomon, had been among them. I had nightmares about this for years.

Caspar:- I often wondered whether we were right to go home without contacting Herod. After all, if we had, it might then have been only one child killed. It really made me wonder what fate was in store for Jesus. We were astonished when Nathaniel wrote to say that Mary, Joseph and Jesus had fled to Egypt because they too had been warned that Herod was desperate to kill the baby.

Balthassar:- We received two or three more letters from Nathaniel but eventually he stopped writing.

Caspar:- The next we heard about Jesus was from travellers returning from Palestine who told us of a wonderful new teacher who was able to heal all sorts of illnesses and was leading a band of followers round Galilee. For a long time we did not connect this with the baby Jesus. There was no reason for us to do so. It was only when we heard people talking of his mother and of the family history that the penny dropped.

Balthassar:- We also learnt about the teaching that Jesus was giving. It was like nothing we had ever come across before. If he was setting out to be a great leader, this seemed an odd way to go about it. What king suggested putting other people before himself? He was not teaching a religion with rules that had to be obeyed but suggesting that it was possible to have a relationship with God which would lead to loving and caring for other people.

Caspar:- From what we understood, his message was not just for Jews. We were told of him talking to Romans, Greeks and Samaritans and visiting places where no good Jew would ever go. He seemed to be setting out deliberately to upset the religious leaders. Whenever anyone came back from Jerusalem, we questioned him about Jesus and his teaching. We were told about him walking on water, feeding vast crowds when there was virtually no food and even raising people from the dead. And he taught the many that followed him round that they must be humble, not proud, and love the people they met.

Melchior:- I know I began to question what type of man this was. The episode in Bethlehem didn't seem so odd after all. I couldn't understand what he hoped to achieve. It was beyond any one person to change the way a whole nation behaved

Balthassar:- For many months returning travellers told us of the strange things that were happening in Galilee and Jerusalem. Some even said that this was God on earth. Others thought he was a great prophet like those who had been around among the Jews many centuries before.

Caspar:- I couldn't believe it. This man, coming from very humble roots, born in a stable and brought up in poverty, was seeking to change a whole nation. Then we heard that the Jewish leaders had taken him prisoner and, with the connivance of the Romans, crucified him. I remember asking myself why someone who could raise people from the dead couldn't save himself. Apparently he made no attempt to protect his own life. Almost he went willingly to his death.

Melchior:- For me a dream was over. The person who was going to change society had been beaten by it. I was very sad. It is not often that you hear of a genuinely good man who wanted above all else to help others. I couldn't help imagining what the world would be like if he had been successful. He wasn't trying to tell us to behave in a particular way but to be ourselves and look after our neighbours. When you think of it, not so radical.

Balthassar:- I always thought that what we were being told was too good to be true and wasn't surprised that eventually the authorities caught up with him. I was disappointed but had never understood how he could succeed.

Caspar:- It was a few weeks before stories began to come back to us of him having been raised from the dead. At first we ignored them but as they persisted, we began to take them more seriously.

Melchior:- We didn't know what to think. I was even tempted to go back to Jerusalem to find out for myself but I'm too old. The rumours kept on coming back to us and the more they persisted, the more confused we became.

Balthassar: - We began to hear reports that the great Jewish prophets had foretold all that had happened to Jesus. I could remember vividly how excited I was when I first saw that little baby in the inn in Bethlehem and I wished I could believe that what was now being said was true. But Matthew what are you hoping to learn from us?

Matthew:- I was one of the ones that Jesus healed. Not physically mind you but mentally. I was a tax collector, the lowest of the low. I had sold my soul to the Romans for money and no normal Jew would speak to me. I was an outcast hated by my fellow citizens and not allowed into polite society. Then I met Jesus and he totally changed my life. I paid back what I had taken illegally and became one of his chosen followers. He was unlike anyone else I have ever met. He had time for everyone and seemed to know instinctively what each person really needed – not just food and some-where to live but their inner needs. Colour, creed and position in society meant nothing to him. An outcast was as important as a priest. I decided that I wanted to write down all I could about his life so that it was not forgotten and try to work out how the events of which he was part fulfilled the ancient prophecies. When he was taken prisoner and killed, my world collapsed. But he did rise again. I met him. In his hands were the marks of the nails where he had been crucified. And it wasn't just me who saw him – on one occasion there were more than 500 present – far too many for me to be making this up. He was the same Jesus but different – somehow he seemed no longer of this world. He had told us he was the Son of God and I don't think any of us understood what he meant until, about two months after he was crucified, he disappeared from our sight through the clouds. He had said he would send his spirit to be with us so that we could do the sort of things he could do; when all his followers were gathered together about ten days later, we felt his unique presence and the power that he used to give us when he sent us out to do his work. Jesus changed my life and, while he was still alive, that of many others. And he is alive today, still changing other people's lives so that, instead of exploiting their fellow men, they seek to serve them. This is what I think his life was about and how he wants us to be. But you must make up your own mind.

Life

Mary

Luke:- So you returned from Egypt to Nazareth two years later than you expected?

Mary:- Yes. When we got home, we found that Jacob, Joseph's father, was growing too old to run the carpenter's shop, so Joseph took over. The next few years were among the happiest of my life. Mum saw Jesus for the first time and was in her element as a granny. She seemed to have forgotten that Joseph was not Jesus' father. We were a real family and my other children started to put in an appearance, four boys, James, Joseph, Simon and Judas and three little girls. Joseph was very good; he never differentiated between Jesus and the rest. Jesus loved going and 'helping' him and in time became a very skilled carpenter. He started whittling little figures for me and they were lovely – made with such care. Later with Joseph's help, he made me a beautiful table. We had the usual number of small accidents and I was often needed to bandage cuts and kiss bumps better. He was always laughing and into mischief but never to hurt or harm anyone. Almost I could forget that there was anything different about him. Nobody ever doubted that Jesus was Joseph's son. Throughout my life Joseph was the only man for me. I never stopped loving him and I believe he loved me till the day he died.

Luke:- Did you worry about what the future held for Jesus?

Mary:- I could never forget the things, which had happened when Jesus was conceived and, later, in Jerusalem. I particularly remembered when Simeon had said in the Temple "This child will cause much change in Israel, some benefiting the people and some harming them. For you too a time will come when it will be as if a sword will pierce your heart". I still couldn't understand how I could be hurt by what had happened. I honestly believed that Jesus was the Messiah but why he had been born to me I had no idea. I didn't feel I could speak about this to anyone both because it would shame Joseph and because no one would believe me. I did go and talk to the Rabbi on several occasions but he was not much help. I wanted to know about any prophecies concerning the Son of God and he couldn't really explain them. Anyway he thought it inappropriate that I, a woman, should be asking this sort of question. I was also aware that Jesus was at risk from deliberate malice as well as illness or accident.

Luke:- When Jesus was twelve, you took him to Jerusalem for the Passover.

Mary:- We used to go every year. It was tremendously exciting going with a group from Nazareth. We all had such fun together. As we went we sang the old psalms and joined with all the other parties setting out for the Temple. When we got there we attended the various ceremonies, met old friends and listened to the learned rabbis explaining the scriptures. I was surprised how interested Jesus was in hearing them. Quite often he stayed on while we went off with friends. Our particular companions were Judah and his wife Rachel and their children, Martha and Mary from Bethany near Jerusalem. Meeting them again was always one of the highlights and it was very sad when Rachel died in childbirth. We also saw Elizabeth and her son John, until he went off to join the Essenes and live the life of a hermit. Zechariah had died some years earlier and Elizabeth was on her own. She was a poor, sad old lady.

On this occasion we set off home with our party and had been travelling all day when we realised Jesus was not with us. We had thought he was with his friends but in the evening we knew he was missing. We had to go back to find him. To say we were annoyed is putting it mildly. We left the other children with friends and set off. When we arrived we searched everywhere for him but, although people had seen him, no one knew where he was. We were at our wits end and on the third day, we went into the Temple to pray. There we found him in a group having a discussion with one of the teachers. He was sitting quietly, not just listening but joining in, asking questions and expressing opinions and the others were paying him attention. We went to him and he was surprised to see us. "Why are you searching for me? Don't you know I need to be in my father's house?" He had completely forgotten on which day we had said we would leave. It put us in a difficult situation as it was unsafe to travel just as a family and we had to find another party going to Nazareth which wasn't easy. Jesus would never tell me where he spent the nights when he was alone in Jerusalem but I imagine it was in the open.

Luke:- So you went home again and resumed normal life?

Mary:- Yes. The next few years were good years. Unfortunately Joseph became ill with a growth and was unable to run the business. Eventually he died and, in a way, I was relieved as he was in so much pain. We all missed him terribly. He was such a sweet tempered man and always had time for the children and me. Jesus took over as head of the family and ran the business. He was wonderful with his brothers and sisters. The thing I remember most about those days was his ability to tell them stories. They used to beg him to do so. Almost I forgot the special circumstances of his birth but I still had this nagging question at the back of my mind, 'Why has he been born'? I knew that, one day, things would change and I was pretty sure that, from my point of view, it would not be for the better. Even then, he used to disappear for long periods so that he could be by himself. I asked him what he was thinking about but he wouldn't answer. He never missed going to the synagogue on the Sabbath.

Luke:- Did you tell anyone about the circumstances of Jesus' birth?

Mary:- No. I suppose I wanted to forget and think of Jesus as being like any other child. I didn't even tell his brothers and sisters as I thought that might lead to jealousy. In any event I was afraid of hurting Joseph. I never spoke to Jesus about his birth, not then or later. I tried to treat all the children equally but Jesus was the oldest!

Luke:- So when did things start to change?

Mary:- The first thing that disturbed our peace was that we heard that John, Elizabeth's son, was baptising people in the River Jordan. A number of the young lads from the village went and they came back telling us how he was preparing the people who he baptised for the coming of the Messiah. Certainly it changed their lives as some of them from our village had been quite rowdy. Jesus talked to them and found out exactly what John was teaching. He told us he too had to be baptised by John and went off to the Jordan. He left James, his eldest brother in charge of the shop. I was told later that, somewhat reluctantly, John baptised Jesus. He felt that Jesus should baptise him. After the baptism a voice out of heaven announced that *"This is my Son whom I love; with him I am well pleased"*. A figure like a dove descended and rested on Jesus.

Luke:- When did you next see Jesus?

Mary:- Not for a while longer. We had no word from him and then about eight weeks later he returned home. I could see he had changed. There was a new sense of purpose about him as if he realised why he had been born. The time when he was just a normal member of the family had gone and Jesus was ready to be about the real business of his life. He brought with him a group of friends who he was teaching. You were among them John.

John:- James, my brother and I shared a boat with Andrew and Simon. It had belonged to Zebedee, our dad, but, when he grew too old to go out each day, he left it to the four of us. Andrew had been going through a rough time and Father told him to go away for a couple of weeks. He had met up with John the Baptist and then with Jesus and he came back to our village of Bethsaida in a state of high excitement. He claimed to have met the Messiah and he persuaded Simon to go back with him and meet him. They came back a few days later convinced that Andrew was right and that Jesus was the Messiah. About a month later Jesus was walking beside the Sea of Galilee. He saw Simon and Andrew fishing and called them to follow him. He then saw James and I and called us also. We were out on the lake with Dad. As soon as we reached shore we too went off with him leaving Dad in the boat with the hired men, shouting at us to come back. Eight others were called including Philip who was also from Bethsaida, our village. Jesus started teaching us as we followed him round Galilee.

Mary:- I remember when you all turned up at my house in Nazareth. John and James I knew of course because we are related. There was no room for you all to stay so you camped outside the village. I had been asked to help at the wedding of a friend's daughter at Cana and Jesus and his friends were invited. It was there that, for the first and only time, I asked Jesus to use his power to help me. During the festivities my friend came to me in some distress. The wine was beginning to run out and, if it did, he would be shamed in front of not only his family and friends but also the bridegroom's family. An inner voice seemed to be telling me that, if Jesus was asked, he could solve the problem. I told Jesus what was happening and asked him to help. I had no idea what to expect. He was, unusually for him, quite curt and asked why I was involving him. I recall him saying, "My time is not yet come". Nevertheless I told the stewards to do exactly what he told them. He instructed them to fill six stone water jars, used for ceremonial washing, each over 6 ft. high and holding between twenty and thirty gallons with water. To my astonishment they did so right to the brim although they must have thought he was mad. Jesus told them to draw some out and take it to the president of the feast. Again they obeyed without question even though they knew what would happen if they served water to the host. He tasted it and pronounced it to be excellent, better in fact than the wine that had been served earlier. Most people served the good wine first and, when people were unable to tell the difference, served poorer quality. Jesus' watching friends were as astonished as I was.

Luke:- What did you think when this happened?

Mary:- I think it confirmed that Jesus' time with the family was over and his real task was about to begin. I still didn't know what this work was as I couldn't imagine why he had come to earth. I was surprised and slightly ashamed of myself that I had put Jesus in a situation where I might have embarrassed him. I apologised later and he told me not to worry.

Luke:- Did he say anything to you later about what you had done?

Mary:- No but I knew it was something I should not do again.

Luke:- So did you see much of Jesus after that?

Mary:- Not that much. I had to stay at home looking after my younger children. Jesus spent his time travelling around Galilee and further afield. We used to hear how he had healed people, restored their sight and their hearing, cleansed lepers and fed large crowds when there was virtually no food available. We also heard some of the stories he had used to teach those who followed him. The main point of his teaching was that we must love and care for each other. Things got very difficult for him because everywhere he went crowds gathered bringing people who hoped to be cured from their ailments. I was told about one occasion when a leper came and knelt by Jesus and told him that if he wanted to, Jesus could heal him. Jesus replied "I want to. Be healed." Immediately all signs of the Leprosy disappeared. Jesus told him to go and let the Priest certify that he was clean. He instructed him to keep quiet about what had happened but the man could not resist telling everyone he met how he had been healed. Jesus told me that, as a result, he and his friends no longer felt able to enter the towns and villages because of the attention they attracted. They had to live outside in the fields and other remote places. How could this happen to my special child?

On one occasion he came home for a few days and we all went to the Synagogue on the Sabbath. He had often been before and was sometimes asked to read the scriptures. On this occasion he did so and then sat down. The passage he had read was from the prophet Isaiah foretelling the coming of the Messiah saying "God's spirit is in me and He has told me to go to tell the poor the good news about my coming. He has sent me to proclaim that prisoners will be set free and the blind will recover their sight, that the downtrodden will be freed from their oppressors and that the year of the Lord's favour has arrived." People looked at him and he got up again and began by telling them "This scripture has come true today in front of you". He spoke with complete authority and the people were wondering how the carpenter, the son of Joseph and Mary, brought up in their town could talk as he did and have the power to cure people from their illnesses. He noticed how disturbed they were and told them that no prophet was ever accepted by the people of his hometown or his family. The people were furious and some Pharisees started screaming that he was blaspheming. Jesus was seized and dragged to the brow of the hill on which the town was built so that they could throw him down the cliff. But he quietly turned and walked away, straight through the middle of the crowd.

Luke:- You and the rest of the family remained in Nazareth. Wasn't life a bit difficult for you?

Mary:- For a few days people felt awkward when they saw me but mainly they were sorry for me and things soon got back to normal. The children had a much rougher time. They, particularly the younger ones, were teased unmercifully and went through a bad patch. Pharisees and Teachers came and asked them about their brother. I didn't understand why Jesus had to antagonise them. However after a bit something else happened and people forgot. The shop continued to prosper as James, Jesus' eldest brother, was the only carpenter in town and he was wonderful at his job. Jesus never went to Nazareth synagogue again.

Luke:- Did you ever follow Jesus on his travels?

Mary:- Very seldom. I had my other children to look after at home. I once went with some of them to see him because we had heard rumours of what he was doing and how his critics said he was possessed by the devil and out of his mind. He was always so surrounded by people that he did not have time to eat and drink. I just could not understand how my special child, given to me by God, could be behaving in this way and I didn't want him to become a laughing stock. We went to bring him home but we could not get near him. Someone told him we were there and he said,

"Who is my mother? Who are my brothers?" and then, pointing to his people surrounding him "These are my mother and my brothers. Anyone who does the will of my father in heaven is my brother and sister and mother". I could understand that he was busy but I was extremely upset. I told him so when I spoke to him later and he reassured me that he would always love all his family and especially me. He gave me a big hug. All the events of his birth and his early life came back to haunt me. How could this 'special' son of mine, given to me by God, be considered mad by his fellows? How could he insult me as he had just done? I hadn't asked to be Jesus' mother and didn't understand how he could treat me as he did. I knew that he had moved away from us and was fully occupied in his own affairs but I had no idea what these were or what his purpose was.

Luke:- Your children went with Jesus to Jerusalem once didn't they?

Mary:- Not exactly. It was the time of the Feast of the Tabernacles and Jesus hadn't made up his mind whether to go to Jerusalem although everyone expected him to. His brothers didn't believe he was anyone special and told him that, if he wanted to prove he was a healer, he had to go to the Feast and show what he could do in front of the crowds that would be there. He told them that the time was not yet right and they went on to the Feast without him. He went later and arrived after the celebrations had begun.

Luke:- What else did you hear of his doings?

Mary:- Much later I heard of the time when Lazarus, the brother of Martha and Mary whose family I had known from childhood, was raised from the dead. This meant a great deal to me as I was very close to them. I knew how much the death of their beloved younger brother would have affected the two girls. I wondered if it was because they had such faith in Jesus' ability that he was able to perform this miracle. Lazarus had been dead for some days before Jesus came so what happened could be described in no other way. The girls were very upset when Jesus hadn't rushed to be with them. I can only imagine their joy when Lazarus came to life again. Mary Magdalene told me all that had happened.

Luke:- Did you understand why Jesus had been born?

Mary:- No. I thought that for him to be teaching and healing people was wonderful but it would not affect anybody other than those who lived in Galilee. Simeon and Anna had talked about Jesus rescuing Israel and I had heard that Simon had said openly that he believed Jesus was the Messiah but this wouldn't happen if Jesus stayed in Galilee. What he was doing was certainly not what I expected. He didn't mix with the rich and famous but with those who, in the eyes of most people, had no importance. They were not the sort of people who were going to change the world. Why did it need the Son of God to do the sort of things he was doing? There had been teachers and miracle workers before and they were human like us As his mother I noticed that Jesus seemed to be frightened of the future. It was as if something dreadful was going to happen which he could not avoid. When he was alone with me there was a sadness about him which I hadn't noticed before.

Luke:- What did you think when Jesus said he was going to Jerusalem for the Passover?

Mary:- I was terrified because I knew that the High Priest and his allies would not accept someone travelling round the country performing miracles and contradicting their teaching. To them religious observance was a matter of pride; to Jesus it was a cause for humility. I knew how much the Pharisees and Scribes hated him. I met up with him at Martha's and begged him not to go to the Feast but he said he must. I did not understand why my special child should put his life at risk. There was enough needing to be done in Galilee.

Luke: - That's enough for the moment. We will go on tomorrow.

Mary's Mother

Ann, Mary's mother died shortly after Jesus began his public ministry. She was not present at the wedding in Cana and she never left her home after that. However John talked to her about Jesus' childhood when he got back to Nazareth and wrote down her story as she told it to him.

I was born in Nazareth, the eldest daughter of a merchant. There were just two girls in the family, myself and Ruth who was two years younger than me. Mum got pregnant again but the baby, a son, was born dead. She was ill for many weeks and I thought she was going to die. Eventually she got better but after this, to Dad's great sorrow, Mum couldn't have any more children. I know from what he told me later how much Dad had looked forward to passing his business over to a son but it was not to be.

Dad's family had lived in Nazareth for many generations. Mum was originally from the hill country of Judea near Bethlehem. Her parents had moved to Nazareth from Judea when she was a baby to avoid the continuous unrest which existed in Jerusalem and the area round the city. She still had numerous uncles and aunts there.

We were a very happy family and both Mum and Dad always treated Ruth and I as people in our own right. They asked what we thought before reaching any decisions which would affect us. We always knew that they were on our side although, if we did something they thought was wrong, they let us know about it in very clear terms. The price for being considered in this way was that, right from when we were young, we were expected to help with the work of the house but Mum made even this fun.

I got on well with Ruth most of the time although she was much more self-willed than me. If she didn't get her own way she could throw a most spectacular tantrum. She was two years younger than me but, as she grew older, instead of becoming more considerate, she became more assertive. The rest of us learned to cope with this and also how to avoid setting her off. Most of the time she was great fun to be with. We were never in any doubt about the love Mum and Dad had for us.

The highlight of the year was our annual visit to Jerusalem for the Passover feast. The journey took about a week and we travelled with many of the people from the village. When we got to Jerusalem the bustle and clamour were a complete contrast to the peace of the village. The Temple was wonderful although, as girls, we were not allowed to go into the inner parts of the complex. Seeing the priests and traders going about their business was fascinating. We stayed with the same friends each year in Bethany, a village about three miles outside the city on the far side of the Mount of Olives.

As I got older I began to take notice of the boys in the village and it wasn't long before James caught my eye. He was apprenticed to his father who was a carpenter. He was gentle and caring and the fact that he was extremely good looking didn't do him any harm. We started to see a lot of each other and, eventually he came round to see Dad to ask permission to marry me. After talking things over with Mum it was agreed that we could become betrothed and be married when he had finished his apprenticeship. This was the only time I can remember when I was not asked about a decision which affected me. James' father was in poor health and he offered to take James into partnership as soon as his apprenticeship was over. James and I got wed as soon as possible. Marriage was every bit as happy as I had hoped.

My sister soon married a coppersmith from by the Lake but she died in childbirth about a year later. We never heard from her husband again. I too got pregnant very quickly and had a daughter Mary. She was followed two years later by Salome but after this there were no more children. Mum often told me how odd it was that the relationship between Salome and I was almost exactly the same as that between her and Ruth. We were a happy family although James would have loved to have had a son. James soon became the sole owner of the carpentry business and we settled down to a quiet life.

Mary was a delightful child. She was always cheerful and had a very lively sense of fun. One of the things I noticed about her was that, whatever she was doing, she still appeared to be clean and tidy. The same couldn't be said of Salome who was a regular tomboy. If there was mischief afoot she was always involved. She much preferred the company of boys to that of girls. You were never quite sure when she came to you if she was showing her love or trying to get round you. The girls seemed to get on together which, considering their different characters was surprising.

Mary was just fourteen when the event which changed her life took place. She had just become a woman and, as many girls are at this stage of their lives, was slightly moody. She went up to bed early and when she came down in the morning, I could see that she was seriously upset about something. She had become betrothed to Joseph, the apprentice who was helping James but I knew that they had not been alone together. Joseph was originally from Bethlehem, a village in Judea near Jerusalem. His parents had moved to Galilee because of the continuous unrest and fighting between the various Jewish factions and also between them and the Romans. Joseph was a lovely lad, very caring and obviously devoted to Mary.

I asked Mary what was wrong and at first she wouldn't answer me. I knew she hadn't had a row with Joseph. I sat down with her and, after making me promise that I would tell no one else – not even James, she told me the most unlikely story, so unlikely that she couldn't have made it up. She had been lying in bed and an angel had come to her and told her she was going to have a baby. He was to be the Son of God and was to be called Jesus. I thought she had had a bad dream but she insisted that she was telling me the truth. I asked her if she was still a virgin and she told me in no uncertain terms that she was. She had asked the angel how, as a virgin, she could have a child and he replied that all things were possible to God.

I didn't know what to do and told her I would think about what she had said and talk to her later. Eventually we agreed that she should go on a visit to an aunt in Judea near my old home. I was quite surprised that Mary agreed to go as it meant being away from Joseph. Elizabeth was very kind but she didn't really understand children and was aged over 50. She was married to a Temple priest and we didn't know her particularly well. Mary had been told in her dream that, however unlikely it might seem, Elizabeth was to become a mother. I told James and Joseph that Mary needed to go away to think about all that had been happening. She was still very young.

Two days later she set off with a group of travellers who were going to Jerusalem. I was worried about this as the roads were not safe and she would have to go on the last part of the journey on her own. I wondered if James or Joseph should go with her but this was not practicable. There was no way in which we could warn Elizabeth that Mary was coming. We were very relieved when a returning traveller told us that Mary had arrived safely.

Mary came back to Nazareth about three months later. There was absolutely no doubt that she was expecting. She had enjoyed her time with Elizabeth who was indeed pregnant as the angel had told her. This was every bit as surprising as Mary's situation as Elizabeth was well past normal child bearing age. One of the odd things about her and Zechariah, her husband, was that he still prayed everyday for a child in spite of this. Elizabeth's child was almost due when Mary set off home.

We now had to plan what to do. Joseph would have to be told what was happening and Mary insisted that she must be the one to do this. I admired her courage. She told him the same story as she had told me and, as you might expect, he was devastated. I watched him leave our house and he looked like a broken man. He felt totally betrayed and as if all his dreams had turned to dust He didn't think he should have anything more to do with Mary. Because of his respect for James and me and to prevent her being publicly disgraced, he would break off the betrothal quietly.

I was not very surprised when two days later he came back to our house and said that an angel had appeared to him in a dream and told her that what Mary had said was true. I began to realise that forces greater than I understood were involved. James couldn't help but notice that Mary was pregnant and I had to tell him the whole story. He was absolutely astonished but seemed to accept the truth of what he was being told. Mary told me much later that he came to her room and said that, whatever happened, she would always be welcome in our house.

The four of us got together and decided that Mary would go to live with Joseph but, as the angel had told him, she would have no marital relations with him until after the baby was born. Mary left with him a few days later. Later that month we were all told of a decree by the Roman Governor that there should be a census and that every man with his wife and children would have to return to his own town for this event. Mary would have to go to Bethlehem with Joseph and the baby would come while they were away. This meant I would not be able to help Mary at the birth. I was completely shattered by this. If this was how the Son of God was to come into the world, I wondered what sort of God I was serving. I was desolate and spent most of my time in tears and it was Mary who had to cheer me up. The day came and she and Joseph set off. She was riding on a donkey that Joseph had obtained for her. My heart broke as I saw her go. She would not be back for two months as the baby would be presented at the Temple while she was away.

I heard nothing for about three weeks until a returning traveller brought a message that baby Jesus had been born and that both he and Mary were well. I became very excited at the thought of seeing the baby and was deeply upset when Mary didn't come back when I expected. I had heard of King Herod's decree that all boys in the Bethlehem area and under three years old should be killed and wondered if Jesus had been one of those caught. Considering how he had been conceived,

I couldn't believe this could be the case. Even if it was, I knew that Mary and Joseph would have let me know.

To my great sorrow I didn't see Mary or Jesus for two years. I was kept busy in this time as Salome formed a relationship with Zebedee, a fisherman, and was insistent that she was going to marry him. James and I both thought he was unsuitable but she got herself pregnant and we had no choice but to allow the marriage. She moved off to Bethsaida on the Lake and we seldom saw her after that.

I had begun to believe that Mary and her family would never come home but eventually they turned up. I had no warning but one day they just arrived. Mary explained that they had been told in a dream to go to Egypt and had had no way of getting in touch. I thought they had panicked but they had always followed these dreams before and things had turned out well. She was more beautiful than ever and it was obvious that she and Joseph were happy together. Jesus was a lovely child, good looking and into everything and Joseph doted on him. Mary was expecting another child. When the first excitement had passed she told me all that had taken place since she left home. I found it difficult to believe, especially the story of what happened when Jesus was presented at the Temple. Life quickly settled into a routine and James was born safely. My husband, James had become listless and was finding his work too much for him and very quickly Joseph took over from him. Jesus loved nothing better than following his father round as he worked and Joseph had limitless patience with him. Unfortunately James' health got worse and he died two years after Joseph's return. Mary and her family being home was some small consolation.

The years went by and Mary's family increased until she had five boys and three girls. Jesus was never treated any differently from the other children but there was something about him. He was totally honest and, whatever mischief he got into, when caught out he would always admit what he had done. He loved going out into the hills either with his friends or on his own and soon knew them like the back of his hand. I don't know how much Mary thought of how he was born but she never made any allowances because of who his father was.

The only time that there were any difficulties was when we went up to Jerusalem for the Passover when he was about twelve. For once Mary was neither pregnant nor nursing and the whole family was able to go. When we got to Jerusalem the children as usual went off together and it wasn't until we stopped after the first day of the return journey that Mary realised that Jesus was not with them. She and Joseph had to go back to Jerusalem leaving the other children with friends. They searched for three days and had almost given up hope of finding him when they saw sitting discussing the scriptures with some scribes. When she told him how worried she had been, he replied that we should have known he would be in his father's house. This was the only time I heard him mention his real father in front of Joseph who was very upset.

Life went on as normal for the next few years. Unfortunately Joseph became ill and was eventually unable to carry on working. Jesus took over the business and, as he was an excellent carpenter, the business did very well. James became his assistant and eventually his partner. There was nothing to remind us that Jesus was different from other children. We were disappointed that, although Jesus went out with a girl from time to time, he never seemed serious about any of them. I know of several who would have married him like a shot if they had been given the chance. Jesus was regular in attendance at the synagogue but didn't spend more time there than a number of other young men. He did study the scriptures and could quote large parts from memory.

One of the happiest things that happened in these years was that we got back in touch with Salome. We went to visit friends in Capernaum and I decided to find where she lived in Bethsaida. When I got there everyone knew where Zebedee and his family lived. I think Salome was lonely and she was delighted to see me. We arranged that Mary and her children would come to meet Salome's sons, James and John. Jesus in particular seemed to get on well with them and from then on we saw them each year, either in Nazareth or Bethsaida. It was lovely to have met up with them.

The other major event in this period was the death of Joseph. There was no dramatic ending. He gradually grew weaker and eventually failed to wake up one morning. I had grown to love and respect him very much. He had had much to put up with but he loved Mary very much and she couldn't have wished for a better husband or father for her children. She was devastated by her loss and took many months to get over it. I don't think she was ever the same person after this.

Life continued peacefully until Jesus was about thirty years old. He suddenly told us that he was going off to Judea. He was gone for around two months and when he came back he had changed. There was a sense of purpose about him which had not been there before. He came back and almost immediately went off to the Lake. He called James and John, Salome's children, and their friends Simon and Andrew together with eight other young men and told them they were going to help him in a great work. Zebedee and Salome were none too happy about this and had a few choice words to say about Jesus next time we met Both Mary and I knew that his real work on earth was about to begin but we had no idea what this was. He must have been pretty persuasive to take James and John from their fishing. All the twelve he picked, except one, were Galileans and their previous occupations ranged from tax collector to wood carver. They all came to stay in Nazareth and Jesus took them with him to the wedding of a friend of the family in Cana. I was not well enough to go to the wedding but I met them all. When they returned they talked about nothing but how Jesus turned water into wine.

Mary told me about the crowds who came to hear Jesus teach and of the numbers who were healed from illnesses ranging from blindness to leprosy and madness. There was great excitement among the people. This was what I expected from the Son of God but I didn't see how he was going to influence any but the locals. Neither could I understand why he seemed to go out of his way to upset the authorities. I thought he would work with them. Things got so bad that, on one occasion, Mary went to fetch Jesus home before he was arrested. He ignored her and she came back alone.

All that had taken place at Jesus' birth came back into my mind and I wondered how things were going to end. If he was the Son of God, I knew that he would have a clear purpose for his life but I couldn't work out what it was. I don't believe it will be anything good. I fear for Mary.

I know that the growth on my breast is getting worse and that I am not long for this world. I am glad that I will not be around to see what happens. I am trusting that what Jesus said about going to be with his father is true.

Ann died before the end of the first
year of Jesus' public ministry

John the Baptist

When John was in prison, he had the time to think back over his life and he told his story to one of his disciples who used to visit him. This disciple gave it to Matthew who in turn used it in writing his gospel.

My first memories are of home and my mother and father. Dad was a priest and when I first remembered him, he was already around 65 years old. He was not in good health, having never recovered from an experience he had undergone just before my birth. He had been enjoying what should have been one of the highlights of his life, having been chosen to burn incense in the Lord's presence in the inner sanctuary of the Temple. While he was there, an angel had appeared and told him that he was to have a son. Since Mum was already past normal child bearing age by then, he found this difficult to believe and he told the angel of his doubts. As he had never stopped praying for a son, this showed a lack of faith but I think, in his circumstances, I might have done the same. Any way he was struck dumb until the time that I should be born. His speech did return but the shock of what had happened undermined his health. He never fully recovered and died when I was only five.

While Dad was in the sanctuary he had been told by the angel what my life would be like. I was never to touch strong drink and I would be full of the Holy Spirit from the day of my birth. My task in life was to be to prepare the way for the Messiah, the one who was to come and rescue Israel. Many people would turn back to God as a result of my ministry. I was to be called John which means 'Gift from God, Apparently this caused quite an argument in the family when I was named following my circumcision but this was what the angel had said I was to be called and so it was. Dad told me all this many times before he died. It was hard for a little tot like me to understand but I did realise that I was not like other children. I don't think it made my behaviour any better as I felt I must enjoy every moment of my childhood until I set out on my life's task.

Mum also was much older than the average mother. She was well over fifty when she had me, more like a granny than a Mum. She couldn't run and jump like some of the other mothers but she did her best to make my life fun. I was never in any doubt that both she and Dad loved me even if they found it difficult to kiss and hug me. After living on their own for so long, Mum and Dad found it hard to adapt to my presence. I spent a lot of time with the family of Ann who I think was Mum's only real friend. She had three sons and we used to get up to all sorts of mischief. We never set out to hurt anyone but we loved playing practical jokes. We always owned up before any real hurt was caused.

One of the highlights of the year was the annual visit to the Temple for the celebration of the Passover. Jerusalem was about 15 miles from where we lived and we went every year. I used to enjoy the excitement and the noise. There were all sorts of entertainment in the city and I took full advantage. It was there that I met Jesus for the first time. His mother, Mary, and Dad were distantly related and Mary had visited Mum when she was pregnant with me. Mary had just recently found out that she too was expecting. She was only fourteen at the time but she managed to calm Mum down and help her to accept what was happening. Until Mary's visit Mum had not left the house for five months because she was feeling ill and because she was frightened the neighbours would laugh at her.

Mary and Jesus didn't come to Jerusalem every year as she was always either expecting or nursing. In the end she had nine children. I didn't know Jesus well but, as we were about the same age (he was six months younger than me), if he did come we spent some of our time together. He was a quiet thoughtful boy who loved discussing ideas but he could be great fun and was keen for adventure. We each had our own friends who we liked to be with.

Mother was a great story teller and she told me all the traditional stories of my people. She had a gift for bringing them alive. I can remember sitting by her knee and, as she finished one story, urging her to tell me another. She used to shake her head and say she hadn't got the time but I knew that there was nothing she liked more. I learned much about the history of the Jews. My particular heroes were the great warriors, David and Gideon and Samson. I also began to wonder why we, as a nation, didn't remember our roots and turn back to the Lord. I didn't enjoy going to the synagogue on Sunday as the Rabbis were full of things we must not do and on stupid rules about our behaviour such as what we could and could not do on the Sabbath. Even then I didn't think our relationship with God was supposed to be an obstacle race. In any event they didn't bring the stories to life like Mum did.

When I was ten years old I began to hear a voice within me telling me it was time for me to leave home. Later I began to recognise this voice as the voice of God which Dad had told me would be part of me from when I was born. I was at liberty to ignore it but somehow it never occurred to me to do so. I knew that I was being told to go and join one of the communities of hermits which lived in the hills and deserts to the North of Jerusalem. I discussed this with Mum and, to her great credit, she said to me that I must do what I thought was right. She didn't try to persuade me to stay at home although she would have known that she might never see me again. She had always understood that I was born for a purpose and that the time she had with me was a gift from God. We made contact with one of these groups and I set out to join them just before my eleventh birthday. I was deeply grateful to Mum that she didn't make a big song and dance when I went although I imagine she cried her heart out as soon as I was gone. What ever people might say about Mum she had courage. I never saw her again and didn't know when she died until much later. I felt guilty about leaving her on her own but I was not my own master.

I was very frightened when I joined the Community. I had no idea what to expect. When I arrived I found the ten or so members lived in a couple of large caves in the middle of the desert. I was by far the youngest there but the leader took me under his wing and I was treated with great kindness. For the first few weeks I longed to be home but I had to put this behind me. We spent our days studying the Law and finding our own food and provisions. This was a thankless task but, if we didn't persevere, there was no other way in which we would get food. We tried to grow crops but usually there was insufficient rain for them to prosper. Our main diet was insects like locusts and honey from wild bees. I was stung so often that I grew immune to the poison. I soon grew out of the clothes I went in and dressed like the others in the community in camel skins held in place by leather belts. The skins were coarse and constantly irritated the skin but, after a while, one grew used to it. I think my biggest problem was the complete lack of privacy unless one went off into the desert. Everything we did was done in the open but there was never any problem about impropriety.

Time passed remarkably quickly. We prayed and talked together but much of our time was spent in silence. There was always something of interest to watch like the birds and the wandering animals and the beautiful flowers which blossomed as soon as there was any rain. We rarely saw any other people and when we did this was a cause for celebration. I remember one occasion when we came across a group of lepers wandering aimlessly in the hills. We tried to come alongside them but they were not able to accept that we were acting out of love and had no wish to harm them. They were always welcome to share in our life although this didn't seem to hold much attraction for many of them. I learned to love the solitude and used to go off on my own over the hills. I could feel God's presence in the wide spaces and the wind and knew his presence with me.

I spent seventeen years in this way, years of great contentment and wondered if there was to be anything more to my life. I didn't think that I had been born in the way I was just to live in the desert so this life must be a preparation for something. As we talked together and I studied the Prophets, I found myself thinking more and more about the promised Messiah. When would he come and how? I never believed as so many did that he would be a great soldier and conqueror but I couldn't imagine how he would get his message across. As time went on I became more and more certain that my role was to be that of one going before the Messiah and telling whoever would listen that he was coming. Eventually I understood this was to be my ministry and I discussed what to do with my companions. They were reluctant for me to leave the community as no one had ever done so before but in the end agreed that I must do what I thought was right. When I was twenty nine I left them and set out on my own. I never went back.

I made my way over to the River Jordan North of the Dead Sea. The world I went back to seemed to have become a harder place than the one I remembered. Perhaps this was because I had been only ten years old when I went into the wilderness and had lived a fairly sheltered life. There was so much noise and bustle and people were desperate to get their own way. There was also a widespread discontent with the way life was led. This was partially due to the increasing domination of the Romans but also because people could see how little the Jewish leadership was maintaining the standards that were expected. There was open talk of corruption in the Sanhedrin. Earning a living was becoming increasingly difficult and there was widespread hunger. Meanwhile taxes continued to increase.

I began to preach. At first there were very few to hear me but gradually numbers built up. My message was always the same. We had all sinned and needed to turn to God in repentance. He will forgive us but he expects us to live our lives as he intended. This involves sharing our possessions with those less fortunate than ourselves and living our lives honestly. I felt there needed to be some action to show that a man had repented of his sins and I heard a voice within me suggesting that I revive the old custom of baptism. If a person was totally immersed in the river, this would symbolise the washing away of all that was past and a new beginning. The crowds coming for Baptism started to grow rapidly and people from all round Judea travelled to hear me.

Someone suggested that I was the Messiah who would come to rescue Israel and I was very quick to deny this.

I was there to prepare the way for the Messiah but I was not him. Indeed I was not worthy to serve him in any way at all even in things as trivial as tying up his shoe laces. When he came the Messiah would baptise with the Holy Spirit and fire. I had to continually repeat this as I was determined that there be no confusion in the matter.

As my fame grew, I began to notice that there were men in the distinctive dress of the Pharisees watching me. They began to ask questions such as "By whose authority are you preaching and baptising?" I am afraid that I turned on them and called them a 'brood of vipers' and many other choice names. I knew that, in spite of their pious exterior, their lives were anything but holy. They never forgave me and later on did nothing to help me when I fell foul of King Herod.

One day, as I was preaching, I saw a dark haired man of about thirty approaching. A voice inside me told me that this was the Messiah. He came to me and asked me to baptise him. I had a dim memory of having met him before and suddenly realised he was Jesus, the son of Mary, Mum's kinswoman. I told him that I could not baptise him; it was more appropriate that he should baptise me. He insisted that it was part of God's plan that he should be baptised and reluctantly I did so. As we were emerging from the river I heard a voice from heaven saying 'This is my beloved son and I am totally delighted with him'. A dove came and perched on his shoulder. The next day I was standing on the bank with two of the young men who had come to learn from me and lived with me. I spoke to them and said

'Look, there is the Lamb of God that I told you about'. Without a word they turned and followed Jesus.

I saw no more of Jesus for two or three months and then he returned with a group of young men who started baptising in his name. One of them was one of the lads who had turned from me and gone to follow Jesus a few weeks ago. The number being baptised by him increased and the number coming to me decreased. When I was asked if I minded this I explained that I was not the Messiah. I was like a friend of the bridegroom at a wedding who rejoices when the bridegroom comes to claim his bride.

The number of people coming to hear me was still considerable so I went on with my ministry and shortly Jesus went off back to Galilee. Still the Pharisees came and soon men sent by Herod, king of Galilee, came to find out what was going on. I knew about Herod and how he was living openly with Herodias who had been his brother Philip's wife. They had gone through a form of marriage although few people thought it legal. I felt the need to express my feelings about this and his many other misdeeds. Shortly afterwards I was arrested and imprisoned in Tiberias. I have been there now for many months. I imagine Herod doesn't know what to do about me as I am too popular to be disposed off. I don't expect to be released quickly if at all. Herod doesn't forgive insults.

I am not treated badly in prison but I hate it. I miss the open air and seeing what is going on around me. I am allowed visits by my friends and I admire the courage of those who come. Inevitably they will become associated with me and their own liberty will be at risk. Sometimes I get very depressed and on one such occasion I began to wonder if what I had done had served any useful purpose. I heard all about the things Jesus was doing but I found it difficult to reconcile these with the idea of the Messiah as a great popular figure. I asked two of my followers who were visiting me to go to Jesus and ask him if he was truly the Messiah or whether we should keep on looking for someone else. When they saw Jesus he told them to come back to me and tell me what they had seen and heard. "The blind see, the lame walk, lepers are cured, the deaf hear and the dead are restored to life. The good news is being preached to the poor and God blesses those who are not offended by me." When I heard these words I was reassured and could endure my captivity with greater courage.

I wait now for the end. I know I will not be released and any day could be my last. I thank God for his goodness to me.

Shortly after this John was beheaded. The circumstances which led to this were unusual. At Herod's birthday Salome, the daughter of Herodias, performed a crude dance which greatly pleased Herod. He promised her on oath that he would give her anything she wanted. Salome consulted her mother who suggested that she ask for the head of John on a platter. The king couldn't be seen to break his oath in front of his guests and so John was executed Most of the guests wept and many were physically sick when John's head was brought back into the hall on a platter.

Andrew

I was born to be a fisherman. Bethsaida, the village on the Sea of Galilee where we lived was a fishing village and Father, named Jonah, shared ownership of a boat with his great friend, Zebedee. Even when I was small my great delight was to go out on to the lake with them. It never occurred to me that I would earn my living any other way.

I don't come from a big family, just my brother, Simon, 15 months younger than me and a younger sister, Leah. We were a close-knit group and enjoyed each other's company on the occasions when dad was not out celebrating with his friends. Any excuse seemed good enough for a party and, as the years went by, it became clear that he was more and more dependant on his drink. Eventually he could not go out in his boat any more and he died when I was 11. Mum was heartbroken because he had always been good to her and, unusually for the village, had never become violent with her or with us. I missed him but Zebedee allowed me to become a member of his crew and I was able to earn a living for the family. Unfortunately Mum did not get over Father's death and she too died a couple of years later. This left the three of us. Simon joined us on the boat and Leah, who was nine when Mum died, did her best to keep house. Our neighbours kept an eye on us and we got along reasonably well.

It was some years later that I started getting restless. Simon had started keeping company with Rachel and spent less and less time at home. Leah had become bosom pals with another girl in the village and, even if she was at home, spent her time talking to Debbie. I felt the responsibility of keeping the family together very keenly and when Simon and Rachel married and settled down together (although settled might be the wrong phrase – I have never seen a less settled pair than they were), I felt that life was passing me by. Zebedee noticed that something was wrong and told me to go away from everything for two weeks and have a break. As it was, I was not helping him or anyone else. His wife, Salome, would look after Leah.

I decided that I would head south down the River Jordan. I fell in with another lad, Saul, who was going the same way. On the third morning we saw in the distance a small crowd gathered by the banks of the river and went to see what was going on. In the river was a huge shaggy bearded man wearing a tunic that appeared to be made of camel skin. It was rough and tufty and, although normally it would have fallen below his knees, it was tucked into a thick leather belt. He was standing in the water and ducking a succession of people who came in to join him. Before pushing them under he was saying a few words to each person. The whole scene gave promise of fun so we decided to stay with him and see what happened. After a bit the line of people waiting to be ducked (or baptised as we later found the proper name to be) dried up (not a good pun). I had never seen a baptism as the only time when this took place was when a Gentile wanted to become a Jew.

The man came out of the river, stood on a natural mound and started talking to the people gathered around. For a big man his voice was remarkably soft but it was very clear and he could play it like a harp. What he said was unlike anything I have heard before and it held me entranced. "I have come to prepare the way for the Lord, to straighten paths and to make his way easy for him. I will baptise you with water as a sign of repentance. But shortly someone far greater than me will come. I am not worthy even to tie up his shoelaces. I have baptised you with water but he will baptise you with the Holy Spirit".

By mid afternoon the crowd had gone and we were left alone with the Baptist whose name was John. He was good company and invited us to stay with him. We shared his meal of honey and locusts, which were surprisingly tasty. We slept in the open but this was no hardship as we were equipped to do so. In the morning the crowds started gathering early. John began to speak and as I listened, I began to understand what he had to say. All of us had done things of which we were ashamed and needed forgiveness. If we were baptised, that would wash our sins away. He had words to say to all the different groups of men who came to be baptised, tax collectors, soldiers and the rest.

About midday a group of richly clothed men appeared. A more unsuitably dressed group I have never seen. John seemed to take an instant dislike to them. He started insulting them and calling them all sorts of names. They watched in stony-faced disapproval and eventually turned and left. Saul and I wanted to know more about John and his teaching so we stayed on. What he said seemed to address my concerns about the pointlessness of life. The next day I decided to be baptised and Saul came with me. The experience brought me some relief from the misery I was feeling.

Two days later a tall, dark man of about 30 appeared at the back of the crowd. For the first time since I had known him, John appeared embarrassed. He said to him, "I need to be baptised by you, and yet you are coming to me?" The man insisted that it was necessary for him to be baptised and in the end John consented. This was the first time I saw Jesus. As he came out of the river a voice could be heard, as if from heaven itself saying "This is my son with whom I am well pleased."

The next day Jesus was passing by at the back of the crowd. John saw him and called out at the top of his voice "Look, the Lamb of God". Saul and I looked at each other and turned and followed Jesus. After a while Jesus noticed us and asked, "What do you want?" In order to start a conversation I replied "Teacher, where are you staying?" "Come" he said "and you will see". So we went and spent that day with him. The next day I started home to Bethsaida. I never saw Saul again.

When I got home I met Simon and told him what I had been doing. "I have found the Messiah" I said and took him to meet Jesus. Jesus looked at him and said, "You will be called Cephas" which when translated is Peter, the rock. Later Jesus chose others to be in his circle of close friends. Among them were James and John, the sons of Zebedee, and Philip also from our village. We came from all walks of life, even including a tax collector. There were twelve of us in all and he called us his disciples. Almost immediately we became involved in baptising the people Jesus had talked to. It was very odd doing for other people the same as John the Baptist had done for us a few days earlier. It became notice-able that more people were listening to Jesus and then coming to us for baptism than were going to John. The Pharisees stood and watched and counted the numbers being baptised by each of us.

We went to stay with Jesus near his home and, three days later he took us to Cana with his mother and his brothers and sisters for the marriage of a cousin. It was a great occasion. It was here that we watched Jesus water into wine. I will never forget the look of dumb resignation on the faces of the waiters as they followed Jesus' instructions. They would pay the price if anything went wrong.

All of us disciples were astonished at what had happened and began to wonder who Jesus was. From that time on we travelled round Galilee with Jesus, going to the villages but never to the bigger towns. The only city we ever visited was Jerusalem in Judea. Wherever we went crowds followed us and the excitement when he was around was like nothing I ever felt anywhere else. If he went into a room, the atmosphere changed and he became the centre of attention. Jesus had time for everyone. The sick and the dumb, the blind, the spirit possessed and the lame were all brought to him and only had to touch his garment for their lives to be changed. I remember when one of Herod's senior court officials came and told Jesus his son was lying at home dying. He begged Jesus to come and heal him. Jesus said that all the people wanted from him was miracles. They weren't listening to what he said. The man repeated 'My son is lying at home close to death'. Jesus looked at him and said very quietly 'Go home. Your son will live.' Much to my surprise, the man went and we heard later that the son was healed at the exact time that Jesus spoke.

There was another occasion which sticks in my mind. Jesus tried, whenever he could, to go to the religious festivals in Jerusalem and once we went to the pool of Bethesda. There was the usual crowd of the blind and lame and paralysed who used to wait by the pool. There was a belief that, from time to time, an angel came and rippled the water and that the first one into the water would be healed of whatever illness he had. Jesus started talking to a man who told him he had been disabled for 38 years. Jesus asked him "Do you want to be healed?" I thought this was quite an odd question as the man wouldn't have been there unless he did.

I suppose Jesus wanted him to think of the results of being made whole again.

The man replied "I have no one to help me into the pool so I can never be first. While I am trying to get in someone always beats me to it."

Jesus spoke. "Get up, pick up your mat and walk." And the man did! While he was doing so Jesus slipped away. It was the Sabbath and the Pharisees noticed the man walking away carrying his mat and told him in no uncertain terms that he was breaking the Law by doing so. I don't know if they recognized that he had been one of those waiting for healing. Anyway he replied "The person who made me well told me to pick up my mat and walk." They asked him "Who is he?" He had no idea and told them so.

There was an odd ending to this story. The next day Jesus went to the Temple and found this same man pretending to be lame and begging. Jesus went up to him and warned him "Look you are well now. Stop sinning or something even worse may happen to you." I had never heard Jesus use such a stern tone of voice before. The man went off and told the Jews who it was that had healed him. They came to Jesus and asked him why he was encouraging people to break the Law. He outraged them even more by saying he was doing his Father's work, thus claiming to be the son of God. I didn't know why Jesus took such delight in irritating the Jews.

Not everyone was made better physically but all went away feeling happier and more at peace with themselves than when they arrived. One of his sayings particularly struck me. "Come to me anyone who is tired and overworked. I will give you rest. Take my yoke upon you. Let me teach you because I am humble and gentle and you will find peace for your souls." There were many times in my life when I found this to be true.

The lengths to which people went to bring their loved ones to him were amazing. On one occasion Jesus was in a house in Capernaum talking to the people who had crowded into every corner of it. It was so full that no one could even turn round. As usual we were watching. I happened to look up and saw a small hole appear in the ceiling. This was no mean feat as the roof was strongly built so that the family could sleep there in the summer. I saw an eye come into view and then the hole was closed again. I went on watching and another hole appeared right over the place where Jesus was standing. Dust went everywhere but no one in the room seemed to notice. The hole grew bigger until it was large enough for a large mat to pass through. Jesus looked and saw four young lads carefully lowering a mattress by cords tied to each corner. On it was a man who was clearly paralysed. It was not easy to keep him from tipping off. Jesus spoke to the man who had appeared in front of him. "Take heart, son; your sins are forgiven." Immediately some of the rabbis who were watching started muttering. "Who does this man think he is? He is blaspheming! Only God can forgive sins."

Knowing their thoughts, Jesus said, "Why do you think this is blasphemy? Which is easier to say, 'Your sins are forgiven' or 'Get up and walk'? I will prove that the Son of Man has authority on earth to forgive sins." Then he turned to the man on the mattress and told him "Get up, pick up your mat and go home." And the man slowly got up, picked up his mat and, as we stood in awed silence, walked out of the room. We could hear his friends yelling and screaming as they tumbled down from the roof, jumping around in excitement as they greeted him. No one came to thank Jesus and we never saw any of them again. I could not understand why he deliberately seemed to antagonize the Pharisees by speaking what to them was blasphemy. He could just as easily have said "Get up and walk". Why couldn't he just live and let live?

Another occasion I remember well, partially because it happened in Bethsaida my home village, was when Jesus was in the synagogue. Among the people listening to him was a man with a withered hand. He was ashamed of this and used to keep it wrapped in his sleeve. It was the Sabbath and Jesus noticed him. The usual number of Pharisees and Teachers were there waiting to see if they could catch Jesus out. If he healed someone on the Sabbath, they could accuse him of blasphemy. Jesus made the man stand in front of everyone. He turned to his critics and said 'Is it legal to do good deeds on the Sabbath or is it a day for doing harm? Is it a day to save life or destroy it?' He glared at them as he was clearly upset by their hard hearts. He turned to the man and told him to stretch out his arm. The man lifted his good arm. 'No' Jesus said, 'the other arm'. The man slowly raised it and the sleeve which covered it dropped back. As it did so we could all see the white wasted flesh grow pink and recover its shape. The look on the man's face as he realized what was happening was wonderful to watch. I can not begin to describe it. The man fell on his knees worshipping Jesus. I saw the Pharisees sneaking out, hoping they would not be noticed.

Even when Jesus tried to spend time alone with us or just needed a rest, he couldn't escape from the crowds. We always had a boat ready so that we could set off across the lake to places where it was difficult to reach on foot. On several occasions, when we got to the other side, people had somehow got there before us.

We saw many remarkable things as we travelled around. We were in Bethsaida again when a blind man was led up to Jesus. I had seen this fellow many times before. Jesus spat in the man's eyes, put his hands on him and asked "Can you see anything?"

The man replied "I can see people; they look like trees walking around."

Once more Jesus put his hands on the man's eyes. Then his eyes were opened and he saw everything clearly. Jesus sent him home telling him not to go into the village.

It was very enjoyable travelling around with Jesus. He was always approachable and he was quick to see a joke. The thing that I liked most about him was his unpredictability. He was astonishingly skilful at dealing with people. He was easily moved by their misfortunes. For example one day we were going to visit friends in

Nain, a small town in the hills of Galilee. As we were approaching the town gate there was a corpse being carried out for burial. A widow was leading the procession of mourners and all the villagers were following her. We learned that the body was that of her only son, still a young lad. Jesus went up to the widow and told her to stop crying. I don't know why but she did. He went up to the coffin and touched it. The men carrying it stood still and Jesus said, "Young man, I command you, get up." The boy sat up and began to talk to his mother. Jesus seemed to understand by instinct what people meant rather than what they said.

I remember the time when a large crowd had been listening to Jesus on a hill near the Lake. As the day drew on we went to Jesus and said to him, "This is a desolate place and it is getting late. Send the crowds away so that they can go to the villages and buy food." I had already asked round to see if anybody had any food and had found that there were only five loaves and two small fish brought by one young lad who was not very keen on giving up his lunch. I told Jesus this and he looked up with the sort of half smile that was typical of him and said, "His food isn't needed. You feed them." We looked at each other wondering what to do next. Eventually I told Jesus that there was only this tiny amount of food available. I didn't think that this would be of any use in feeding such a crowd and was not expecting to be taken seriously. He asked me to bring it to him and, when I did, he looked up and gave thanks. He broke it up, put it into baskets and told us to take it round to the people. Everyone there had enough to eat and there were twelve baskets left over. We estimated that five thousand men together with women and children had been fed. The crowd was awestruck by what had happened and we began to hear murmurings that they wanted to make Jesus their king. When we looked round we found that Jesus had gone off by himself into the hills. We caught up with him and went with him to Caesarea Philippi. There were no crowds following this time.

When we were alone, Jesus asked us who the people thought he was. We all gave different answers which included John the Baptist, Jeremiah and Elijah. Out of the blue Jesus turned to us and asked, "Who do you think I am?" Without any hesitation Simon replied, "You are the Christ, the son of the living God." As he said it, I knew it was true. Jesus turned to Simon and said "You are truly blessed for you must have been told this by my father in Heaven". He then repeated what he had said when he first met Simon. "You are Peter and on this rock I will build my church." In Greek Peter means rock. I think many of us were at first jealous. This was especially true of me as it was my younger brother and I did not see why he should be picked out in this way. It took a little while for me to accept that he was far more of a leader than I was. Jesus later warned us of the sacrifices required to follow him.

One of the most amazing things about Jesus was his control of the elements. I remember two examples particularly. Once Jesus asked us to take him across the Lake in our boat. Without any warning, a violent storm blew up and waves broke over the boat. It was the worst storm I have ever been in on the lake with the waves actually breaking over the sides of the boat. Jesus was in the stern sleeping on a cushion. How anyone could sleep in the deafening noise and while getting soaked to the skin I do not know. Even I, a fisherman, thought my last moments had come. We woke him up screaming, "Lord save us, we are going to drown." He stood up and commanded the waves "Quiet, be still." He seemed to have no doubt that what he wanted would happen. Immediately the wind dropped and the sea calmed. He turned to us, almost with a pitying look, and said "Why are you so afraid? Do you still have no faith?" It was almost as if nothing could hurt him unless he permitted although later we realised how wrong this was. Even the elements could not harm him unless he allowed it. As we said at the time "Who is he? Even the wind and waves obey him." I remember that he went back to sleep.

On another occasion Jesus again told us to get in our boat and return across the lake to our home in Bethsaida. He would meet up with us later. It was hard work rowing against the wind and we were tired but many of us were experienced fishermen. Suddenly we saw a figure walking across the water. We thought it was a ghost and were terrified. At one stage the figure seemed to be walking right past us and we shouted out to it. The voice of Jesus called back to us "It's all right! It is me. Don't be afraid." Simon, well it would be him wouldn't it, answered "Lord, if it is you, ask me to walk to you on the water." We heard him say "Come" and Simon stood up, took off his robe, got out of the boat and started walking towards Jesus. Suddenly he realised what he was doing and, instead of looking at

Jesus, he looked down and began to sink. He screamed out "Lord save me" and Jesus reached out and caught him by the arms. Holding Simon in front of him, he said to him, "You don't have much faith do you? Why do you doubt me?" He lifted him back into the boat and Simon stood there, bedraggled and ashamed, looking very sorry for himself. In other circumstances it would have been funny. Jesus followed Simon into the boat and immediately the wind died down. We were thunderstruck and began to worship him saying, 'You really are the Son of God.'

All the time we were with Jesus he was teaching us. Mostly he used stories to illustrate his point and they were often very funny but they were always there for a purpose. My favourite was the one about a man with a log in his eye complaining about another who had a speck of sawdust in his. Often we didn't understand what he was trying to say until much later. What seemed to irritate Jesus most was pretence. He was critical of the Pharisees because, although outwardly very religious, inwardly they were full of their own righteousness. They followed him round trying to catch him breaking the Law, particularly in respect of the observance of the Sabbath and ritual cleanliness. They could not understand that he would sit and eat with people they thought of as unclean and, at first, I shared their view. He used to tell us the Law was made for man, not man for the Law. On one occasion towards the end of his life he called the teachers of the Law and the Pharisees 'white washed tombs' because their clean exterior hid so much that was empty and dirty. He was always opposed to outward display. He even once condemned Bethsaida, my hometown, for the lack of faith shown by its people in spite of the miracles that had taken place there.

His teaching could be hard. I remember when he told us that we should envy the poor, the hungry, those who mourn and the outcast from society. The rich and popular should be pitied. It took many years for me to understand what he meant. Early in his ministry he told a group of people listening to him who he was and what it would cost to follow him. Many of them went away because what he asked of them was too demanding. He was always asking his hearers to decide whether they believed in his teaching or not. When he was teaching, Jesus was a very fiery speaker. He used to get really worked up and no one was left in any doubt about the strength of his convictions. There was a huge contrast between his aggression as a speaker and his gentleness in dealing with people in need. I never saw him become impatient with anyone who had a real problem although he could give as good as he got with those who were trying to exploit him.

These were truly the golden days of our time with Jesus. We all got on well together. Simon became our spokesman if only because no one could keep my brother quiet. If ever a man spoke and acted before he thought, it was Simon. He, James and John became an inner group and occasionally went off alone with Jesus. For some reason this did not cause any jealousy but when Salome, the mother of James and John and Jesus' aunt, asked Jesus if they could have the best places in his kingdom, this was too much. To give them their due I think they were pretty fed up with what their mother had done but Salome was an ambitious woman Of course there were times when all was not sweetness and light like the occasion when we started discussing which one of us would be the most important. Jesus seemed to know our thoughts. He took a little child and said "Whoever welcomes this little child in my name welcomes me and whoever welcomes me welcomes him who sent me. The least among you will be the greatest." Jesus loved being with young people. He told us that if we wanted to enter the Kingdom of God, our faith must be the same as children have in their parents.

The only one of us who didn't really fit in was Judas Iscariot. He was obsessed by the idea that Jesus would drive Herod and the Romans out of his country. He was an outsider, a Judean, whereas the rest of us were from Galilee, and he seemed to hover on the edge of the group, impatient and angry. Judas looked after the money given to Jesus and we began to suspect that he was using it for his own purposes. In spite of this, it was amazing that people as different as we twelve got on so well.

My particular role seemed to be introducing people to Jesus as I had Simon. I remember bringing to him a party of Greeks who wanted to meet him. Jesus spent some time talking to them. At the end of their conversation something happened which none of us could understand. Jesus said aloud "I am deeply troubled. I could pray, Father save me from what lies ahead but that is the reason why I came to earth in the first place.

Father, bring honour to your name." As we listened we heard a voice from heaven saying, "I have already brought it glory and I will do so again." Some of us thought it was thunder and others that an angel had spoken but I had heard this voice before and was and still am sure that it was the voice of God.

Sometimes the twelve of us were sent out in pairs to do his work on our own. We were given very exact instructions about how we should behave. For example we were not to go into the houses of Gentiles or Samaritans or to stay in any village where we were not welcomed. We were told to say that the kingdom of God was near and to heal the sick, raise the dead, cleanse those with leprosy and drive out demons. We were always to heal people in his name. I will never forget the joy on people's faces when they realized that the problem they had had to bear for so long had gone. I will never tire of the honour of being able to help people in Jesus' name. None of us could understand how he was able to give us such power but we all knew that it was through him that we were able to do the things we did and we told those we helped that this was the case. We were to rely entirely on those we met for our food and accommodation. When we talked about our experiences with each other, we all seemed to be in a state of disbelief that we had been chosen for this work. It was an unimaginable privilege.

Although he was always pleasant to us, he could be very difficult when he felt people were trying to patronise or exploit him. On one occasion Simon, a Pharisee, invited Jesus to dinner with him. It would be difficult to imagine a less gracious host than Simon. He hardly greeted us and immediately went back to talking with his friends. We were in no doubt that Jesus was being set up for something. Anyway Jesus went and was reclining at the table. Suddenly a woman ran in. She was known to many there as a prostitute. She stood behind Jesus crying and she was in so much distress that she began to wet his feet with her tears. She then produced an alabaster jar of perfume. She dried his feet with her hair, kissed them and anointed them with the perfume.

The Pharisee, taken aback, said to himself, "If this man was a prophet, he would know what kind of woman she is and stop her touching him."

Jesus saw what the other guests were thinking and said to Simon, our host, "I have something to ask you. Two men owed money to a certain moneylender. One owed him 500 pieces of silver and the other 50. Neither of them had the money to pay him back, so he cancelled the debts of both. Now which of them will love him more?"

Simon replied, "I suppose the one who had the bigger debt."

"You are correct," said Jesus. Looking at the woman he said to Simon "See this woman kneeling in front of me. I came into your house. You did not give me any water to wash my feet, but she wet my feet with her tears and dried them with her hair. You did not give me a kiss of greeting but this woman, from the time I entered, has not stopped kissing my feet. You did not put oil on my head, but she has poured perfume on my feet. I tell you her many sins are forgiven – for she has shown me so much love. But a person who has little to be forgiven shows only little love." Jesus turned to her and said, "Your sins are forgiven." Other guests began to say among themselves "Who does this man think he is going round forgiving people their sins?" Jesus turned to the woman and told her "Your faith has saved you; go in peace."

Throughout the years I followed Jesus round I had tried to identify who Jesus was. Right from the time that John the Baptist had seen him when he came to be baptised, it was clear that he was someone special. If I had had any doubts, these were taken away when I heard that voice saying "This is my beloved son." The wonderful things he did at Cana and on so many occasions later confirmed that this was no ordinary man. What I couldn't work out was, if he was the Son of God as he claimed, why he had come to earth. When Simon responded to Jesus' question that he thought he was the 'Promised One', there was no denial. I learned, after Jesus' ascension, of the time about a week after Simon's declaration when he, James and John had gone with Jesus to the mountain top and seen Jesus as the Son of God living on earth. They heard the same voice I had heard on the banks of the Jordan saying "This is my beloved son." They were told they must not tell anyone of this experience until after Jesus had been raised from the dead. What they made of this instruction at the time I have no idea.

I remember that time well. The nine of us who were left were surrounded by a great crowd who expected us to be able to work the same sort of miracles as Jesus. One of them had brought his son who had been struck dumb for healing. He was possessed by a demon and threw himself on the ground, foamed at the mouth and gnashed his teeth. We were unable to help him. A crowd had gathered and some Teachers of the Law were arguing with them. The situation was getting out of hand. When Jesus came back and saw what was happening, he said "You faithless people. When will you learn to believe? How long must I put up with you?" He called the boy over and immediately he fell to the ground foaming at the mouth.

Jesus asked the boy's father "How long has this been happening?"

"Since he was very small" he replied. "Have mercy and help him. Do whatever you can."

"What do you mean 'Do anything you can'? Anything is possible if a person believes."

"I believe. Help me not to doubt." the father answered. Jesus turned to the boy and commanded the evil spirit to come out of him. The spirit screamed, threw the boy into another convulsion and left him. The boy lay completely motionless and those watching thought he was dead. Jesus took his hand and pulled him to his feet. Later, when we were alone with Jesus we asked why we couldn't help the lad. "This kind can only be brought out by prayer" he explained.

I don't think any of us believed Jesus, when he repeatedly told us that he must suffer rejection and other terrible things and then die. He was still telling us this the week before his death. We ignored him when he said that, after three days, he would rise from the dead. Simon even took him aside and told him not to talk nonsense. If he could do the sort of things he was doing, he could certainly prevent his own death. We all knew something extraordinary was going to happen but none of us knew what. As time went by our sense of anticipation grew stronger. It wasn't until after his resurrection that I began to understand why he came to earth.

This was not the only time Jesus did things which there could only be explained as a miracle. One occasion that sticks in my mind is when we went across the lake to the country of the Gerasenes. For once we seemed to have escaped the crowds. As Jesus was getting out of the boat a man called out to him "Why are you bothering me Jesus, Son of the Most High God? I beg you, please don't torture me!" As he screamed this out he fell to the ground in front of Jesus. We heard later that this man was demon possessed and lived in the cemetery. Often he was chained up but he snapped the chains and broke free. He was naked and uncontrollable.

"What is your name?" asked Jesus. "Legion" he replied for the man was filled with many demons. The demons kept begging Jesus not to send them into the bottomless pit. A large herd of pigs was feeding on the hillside nearby and the demons pleaded that Jesus would let them take possession of the pigs. Jesus agreed. The demons came out of the man and entered into the pigs and the whole herd plunged down the hill and into the lake where they drowned. The sight of the pigs suddenly breaking out of their pen, charging headlong down the field and jumping off the cliffs far out in to the sea is one I will not forget. I often wonder what the owner of the herd made of it all.

When the herdsmen saw this they rushed into the town to tell the people what had happened. A crowd gathered and they saw Legion sitting clothed and quiet at Jesus' feet. They talked among themselves about what the herdsmen had seen and in the end begged Jesus to leave their country. Jesus went to get into the boat and Legion asked if he might come with him but Jesus told him to go back to his family and tell them of the wonderful thing God has done for him. The man did exactly what he was asked telling everyone in the city what had happened.

This was not the only occasion that Jesus healed someone who was not a Jew. We remembered the healing of the deaf and dumb man and the feeding of the four thousand in the Decapolis, the Samaritan Woman at the Well and the expulsion of the demons from Legion into the herd of swine. We didn't understand until much later why Jesus was interested in them. It was only after his death that we realized that he came to save everyone, not just those of our faith.

This life went on for nearly three years. As time went on it became clear that it was his intention to go to Jerusalem for the feast of the Passover. The twelve of us were much opposed to this as he had violently upset the Pharisees and the Priests. In Galilee we were relatively safe but this would not be the case in the city. However nothing would make him change his mind. We dreaded what was going to happen.

I have talked for enough now. I will tell you what happened when we went up to Jerusalem for the Passover another time.

Martha

I was ten years old when Mother died giving birth to Lazarus. She was a wonderful woman who had given Mary, my sister and me a very happy childhood. Because I was keen to help, she had involved me in the housekeeping and I was very domesticated for my age. I preferred helping Mother with the cooking to going out with my friends. Mary is 18 months younger than me. She was and is dark and slim and very attractive. Beside her I am plain with short curly hair, slightly plump but with a smooth clear complexion that is my best feature. Mother and I had been such friends and we had been so looking forward to the new baby's arrival. I had promised her that I would help to look after him for we were both certain that it was going to be a boy. Mother and Father had been trying so long for a son to complete the family. Lazarus was everything we had hoped for but Mother was gone. I was really going to have to help with bringing him up. My aunt lived nearby and would be there as much as she could but she had her own family.

Father called Mary and me into a family conference. We were all shattered by what had happened but we had to be practical. Mary had never helped much in the house, partially because I gave her so little chance. Father of course had to go on earning a living and he asked me if I could cope or if he should employ a house-keeper. Neither Mary nor I were keen on that idea and in, any event, the chance to run my own home was very inviting. We employed a wet nurse from the village and I took over the housekeeping; never did anyone keep a home so clean and tidy. Father sometimes said that I was overdoing it but I took no notice. Meals were on time and I put my soul into preparing them. Initially Mary offered to help but I am afraid I didn't encourage her. I was proud to be coping on my own and I used to boast about it. Mary was better at playing with Lazarus who grew to be a lovely kid. He was good-looking but, more important, good-natured. He was happy amusing himself and had lots of pals. Mary spent her time painting and with her friends.

Mother and Father had met Mary and Joseph when they used to visit us on their way to and from their visits to the feast of the Passover in Jerusalem. They lived in Nazareth in Galilee and Joseph was a carpenter. Mary was lovely, very pretty with shiny brown hair just begin-ning to go grey. She made a huge fuss of my sister and me. When Mother and Father first met them, she had only one son, Jesus. As the years went by her family increased and she ended up with five sons and three daughters. Joseph was a quiet man but you could see by the look in his eyes that he adored Mary. I grew very friendly with Jesus. He was 7 years older than me but never made me feel I was too young to bother about. He tried to persuade me to go on walks with him but I was usually too busy with my domestic duties. Mary, my sister, always jumped at the chance if she was asked. He was far too attractive to waste himself on someone like me. Mary and Jesus, with the rest of the family, visited soon after Mother died and they were so sweet. Mary did all she could to help although there was no real need and Jesus made a big fuss of me.

The annual visit was a highlight of each year. Father died when I was 20 and Mary and Joseph came down specially to see what they could do to help. They offered to find us a house near them in Nazareth but my sister and I decided to stay where we were. Mary in particular wanted to stay near her friends. Life went on as normal but as I grew older; I began to feel that I was missing out on life. My whole existence was bound up in the house and I began to resent it. My chance of having a family of my own was passing by. But what would happen to Lazarus if I moved out?

Mary was very attractive to men, good looking and lively company, and there was a constant succession of callers. However they all went away disappointed. She didn't want to move from home and leave me on my own but I think the real reason was that she was in love with Jesus and found nobody to measure up to him. He was very happy to treat her as a friend but didn't want to settle down with her. I too was in love with Jesus but in a helpless sort of way. I was content just to be in his company. I sometimes imagined that Jesus would come to where I did the cooking and say that he could not live without me but I knew this was a dream. It helped pass the time pleasantly though. Only once was there anyone else and he lived by the coast. I sent him away as I couldn't leave Mary and Lazarus on their own.

When Jesus was 30, he gave up his work as a carpenter to be a full time teacher and healer. He started travelling round Galilee and soon gathered a band of followers round him. Even in Bethany we heard stories of the healings he achieved and of his teaching. He became a well-known figure. Twelve of his friends were particularly close to him and sometimes they used to come with him on his visits. Of course they could not stay in the house but we gave them most of their meals. On one occasion when they came I was not feeling myself. The work seemed never ending and, while Mary sat at his feet and talked with him, I was busy cooking. It all got too much for me and I went and asked Jesus to tell Mary to come and help me. I can remember his reply as if it was yesterday. "Martha, Martha, you are worried and upset about many things, but only one thing is needed. Mary has chosen the better path and it will not be taken away from her." I felt as if I had been kicked in the teeth. Everything I was good at was being thrown in my face by the one I loved. For a time there was a coolness between Jesus and me. I am afraid I began to be jealous of Mary. She was so much at ease with people and I found it difficult to relax with those I did not know well or to know what to say when in company.

Fortunately neither of these slight estrangements lasted and Jesus continued to visit us. Two years later Jesus came to stay on his way back from a visit to Jerusalem. He brought his friends including a number of women who followed them around looking after them. Mary, his mother, also came with her friends from Nazareth. Soon after Jesus and his friends left, Lazarus was taken ill with a fever. At first it did not seem serious but it grew steadily worse. We sent messengers to Jesus asking him to come and heal Lazarus. He did not arrive back in time and Lazarus grew steadily worse and died. That was a terrible day. Mary and I clung to each other in total despair. We buried him in the family tomb on the day after his death. Both Mary and I felt badly let down, as we were sure that, if Jesus had arrived in time, he could have healed Lazarus. He, our beloved friend, had not been there when we needed him. The neighbours were wonderful and there were always some of them with us sharing our grief. For the first time in my life I let them look after me. I was in a state of despair. I had given up the best years of my life to bring up Lazarus and now he was dead. I just did not understand and I could not stop crying.

When Jesus came four days after the death, I went out to meet him outside the village. You know the old saying that, when someone dies, for the first three days his spirit stays by the body. After that the spirit went to the hereafter and the body started to decay. I was very angry that Jesus had not come sooner and could not prevent myself being short with him as I told him "Lord, if you had been here, my brother would not have died. But I know that even now God will give you whatever you ask." I really believed what I said although there was no good reason why I should. Jesus turned round to me and said quietly so that only I could hear "Your brother will rise again". As he said this I could see tears in his eyes. I thought that Jesus was talking about the life to come and that I was being mocked but he seemed to have read my mind. "I am the resurrection and the life. Anyone who believes in me, even though he dies naturally, will live; whoever believes in me will never die but enjoy eternal life. Do you believe this?" The answer came almost without thought. "Yes Lord. I believe you are the Christ, the Son of God, who was sent by God into the world." I had never thought in these terms before and was surprised at what I said but I realised that I truly did believe that Jesus was the Messiah.

I went in and called for Mary, my sister, telling her that Jesus was asking for her and she ran to Jesus. Jesus had not entered the village but was still at the place where I had met him. The people who had surrounding Mary all trailed after her. When Mary arrived she fell at his feet and told him "Lord, if you had been here, my brother would not have died." When Jesus saw her and those with her, he was visibly moved and asked "Where have you laid him?" "Come and see" we said and led him to the tomb. By now he was weeping openly. Some of the mourners commented on how much Jesus must have loved Lazarus but others blamed him for not preventing him from dying.

We got to the tomb. Jesus instructed that the stone at the entrance be rolled away. I reminded him that the body was already four days old but Jesus quietly reminded me of his promise that I would see the glory of God if I trusted him. The stone was removed and the smell of death was all around. Jesus spoke "Father, thank you for hearing me. I knew that you always hear me but I said this for the benefit of the people standing here, so that they will believe that you sent me." He then called in a loud voice "Lazarus, come out." A few moments later he struggled out, his hands and feet still wrapped in strips of linen and a cloth around his face. There was utter silence followed by gasps of amazement as Lazarus emerged and then a buzz of excited conversation. You could hear the "Did you see that?" and "How did he do it?" all round the people gathered there. All Jesus said was "Take off the grave clothes and let him go."

I just did not know what to do, whether to go to Lazarus or to thank Jesus. I went to my brother who was being helped out of his grave clothes and into normal clothing. Fortunately this had not yet been burnt. I embraced him with tears running down my face. Mary and I danced round together in total ecstasy. Jesus seemed to have disappeared and it was only later that we could find him to thank him. I think we both felt guilty because we had not trusted him. He looked at us as if he understood and, as we hugged and kissed him, he seemed to understand exactly what we were thinking.

What a party we had that night. All those who had come to mourn stayed to share our joy. Jesus himself seemed as happy and relaxed as I ever saw him. His party set off again next morning. Some of those who had been there when Lazarus walked out of the tomb were still around and they could not believe what they had seen. Explanations ranged from him having been asleep to Jesus being possessed by the devil. Mary and I both said that Jesus was the Son of God but no one would listen to us. We were worried because we knew that what had taken place might cause trouble for Jesus if he returned to Jerusalem. The High Priest and the Pharisees would certainly hear about the raising of a dead man and would put the worst possible interpretation on it.

One of the women who had come with Jesus was Mary Magdalene. She came to help me with all the work and we became very friendly. I asked her what had happened when Jesus got the message about Lazarus' death. She said that he told them "This sickness will not lead to death. It is for God's glory. I, God's son, will be glorified through it." Jesus loved the whole family, yet he stayed where he was two more days. She said that this had astounded them all. He then told them he was going to return to Judea. Some of his followers warned him that his life was in danger there but he would not change his mind. He explained that he could let others determine how he should live his life and told them "Our friend Lazarus has fallen asleep and I am going there to wake him up." Some of his disciples misunderstood and thought he was talking about sleep at night but he meant that Lazarus had died so he told them so. Thomas, one of the disciples thought they would all be killed by the Temple authorities but they came anyway.

I spoke to Lazarus later and asked him what had happened while he was away from us. He told me how he had felt ill and gradually grew less able to stay awake. He went into a deep sleep and passed into a different place. All was light and there was the sound of beautiful music. He was seated on grass beside a river that flowed slowly past. There was no time, no hunger, just rest and peace. Suddenly he heard Jesus calling his name "Lazarus, come out". He woke up and found himself lying in a tomb wrapped in funeral clothes. He struggled to get up and go to Jesus and heard him tell the mourners to free him from his bindings. He walked out into the sunlight where Mary and I met him. Some of the neighbours told me that Lazarus would never die as he had already been raised from the dead but I didn't believe this.

For a while Lazarus was a bit of a freak show but soon people were treating him normally again. The news of Lazarus being brought back to life rapidly reached the High Priest and we later heard that a special meeting of his Council was called. There was great concern about the miracles being performed by Jesus. They were worried that everyone would believe in him and the role of the Temple and Sanhedrin (The Priestly Council) would be brought into disrepute. Caiaphas, the High Priest, told them that it was better that Jesus die as a sacrifice than that many others did so because they rebelled against Roman rule as a result of Jesus' teaching. He also thought that, if Jesus died, it would unite all the Jews throughout the world. The Priests began to lay traps for Jesus and he could no longer travel openly around the country.

The last time we saw Jesus was some months later. He came to visit us with his disciples on his way to Jerusalem to celebrate the Passover. He appeared preoccupied as if there was a great weight on his shoulders. I asked him what was wrong but he just gave that gentle smile that was characteristic of him. We were all invited to dinner with some friends and I helped serve while Mary and Lazarus sat down at table with the guests. I noticed Mary watching Jesus and suddenly she got up from her place and left the room. A few minutes later she came back. Mary went up to Jesus, fell on her knees at his feet and poured a bottle of scent over them. It was pure Nard, a very expensive perfume; there must have been about a pint and, used normally, it would have lasted for months. She then used her lovely, long, lustrous hair, her pride and joy, to dry his feet. I can still feel the stunned silence followed by the babble of excited comment as Mary got up. She told me later that she could see that Jesus was terrified of what would happen in Jerusalem and she wanted to show that she understood who he was and what he must go through. This was the only way she could think of to show her love for him and her gratitude to him for raising Lazarus from the dead.

Some of the disciples, Judas Iscariot in particular, complained saying that the perfume should have been sold and the proceeds given to the poor. Jesus told them, "Leave her alone! She meant to keep it until the day of my burial. You will always have the poor among you, but I will not be with you much longer." A large crowd had gathered outside not only to see Jesus but also my brother who had been raised from the dead.

Later I heard that the Chief Priests began to plot to murder both Jesus and Lazarus from that day.

As he had done before, Jesus stayed with us when he was visiting Jerusalem. This didn't mean we saw much of him. He left early in the morning and arrived back late at night. I left food out for him and when we looked next morning it was gone. We did not go to Jerusalem that year because we were worried about Lazarus' safety and so we only heard what happened second hand. The news of Jesus' death was not entirely a surprise although it was still a great shock. We were told of his resurrection by a number of pilgrims travelling back to their homes from Jerusalem. Both Mary and I truly believed that Jesus was the Christ, the Son of the Living God. In spite of all we had heard him say, we had not grasped that he must die so that others might receive eternal life. In a sense Caiaphas had been right in saying that Jesus must die so that many others might live. We were able to comfort each other in the dark times and, as we began to understand the purpose of Jesus' life, to rejoice together. We continued to live in Bethany using our home as a refuge for those in danger or those needing to rest. I even let Mary help with the catering and it was much better working together. She told me how upset she used to get when, every time she offered to help me, I brushed her off without even thanking her Most of the disciples came to visit us at one time or another, as did Mary, Jesus' mother.

Lazarus went up to Jerusalem to live with Jesus' followers but was unable to stay as the High Priest and his advisers still believed that they needed to kill him because of his miraculous recovery. Eventually he made his way to Cyprus and we heard from him from time to time when someone from there travelled to Jerusalem. He helped to start a group of disciples of Jesus and it was exciting to hear how this grew. He got married but we never knew if he had any children.

Friends kept us in touch with what was happening in Jerusalem. We heard about the early church, of how they shared their possessions and food and giving their time praying and helping the needy. We heard about the coming of the Holy Spirit and the wonderful things being done in Jesus' name. We listened to the news coming from the city and praised God for all that was happening. We had seen what Jesus could do and were not surprised that his disciples were now able to use his power.

Mary Magdalene

If someone had told me that I would end my life following a religious teacher and trying to copy his lifestyle, I would have thought him mad. I was born in the poor section of Magdala on the Sea of Galilee and Mother was never certain who my father was. She was a lady of the streets. I learned early that, as soon as I was old enough, I would be sent out to earn my living like her. Being reasonably attractive with unusual thick red hair, I would have had little difficulty in doing so but I was determined not to follow in my mother's footsteps. From time to time men came to stay with us but never for long. Their departure was usually noisy and, more often than not, Mother was in a sad state physically and mentally after they had gone. At least none of them came after me but I was very careful. At just over thirty Mother seemed like an old woman and had nothing to look forward to. If I did become a prostitute the chances of my keeping anything I earned and being able to change my way of life later were small. Either my mother or a pimp would make sure of that.

When I was fifteen I took what few clothes that I had and ran away around the lake to Capernaum. I had no idea how I was going to manage but anything was better than earning my living on my back. I slept in the open and spent my days scavenging and begging. I was at constant risk from the fishermen but somehow managed to stay out of their clutches. However this limited my chances of finding food. I was permanently hungry and always tired and I knew I would not be able to go on as I was for much longer. I once saw my reflection in some water and the hopeful young girl had been replaced by a drab lank-haired shadow. I had no hope and I prayed to whatever God there was out there that my life might be ended.

One morning when, as usual, I was out on the streets trying to find food, a group of young men came past me. As they passed I called out asking for help and they naturally thought I was offering myself to them. Their leader, a good looking fellow of about thirty, turned and looked at me. The time when anyone would see me as an object of physical desire had long gone but he studied me and seemed to be looking right through me. I felt cold and ashamed and waited to be condemned. Instead he gazed straight into my eyes and told me to follow him. There was a sort of magnetism about him and, as I had nothing to lose, I obeyed him. They stopped for their lunch and, without any action on my part, I was given food. None of them, men or women, patronised me and none of the men looked at me suggestively.

I stayed with them and made friends with a group of women who were travelling around with him. All of them were older than me and fairly well off. They treated me with kindness and made a point of looking after me. I became especially close with two of them, Susanna and Joanna, over the next few weeks. Joanna was the wife of a high official in King Herod's household.

I stayed with this group for a while and was amazed at what I saw. As they went round the country, their leader who was named Jesus taught people and healed those who were in need. He never put pressure on them to accept what he said but he spoke with such authority that the natural thing was to obey. I longed to talk with him but did not have the courage to approach him. As I got properly fed and, for the first time in my life felt secure, some of my good looks returned. I wondered what the catch was but no one even looked at me suggestively, let alone propositioned me. Yet these were real men with as much vitality as any I had ever seen. Up to then most men had only looked at me as an object of lust.

One day Jesus himself came to talk to me. He asked if I was feeling rested I managed to answer yes. I was almost dumb in his presence. He explained that he would not talk seriously to me until I was myself again. If he had spoken earlier, he said, I would not have been able to respond. I told him about my life to then in as harsh a way as I could, intending to shock him. There was never a look of shock or condemnation on his face. When I had finished, he looked straight at me and told me that I was free from any guilt for my past life. Later it was said that seven demons had been driven out of me and I think it was because of the sort of life that I had lived. Anyway I knew that I had been changed for ever. If Jesus had taken the time and trouble to help me, I couldn't be completely worthless.

Jesus told me that it was up to me what I did with my future. I could if I wished follow him. He would understand if I decided to go my own way although he would be disappointed. He would make arrangements for me to go to a good home as a maid. He touched me on my hair and it was as if I had been struck. I cannot describe the feelings that surged through me but I felt different. All the past hurts seemed to leave and I became the woman that I was meant to be. I no longer felt ashamed of my past – it was as if it had happened to someone else. I did not doubt the truth of what he was saying. It did not take me long to choose. I thanked him for his love and begged him to allow me to stay with him and learn from his teaching. I had nowhere else to go and the women especially had been really friendly. I was not used to this and told him so.

He smiled, a smile like a sunbeam breaking through the clouds, and told me to follow him but warned me that hard times were coming and that my resolve would be tested to the limit. He said no more and passed on. We spent the next few months travelling around Galilee. The crowds following him seemed to grow daily. Occasionally he and his close friends disappeared into the hills but we always found him again. The thing that most struck me about him was his consideration for other people. I remember him saying "Come to me anyone who is tired or unable to cope with life's difficulties and I will give you rest. The load I place on you is light. Let me teach you as I am humble and gentle and you will find ease for your souls. What I ask you to do is tailored to meet your personal needs and will not overburden you." He never told us that following him would be easy. He once said "Shoulder your cross and follow me." It wasn't until later that the real significance of this dawned on us. He warned us that, if we wanted to serve him, this would be costly. If anyone tried to do what we wanted with his own life, he would waste it. If he gave his life to Jesus, he would discover what its real purpose was.

To Jesus everyone was an individual and, as he had dealt with me on my own, so he treated each person he met. He went where he was really needed. It was some time before I realised he was not universally popular. Groups of priests and Pharisees in their odd robes and ridiculous hats used to appear, listen and make notes about what he was saying. Often they questioned him and it was as if they were trying to catch him out. On the Sabbath they watched him more closely to see if he obeyed the Sabbath Laws. I began to realise that things could not go on as they were.

I remember the stories he used to tell. Some of them were very funny and some sad. All of them had a point that he wanted to draw out. My favourite was about the Good Samaritan who helped his neighbour when no one else would. Jesus was always careful to ensure that the people with him were looked after. On one occasion when we were up in the hills, he fed a crowd of about five thousand from five loaves and two fish brought for his lunch by a young lad. I was surprised sometimes by the ingratitude of some of those he healed. They came blind, dumb, lame or mentally disturbed and he cured them. Some went away with hardly a word of thanks. I remember a group of ten lepers who were cleansed by him; only one came back to thank him.

There was one incident which stuck in my mind. To get away from the crowds Jesus had led the disciples and the women who travelled round with him round the Lake to the region of Tyre and Sidon. Normally Jews did not go to these areas. A Gentile woman approached him calling out, "Lord, Son of David, have mercy on me! My daughter is possessed by a demon and is suffering terribly." I remember thinking how odd it was that a Gentile should call Jesus Lord and Son of David and that she should ask mercy for herself when it was her daughter who was suffering.

Jesus didn't say even a word to her. His disciples urged him to send her away because she was bothering us all with her begging. Jesus turned and looked at her. "I was sent only to help the people of Israel – God's lost sheep – not the Gentiles." I remember thinking how fortunate I was that Jesus had bothered with me. The woman would not be put off and pleaded again, "Lord, help me."

"It isn't right to take food from the children and feed it to the dogs", he said, meaning that he had come to help the Jews. She immediately replied, "Yes Lord but even dogs are allowed to eat the crumbs that fall from the master's table."

I could see that Jesus was startled by what she said and he turned to her again. "Woman, your faith is great. Your request is granted." We heard later that her daughter was healed at the very moment Jesus spoke. Some of those with me explained that, if the Pharisees heard about what had happened and how he had healed a non-Jew, they would use it to discredit Jesus.

On one occasion on our way back from Jerusalem where we gone for the Feast of the Tabernacles, we visited the home of Martha and Mary in Bethany. Jesus had been a friend of the family for many years. A large party went including the twelve disciples and a group of us women who looked after him. Soon after we left, we were caught up by a messenger who told Jesus that Lazarus was very ill. We all expected that Jesus would rush back to Bethany but he stayed where he was for two more days. To say the least of it, this seemed perverse. Jesus told us "Our friend Lazarus has fallen asleep; but I am going to wake him up." Someone said to him that if Lazarus was asleep, he would wake up naturally but Jesus knew Lazarus was dead. Yet when he did arrive, he wept when he was told the news. He went to the tomb where Lazarus had been laid and asked that the stone covering the entrance be removed. Martha told him that he had been in the tomb four days. I saw the servants looking at each other before, reluctantly, they moved the stone. The stench of death as the tomb was opened was overpowering. Jesus prayed and called on Lazarus to come out. Shortly afterwards he emerged, still wrapped up in the burial clothes and with a cloth over his face. In any other circumstances it would have been a hilarious sight. Many people saw this miracle including some of the priests.

It was there that I met Mary, Jesus' mother, for the first time. She and some of her other seven children had come back from the feast in Jerusalem with Jesus and our group. Her husband had died some time earlier. She was a beautiful woman who often seemed totally lost in her thoughts. There was a sadness about her as if she knew something we didn't.

Jesus was by far the most attractive man I ever met – not only good looking but also a wonderful companion. If he had asked me I would have gone with him without hesitation but I knew it would never happen. There was something separate about him which prevented him forming this sort of relationship. He was always cheerful and the comments he made were unexpected and challenging. He had a keen sense of humour. Some of the remarks he made about the people he met were very funny but I never heard him say anything hurtful about any one. Normally he was calm and self possessed although on occasions he was extremely angry with those who he thought were harming other people. When he was speaking to large crowds he was at times very direct and forceful. He could use his voice like a musical instrument, alternately shouting and speaking in a whisper. He was determined to get his message across, a message he considered of vital importance. He put his whole body and soul into doing so, gesticulating and shaking his head to give emphasis. When he was teaching just his friends he always spoke quietly.

We went back to Jerusalem some months later. Although Jesus had not told us he was definitely going to the Passover in Jerusalem, we started to move in that direction. We went through Jericho and two amazing incidents occurred there. As we went through the town we suddenly saw a man hanging out of a sycamore tree. He was a comical sight, well dressed and not sure if he wanted to be seen or not and he looked as if he would fall out of the tree at any minute. The people around us told us that he was a tax collector but Jesus didn't hesitate to call up to him. He hurried to come down. He was a tiny little man, only about four and a half feet tall. Jesus spoke to him and we went to his house for the night. He immediately promised to give half of his money to the poor and to repay any money he had collected illegally four fold. When we left next morning he was already planning how to contact those he had swindled.

On our way out of the town there was a blind man sitting by the roadside begging. He asked why there were so many people around and was told that the teacher Jesus was passing by. At once he started calling out. "Lord, Son of David, help me." The crowd yelled at him to be quiet but he shouted all the louder. Jesus stopped and called to him.

"What do you want me to do for you?" This seemed an odd question because it was obvious what he wanted but Jesus always respected a person's right to choose. It was only later that I realised the courage the man would need to set out on a new life if his sight was restored. He made a comfortable living from his begging. Jesus touched his eyes and immediately he received his sight. Jesus told him not to return to his village. The man was called was named Bartimaeus and he came with us to Jerusalem. I asked him why he continued to call out when the crowd was telling him to shut up. He replied that he was not going to miss the one chance he had to get his sight back and no one was going to stop him calling out. He had become blind when he fell and banged his head when he was ten years old.

We returned to Bethany for a few days and on our last evening there we were sitting having dinner. Suddenly Mary, Martha's sister, rushed in and knelt by Jesus. She produced a large jar of expensive perfume, poured it over his feet and wiped them dry with her hair. Some of the apostles, particularly Judas, regarded what Mary had done as waste but I was moved to tears by what I thought was a gesture of pure love. Jesus too was moved by what Mary had done and told those who were complaining that she had anointed him in preparation for his burial. "The poor would always be there but He was only with us for a short time." What they made of this I have no idea.

The next day we left for Jerusalem.

The Centurion in Galilee

It was the best posting I ever had. The people were mostly friendly and the duties were light. So long as there were no problems, nobody interfered with me. Occasionally the procurator came from Caesarea for a holiday by the lake but usually he brought his own bodyguard. It was very rare for any of my men to request a move which showed just how good a billet it was. We were based in a camp by the lake just outside Capernaum but most of us lived out and only went there when we were on duty.

I had been in Palestine with my legion for about ten years. Previously I served in Gaul where I had been brought up. My father was in the army before me and had been sent from Rome while still young. I don't think he ever went back to his home. He had a good life but in Gaul there was always fighting. If it wasn't the locals rising up against us, it was invaders from across the border. The commanders in Gaul tended to be ambitious so it suited them to be involved in military action. Things were very different in Galilee. It was regarded as a pre-retirement posting where an officer who had served the empire well was sent to spend his last few years of service. It gave him the chance to make money for himself.

This isn't to say that everything in Galilee was easy. There were two main provinces inhabited by the Jews, Galilee where I was and Judea including Samaria further to the South. The people in each province were very different. In Galilee it was live and let live. In Judea and particularly in the main city of Jerusalem, the people were controlled by the priests from the Temple. They were a touchy lot; they had a very strict set of laws handed down to them through many generations. For example they had one day a week called the Sabbath that was special. No one was allowed to do any sort of work or to travel more than a short distance from home on the Sabbath. The strictness of the rules that were applied was absurd. In Galilee, at least away from the towns, things were fairly relaxed but in Judea the Law was much more closely observed. There was a partic-ular sect known as the Pharisees who prided them-selves on their strict observance of the Law and they constantly stirred up trouble among their own people and also with the Romans about what in their view was failure to observe it. These Pharisees went round in the most extraordinary clothes and seemed to have set themselves a divine obstacle race that, if success-fully completed, would lead them directly to heaven. It didn't stop them being totally unscrupulous in their dealings with the Romans. We had learnt never to trust anything they told us.

I settled in Galilee very quickly. It was always interesting to get to know the natives and there were many opportunities for doing so. However one first had to learn the language, which was a local dialect of Aramaic. When a visitor from Judea came, it was as if they were speaking a different tongue although in fact they were using the same vocabulary. I set about teaching myself to speak the Galilean version and made quick progress, as I seem to have a gift for languages. This had two benefits; firstly I could go out and have conversations with the locals and secondly it impressed my superiors. I was promoted to centurion which was a big step up for me. I was no longer required to do the dirty jobs that fall the way of the ordinary soldier and I got better pay, rations and quarters.

We were not responsible for policing in Galilee. Law and Order was the job of Herod Antipas, the King, who had his own police force to help him. Now here was a real nasty specimen. He was as treacherous as a whole barrelful of snakes. He traded on the fact that according to him he had been a friend of the emperor and he had certainly spent a period in Rome. If we displeased him he would threaten to report us to his friend although I never heard of him actually doing so. Totally unscrupulous he was a man to be avoided. He controlled his territory with great strictness and, if he considered we had interfered with his authority, would immediately complain to the procurator, with whom he was not on speaking terms. He had built himself a vast palace by the lake and renamed Gennesaret, the town nearby, in honour of the emperor Tiberius. The town was growing rapidly as his whole government moved there with him. Antipas was loathed by the people. He was reputed to have cut off the head of a Jewish prophet because of a commitment he made to Salome, a dancing girl and the daughter of Herodias, Antipas' current mistress who had previously been the wife of his brother Philip.

Our task was to ensure that there were no rebellions against the emperor and to help in collecting taxes. So far as Rome was concerned we were detached from the garrison at Caesarea in Judea. We had time on our hands so I spent my time learning about the local way of life. I was especially interested in their religion. The Jews believed they were a 'Chosen' people who had been led by God to their promised land where they now were. When they had first arrived many centuries before they had been in total command but a combination of failure to worship their God as the one and only deity and poor leadership had destroyed this relationship. There had been long periods when they had been taken captive and forced to live in foreign countries and, of course, the Romans now occupied their country. The High Priest and the Council in Jerusalem were preparing for their saviour, the Messiah, who would lead them to victory over their enemies and restore to them control of their country. This 'Messiah' was expected shortly. Meanwhile they tried to observe the Law, the strict code of conduct that had been handed down to them although they didn't seem to observe it in their dealings with us. I used to hear at the regular meetings of the centurions in the province of what they got up to. Nothing was off limits in their efforts to exploit the Romans. One of their problems was that they were always looking back rather than forward.

I began to have some sympathy with their religion. I preferred the idea of one all-powerful God who had made and was in control of heaven and earth, to our pantheon of deities. We could never be sure we had addressed the right one. The Jews, his 'chosen people', had been given the gift of free will and had used it to ignore the Law. If only they could obey this Law, their position in the country would be restored. As a soldier I was keen on the idea of a set of rules but I recognised that it was impossible for anyone to follow them completely. The answer to this was that once a year in the Temple in Jerusalem which was the centre of their religion, on the 'Day of Atonement' a big ceremony took place. Sacrifices were made and, as a result, all the misdeeds of the Jews were wiped away. This was far better than worshipping a God who did not seem to do anything for you. Our gods were supposed to guarantee us victory in battle but, as far as I could see, the things that really mattered were discipline and training.

I began to go to the synagogue and was impressed by what they did. They really tried to look after each other and there was a true spirit of companionship. The synagogue I went to was in Capernaum. They were trying to raise funds to put up a new building as the existing one was falling down and past repair but times were hard and there was not much money around to buy materials. I was able to help by getting them bricks from our camp, which we would never use, and by giving some of my own savings. The new building was completed and was a great boon to them. The community gradually accepted me although I could not become a full member of their religion without going through some ceremonies including circumcision which did not appeal to me at all. I became friendly with a woman who went to the synagogue and we started a relationship although there was never the possibility of marriage

After I had been going to the synagogue for some time a new teacher started to come. His name was Jesus and he was a remarkable man. He spent his time going round the villages near the Lake and had a reputation as a healer. My servant Joseph, a remarkable man who always knew what was going on, told me about him and I saw him with my own eyes cure people of blindness and lameness It was difficult to talk to him as a crowd of his followers always surrounded him. He used to teach on the Sabbath. He taught as one who had authority with none of the 'perhaps' and 'maybes' that peppered the teaching of the other rabbis. I used to look forward to him speaking as he had a real message to get across.

Joseph was a great help to me and our relationship was more that of friends rather than master and servant. He ensured my life ran smoothly and that I knew what was going on in the area for which I was responsible. He was only a young man and he was suddenly taken ill. He was paralysed and his skin was covered in boils. I had all the best doctors, both Roman and local, to see him but none of them were able to help. Joseph begged me to have Jesus fetched and in desperation I set out to find him. Eventually I met with him on the beach just outside Capernaum. Jesus was about 30 years old, dark haired and good-looking. His most striking features were his eyes, which were deep brown and seemed able to penetrate into my inner being. He had a mouth with turned up corners, always seeming ready to laugh. I was with one of the leaders from the synagogue and he introduced me and was good enough to tell of how I had helped in his synagogue. I plunged straight in. "Lord, my servant lies at home paralysed and in terrible pain."

Jesus didn't hesitate in saying he would come and heal him. This was not what I expected to happen, as I was sure that Jesus did not need to see him to make him better. I replied, "Sir, I do not deserve to have you come and visit my home. Just say the word, and my servant will be healed. For I am a man used to accepting orders and having my own commands obeyed without question."

Jesus looked astonished and I wondered what I had done. He turned to his followers. "I tell you the truth; I haven't seen faith like this anywhere in Israel. Many will come from all over the world and will enter the kingdom of heaven with Abraham, Isaac and Jacob. But numerous Israelites, the people for whom the kingdom was prepared, will never become members of this kingdom and will spend eternity wailing and gnashing their teeth." Then turning to me he said, "Go! It will be just as you asked it should be."

I am not sure I understood what Jesus had said to his followers but I turned and left for home. When I got there I found that my servant had been healed at the very same time that Jesus had spoken to me.

Obviously after this I followed the doings of Jesus with great interest and met him from time to time. My colleague in Jerusalem told me of how very distressed the High Priest was with how this new teacher was behaving and, when Jesus said he was going to Jerusalem, I tried to dissuade him. I was unsuccessful and I was not surprised to hear that the High Priest had captured him and persuaded Pontius Pilate, the procurator to have him executed. I was very disappointed in Pilate for letting this happen when as far as I could see, he was no threat to anyone but we all knew that the Governor would do anything for a quiet life. A few days later we got the first message asking us to keep watch because someone had stolen Jesus' body. The requests got increasingly urgent as the rumours that he had risen from the dead started to circulate. Some of Jesus' close followers had been seen in Galilee and it was suspected that they had stolen the body for burial in his home district.

I went out with a squad of men to see what I could find out and came across his followers by the village of Bethsaida. They told me that Jesus had risen from the dead. Not only they but many others had seen him and they were expecting to meet him by the lake. Later I met John, one of them, and he told me how he and his companions had been out fishing. They had had a completely blank night and, when they were coming back to shore in the morning, saw a stranger standing there. They didn't recognise him in the half-light but he told them to cast their net on the right side of the boat. The results were astonishing. The net was so full that they were unable to pull it on board and the weight of the catch was that great that it threatened to capsize the boat. They recognised the Lord and as they spoke, I thought of the Jesus who liked to laugh. He would have enjoyed this sort of situation. I reported back to Jerusalem that I had found no trace of the body which was true as far as it went.

I was convinced by now that Jesus had risen from the dead and that he must be the Messiah for whom the Jews had been waiting so long. I used to meet together with others who shared this view and we talked about what he had done and how we had come to know him. I tried to live my life in accordance with his teaching – "Love God with all your heart and mind and love your neighbour as yourself."

The good times had to end. Eventually I was ordered back to Rome for retirement. The lady from the synagogue came with me as my wife. We sought out other believers in the city and started telling other people about Jesus. Two of the great leaders of the faith came to Rome, first Paul and then Peter. With their help the number of believers rose rapidly. Under Tiberius and Claudius we were generally left alone but, when Nero came to the throne, real persecution began. I am now in prison awaiting execution. I am lucky that, as a Roman citizen, I will have a quick death but many others have to endure the most dreadful tortures. I regret nothing. Meeting Jesus gave meaning to my life and I know I will go to be with him.

Simon's Mother-in-Law

We lived along the coast from Capernaum at Bethsaida on the Sea of Galilee – a whole community of us where the men earned their living by fishing. It was a good living as there was always an abundance of fish to be caught and plenty of people to buy the catch. The fleet consisted of about fifty boats each of which took two or three people to man them. Mostly family members joined together to run their own boats but this was not necessarily the case. It wasn't easy work as the storms that frequently blasted across the lake were fierce and destructive. Suddenly the skies would go dark, the wind would rise and torrential rain would lash down from the skies. I have been out in a storm like this and there is very little warning. It would be upon you before you had any chance to prepare. This is what happened to John, my husband, and we never saw any trace of him or his boat again. He left me with three girls all under 10.

Of course we all knew each other in the fishing community. It was very rare for any of us to marry outside.

When a tragedy such as happened to John occurred, everyone rallied around. I never felt that I was deserted or isolated. Mother and Father were still alive but unable to give much practical assistance. Other families helped by giving us food and helping to keep the house in repair. I missed John though. He was a good man and looked after us well. He loved us and it was difficult without him. I have never been tempted to take another husband though that is not from a shortage of opportunity.

As girls are when they get to the age when boys are all important, my three began to be more difficult to keep under control. The oldest, Esther, quickly settled with Judah who was a fisherman and already had his own boat. He was slightly older than most of the available men and this had given him time to establish himself. There had been rumours about him being a little wild but he was always very pleasant to me and took good care of Esther. Ruth went off with Benjamin. She was a born organiser and she soon had him doing what she wanted. This was good because, truth to tell, I found him a bit slow in the upper regions.

That left Rachel. She was by far the most headstrong of the three, always determined to get her own way. They say like goes for like and she picked on Simon. Of all the boys in the village, he was the most wild. Whenever there was horseplay, you could guarantee that he would be in the middle of it. I tried to persuade Rachel that there were better fish in the sea than him but the more I talked about others, the keener she became on Simon. I had great doubts as to whether the two of them would settle down together but in the end they left me with few options. They were going to be together whether I liked it or not. So with my somewhat qualified blessing, they set up home together.

The first year was tumultuous. I couldn't begin to count the number of times Rachel returned home in tears but always Simon came to fetch her and they went off happily together. I grew quite close to Simon whose mother had died some years earlier. About a year after they set up home together, Rachel came home and told me she was pregnant. She was both happy and scared at the same time. There were no such doubts with Simon. A child would be a great addition to the family and things could go on just as before. He seemed to have no concept of the changes a baby would bring. He was excited about the prospect of being a father and hoped for a daughter that he could spoil. Rachel hated being pregnant and losing her figure. The summer heat was almost too much for her. Eventually the time for the baby to be born came but it was no good. In spite of all our efforts we lost both mother and child. I was devastated but Simon was almost beyond grief. I have never seen a grown man so distraught. He used to come and talk to me for hours blaming himself for not having looked after Rachel better. We shared our grief and I think it helped both of us. In the end we got some sort of normality back into our lives.

Andrew was Simon's older brother, as quiet as Simon was noisy. He had taken the responsibility of looking after Simon (if that was possible) and their younger sister Leah very seriously and never had any time to himself. A number of us said we would look after Leah and that Andrew should go off on a trip by himself. He went down to Judea and became interested in the teaching of a man named John the Baptist. He was attracting large crowds to hear him as he preached by the River Jordan and he would then baptise those who believed what he said. There seemed to be two main themes to John's preaching. First we all needed to repent of our misdoings and the symbol of this was baptism. Secondly someone greater than him would shortly be coming to live among us and lead us into righteousness. Some of the claims that he made about this man seemed very extravagant. He was the Son of God come to dwell in the world. I thought it was just a phase Andrew was going through. There had always been prophets of this type in Israel.

Andrew came home in a state of high excitement. A man had come to John to be baptised and John had recognised him as the one whose coming he had fore-told. John had, somewhat unwillingly, baptised him and, as the man whose name was Jesus climbed out of the river, Andrew claimed to have heard a voice from heaven saying "This is my beloved son: I am delighted with everything he has done and said." The next day Andrew and his friend were with John. He saw Jesus passing by pointed him out to Andrew and his friend saying, "Look the Lamb of God". The two lads turned and followed Jesus. He stopped and asked them what they wanted. "Teacher, where are you staying?" they asked and he told them to come and see. They spent the day with him and Andrew rushed home to tell Simon that he had met the Messiah. The two of them went off immediately to meet him. They came back and, after this, they too to going off with Jesus for days at a time.

Simon used to tell me what they did. I remember him telling me about one night when he and Andrew and their partners James and John had gone out in their two boats and had fished all night without any success. At dawn they came back and were sitting on the sand washing their nets. Jesus arrived followed by the usual crowd, stepped into one of the boats and asked Simon to push it out into the water so that he could talk to the people who had gathered. When he had finished Jesus turned to Simon and told him, "Go out into the deep water and let down your nets and you will catch many fish." Simon said to him "Master we have worked all night and caught nothing. However if you say so, we will try again." I waited for the explosion. I knew how Simon and the others were feeling as I remembered the state John, my husband, was in if he had been out all night without catching anything. Anyway everyone knows that fishing is a night time activity; in the day the fish go deep to find cooler water. How Simon, tired and disappointed as he was, could be persuaded to do something as stupid as this was beyond me. He was about as obstinate as a man could be and he was the fisherman. I was amazed to hear Simon, who had little respect for anyone, call Jesus Master.

Simon and Andrew went out and the catch was so great that their nets began to tear. They shouted to James and John for help and soon both boats were full and on the point of sinking. When Simon realised what had happened, he fell on his knees and said, "Lord please leave me. I am too wicked to be near you." He and his friends were awestruck by the size of the catch. Jesus was chuckling aloud as he said to them "Don't be afraid.

From now on you will be catching people not fish." I remember thinking how much I wanted to meet this Jesus.

The next day they went away again with Jesus saying that they didn't know when they would be back. I was not best pleased. I had grown very close to Simon and I missed him, particularly as the girls were almost totally involved with their own affairs. Simon and Andrew were away with Jesus, the new teacher, more and more and I became very lonely. In the end I became ill with a fever and was forced to take to my bed. I really felt very sorry for myself, especially when I heard a commotion outside and Simon rushed into my room saying that Jesus and some of his friends were with him and needed feeding. I said that I was far too ill to cook for them but as I was speaking Jesus came in. He was a young man of about 30 with long dark hair and a real glow about him. His look was one of infinite kindness. He came to my bedside and laid his hands on me. They were cool and radiated power. Somehow, mysteriously, I felt better and full of energy. I got up from my bed and straight away went and started preparing refreshments for them. At first I felt resentful because I thought he had only made me better so that I could feed him and his friends but I soon realised how unreasonable this was.

During his stay, he made time to talk with me and I found that he really cared for those he met. There was a great compassion about him and a feeling that he knew everything about you, even the things that you would rather he didn't. Simon and Andrew were certainly in no doubt that he was someone truly special and James and John, the sons of my friend Zebedee and Simon's partners, were also travelling round with Jesus. They were still young and I thought that a period away from the fishing would do them good.

During their travels round Galilee over the next three years, Simon and the others, occasionally with Jesus, came and visited and I was always pleased to see them. On these occasions Jesus usually stayed with me. Simon had changed. He had become much more thoughtful. At the end of this time, he was worried that Jesus had decided to go up to Jerusalem for the Passover and that there he would be at the mercy of the religious leaders who had taken against him because he had derided their teaching and called them hypocrites. They had made several attempts to trap him so that they could accuse him of blasphemy and have him put to death but had so far failed. No one could persuade Jesus not to go. The people in Galilee worshipped him because of his teaching and the number of people he had healed.

I did not see Simon for some weeks and when he did come back, he was in a state of total distress. Apparently as he had feared, Jesus had been accused by the High Priest and condemned and crucified. This was bad enough but before this Simon had completely disgraced himself. Jesus had always taught peace and non-violence. When he was arrested, Simon had drawn a sword he was carrying and cut off the ear of one of the High Priest's servants. Jesus had stretched out his hand and healed him telling Simon not to be stupid and to put his sword away. Jesus had often said that he would be captured and put to death and that his close followers who called themselves the apostles would forsake him. Simon had said that this would never be true of him but, within a few hours, he had denied knowing him three times. And Jesus knew. The shame was too much for him to bear and I was frightened Simon would harm himself.

Jesus had more than once told the apostles that not only would he be killed but that he would rise again from the dead three days later. None of them wanted to believe this and they ignored what they had been told. Now Simon remembered. On the morning after the feast he and John went to the tomb in which Jesus' body had been placed wondering what they would find. While on their way they were met by Mary Magdalene and told that the tomb was empty and that the body had vanished. They ran to the burial place as fast as they could. John was small and thin and got there first. He looked in and saw the burial robe lying there but didn't enter. Simon, big and burly, arrived and didn't hesitate but went straight in. The body wasn't there. They went back to where they were staying beginning to believe that Jesus had risen from the dead. Their sense of excitement was overwhelming.

Later that day when Simon was with the other apostles, Jesus appeared and told them to go back to Galilee where he would meet them again. Simon did not know how he could face this. Jesus had done exactly what he said he would do and Simon had completely let him down. There could be no forgiveness for that.

Simon arrived at my house in a terrible state but eventually I managed to quieten him down. The day came when the apostles were to meet Jesus and with great difficulty I managed to persuade Simon he must go. I told him that he would be letting Jesus down again if he didn't do as he was asked. No one could have imagined that Jesus would rise from the dead. I don't know why but I was sure Jesus would forgive him for forsaking him. After all he would not have spent so much time training them for it all to be wasted. That evening Simon returned. He was a different man. Jesus had not only accepted him back but had told him that he would become the leader of those who believed Jesus to be the Son of God. I have never seen such a change in a man. I knew that he would return to Jerusalem and that I would be lucky if I saw him again. It was what he had to do and he believed that he would suffer the same sort of death as Jesus.

When this happened I was an old woman. I never saw Jesus again. I heard of how he was taken up to heaven and of the way Simon spent his life in the service of his master. He occasionally found the time to come home and told me of the great things the Lord had enabled him to do. It was as if the same strange power that worked through Jesus was now present in Simon. I was in no doubt that Jesus had risen from the dead and was who he claimed to be. I never tired of telling of the great events in which I had been slightly involved and felt greatly privileged to have met him. God truly was good.

Nicodemus

I never did know why I was invited to be a member of the Sanhedrin. I didn't come from an influential family and I was only an ambitious rabbi and teacher of the Law whose classes seemed to be highly popular. I had been a teacher for many years. I didn't even know Caiaphas, the High Priest well although I had come across him at a few Temple functions. I was surprised he even knew my name.

I accepted the job of course. It would have been professional madness not to do so. I didn't really know what it involved but it meant meeting many important men who might be helpful to me in my career. I started going to the regular meetings and I was surprised. In as far as I had thought about it all, I had imagined the Sanhedrin to be mostly about the running of the Temple but the bulk of their discussions centred on ensuring that the Law was strictly observed. The meetings were advisory and Caiaphas had the last word but he obviously did not want to upset as influential a group as most of my colleagues were. Two things particularly struck me. Firstly a great deal of time was spent in discussing how to manipulate the Romans and particularly the procurator, Pontius Pilate, into doing what they wanted. Secondly they took extremely seriously any deviation from the interpretations about the observance of the Law laid down by the High Priest. There was never any attempt to see if there was virtue in any variation that had been introduced; it was immediately condemned out of hand.

I would not even then have regarded myself as a strict observer of the Law. As with everyone else I did enough to demonstrate my adherence. I did not go to the extraordinary lengths that some of the members did to demonstrate how righteous I was. For example I didn't bother to tithe the small amounts of herbs I grew for my own use nor did I observe the Sabbath laws with the rigidity of some others. To tell the truth, some of the behaviour sickened me. How they could go to such effort to prove their piety and yet be so underhand in their business activities escaped me. Being a member of the Sanhedrin did not add to my sympathy with the way in which the Law was enforced.

I first heard of Jesus of Nazareth at one of our meetings about two years after I became a member. It was strange because there were two men who came on the scene at roughly the same time who caused concern. The first was a man named John. He was the son of a former Temple priest, Zechariah who had died some time previously. John spent his time baptising men and women in the river Jordan. He claimed that if they repented of their sins and were baptised, they would immediately be cleansed from all guilt. He made no claim to be the Promised One himself but said he was preparing the way for the Messiah who was about to reveal himself. John had been extremely unpleasant to a group of priests who had gone to question him, accusing them of being hypocrites and worse but he was not seen as a major threat. In any event Herod and Salome solved that problem for them in due course.

The second newcomer to the scene was this Jesus. He started going round Galilee, teaching and healing the sick. He quickly built up a following and at every meeting there were further stories of his exploits. He called himself the Son of Man and on several occasions had been into local synagogues and caused uproar. He went into Nazareth and claimed to be the fulfilment of the prophecies made by Isaiah about the coming of the Messiah. He encouraged his followers to ignore the Law. For example he allowed his followers to pick grain on the Sabbath to satisfy their hunger. It was agreed that he must be stopped but it was difficult to do so while he remained in Galilee surrounded by his followers. On several occasions attempts were made to trap him into making statements that could be used to arrest and condemn him but he was clever enough to evade them.

I liked what I heard of this Jesus. He seemed to understand that the Law was made for man, not man for the Law. I had more sympathy with that than with the self-congratulatory behaviour of the High Priest and his acolytes. They were exceedingly proud of the way in which they behaved and considered themselves better than their fellows. I found this view difficult to share when I saw them at the Sanhedrin meetings. There were one or two other members who, I believed, thought the same way as I did including my friend Joseph from Arimathea.

I decided that I had to meet Jesus. I couldn't do so openly as I knew that Annas, Caiaphas' father-in-Law and a former High Priest, had informers and watched what the members of the Sanhedrin were up to. Annas was no longer a member himself as he had been caught up in a scandal concerning the Romans but he was still the power behind the throne. The difficulty therefore was how to arrange a meeting. Fortunately I knew one of Jesus' close disciples, a former tax collector named Levi and he owed me a favour. I contacted him and he arranged a meeting with Jesus on a visit to Jerusalem. It was just outside the City and late at night.

I went to keep my appointment planning that I would keep control of the meeting and would be the one asking the questions. Levi took me to where Jesus was staying and he left us alone together. Jesus was a strikingly handsome man with long dark hair and dark brown eyes. There was nothing of the fanatic about him. He seemed calm and remarkably self possessed. I approached and began as I had planned.

"Rabbi, we all know that God has sent you to be our teacher. The miraculous signs you do prove that God is using you for his purposes."

He interrupted. "I tell you unless you are born again, you will never enter the Kingdom of God".

Taken by surprise I asked, "What do you mean? Can a full grown man go back into his mother's womb?"

"The truth is no one can enter the Kingdom of God without being born of water and the spirit. Humans can only give birth to flesh, but the Holy Spirit gives new life from heaven. You should not therefore be surprised be my saying 'You must be born again'. The wind blows wherever it pleases. You hear its sound but you cannot tell where it comes from or where it is going. In the same way you cannot explain how people are born of the Spirit."

This conversation was not going to plan and I did not know how to respond. Surprised I asked again "What do you mean?"

"You are the leading teacher in Jerusalem and yet you do not understand these things. I am telling the truth. I am speaking of what we both know and describing what we have both seen but still you will not believe me. I have spoken to you of things that happen on earth and you do not believe; how then can you possibly understand if I try to tell you what is happening in heaven? Only I, the Son of Man, having come to earth, will return to heaven again. Just as Moses lifted up the snake in the desert, so I, the Son of Man, must be lifted up so that anyone who believes in me will have eternal life".

I had to regain control of our meeting. Instead of my asking the questions, I, an expert in the Law, was being lectured in it. I needed to think about what he was saying and make sense of it. He went on "God so loved the world that he sent me, his only Son, so that anyone who believes in me will not perish but have eternal life. I wasn't sent into the world to condemn the world, but that, through me, it might be saved. There is no judgment awaiting those who trust in me but those who do not believe in God's one and only Son have been judged already because of their disbelief. This is the basis of that judgment: The light from heaven came into the world, but men loved darkness instead of the light because their deeds were evil. Everyone who does evil hates the light, and stays away from it for fear that his deeds will be exposed and he will be punished. But those who do what is right come into the light gladly, so that everyone can see that they are doing what God wants."

These words were spoken quietly but with complete authority. I had never listened to anyone who was more sure of the truth of what he was saying. I needed time to understand his meaning. I thanked him and took my leave. Small talk was not part of his armoury.

I returned home full of his words. They rang in my ears and fortunately I could remember them. As soon as I got in I wrote them down. One thing was clear – he spoke with such authority that I had to take him seriously. Either he was right or he was mad. For the time being I was not sure which but I needed to decide.

The name of Jesus came to dominate the meetings of the Sanhedrin. More and more stories of healings and miracles were reported. He even visited Jerusalem again at the Feast of the Tabernacles although initially he came in secret. The people were watching for him but he didn't go to the Temple until halfway through the Festival. When the crowds heard his teaching they were amazed. It was like nothing they had been taught before. Many of them believed him and could not understand why the High Priest was trying to kill him. Caiaphas sent out the Temple Guards to arrest Jesus but they returned without having done so. When asked why, they replied that they had never heard anyone speak as Jesus did. Meanwhile the crowds were becoming more and more excited and were openly saying that this man must be the prophet foretold in scripture.

Caiaphas and the Pharisees were appalled. They accused the guards of having fallen under Jesus' spell. "Do any of the leaders of the Pharisees believe in him? These ignorant people in the crowd do but what do they know about things anyway? A curse on them." I asked my colleagues "Does our Law condemn a man without first listening to him and giving him a fair hearing?" I got short shrift for my pains. "Are you from Galilee too? Search the scriptures and you will find for yourself that no prophet has ever come from Galilee." All the old prophecies said that the Messiah would come from the tribe of Judah and from the city of Bethlehem. Looking back it is astonishing that none of those learned men bothered to find out that Jesus had in fact been born there. Eventually Jesus left Jerusalem at the end of the festival. The High Priest was unable to do anything to stop him because of the riots that any attempt to seize him would have sparked off. I knew however that he had heard that I had visited Jesus secretly and I was never trusted again.

My mind was in a maze with all that was going on. I could still hear that clear, confident voice speaking to me. In my heart I think I believed that Jesus was the Christ but to acknowledge this would mean a total change in my life. I could no longer stay on the Sanhedrin or indeed in Jerusalem. I was under no illusions about my fate if I acknowledged Jesus. Already I was under suspicion for what I had said and for having seen Jesus privately. I convinced myself that I needed more time and that I was of more use on the Council than off it. I knew I was fooling myself but that is how I was. I continued to study the scriptures to see what they said about the Messiah and could find nothing that persuaded me that Jesus could not be him.

Things returned to normal until shortly before Passover the next year. We then received news of Jesus having raised a man named Lazarus from the dead. Caiaphas was growing desperate and gave orders that Jesus must be taken, dead or alive, whatever the consequences. The same problem remained. There was never a time when his supporters did not surround Jesus and to take him prisoner under those circumstances would cause a riot. That would draw retribution from the Romans and might endanger Caiaphas' position. Jesus duly arrived in Jerusalem for the feast and was greeted like a hero. People were worshipping him and so openly breaking one of the commandments. The next day he caused havoc in the Temple courtyard by upsetting the money-changers' tables and driving them out of the building. Caiaphas and the Sanhedrin were at their wits end. They were only saved when one of Jesus' disciples, who wanted him to lead an armed rebellion against the Romans, offered to betray him. In secret, at dead of night, Jesus was arrested on the night before Passover.

He was initially taken to Annas a former High Priest and a real hard man who tried to bully Jesus into condemning himself. This proved unsuccessful so he was brought before the Sanhedrin and accused of blas-phemy. When he was accused of being the Christ, he made no attempt to deny it. This was enough for my colleagues. Such a claim warranted the death penalty. Unfortunately only Pilate, the Roman governor, could authorise executions and he would not be very impressed by what he would see as a religious argument. I saw Annas coaching false witnesses to say they had heard Jesus insult the emperor by disputing his right to tax them. They also said that he had threatened to destroy the Temple and rebuild it within three days and at least two witnesses were agreed that they had heard Jesus say this.

We all went across to Pilate's palace and he came to us in the courtyard. Caiaphas and his helpers made their accusations and the false witnesses were called. They made such a mess of things that we were all laughing at them. Pilate heard Jesus was from Galilee and sent him to Herod for judgment but that sly man would not take the responsibility and so the decision was left to Pilate. In the end, as Caiaphas had always said, Pilate would do anything for a quiet life. Before condemning him, Pilate washed his hands in public to show that what was happening was not his fault. I knew how he felt.

The guards rushed Jesus off to be crucified. Later in the day Joseph, another member of the Sanhedrin from Arimathea, and I went to see Pilate to ask if we could have Jesus' body for burial and he gave his permission. Joseph, like me, had become a believer in Jesus but had not told anyone because he feared for his life if the High Priest found out. Neither of us could face watching the crucifixion so we waited until late afternoon before we went to the execution ground. Joseph came to my rooms but we didn't have much to say to each other, as we were both aware that a great injustice had been done. If I had been a different type of man I think I would have got very drunk so that I forgot what had happened.

When we got to Golgotha, the execution ground, all the three who had been crucified had been pronounced dead. We were given Jesus' body for burial and we laid it with every care in a new tomb originally intended for Joseph himself. I had bought a large quantity of embalming ointment made from myrrh and aloes. As is customary we wrapped the body in a long linen cloth with the spices. A huge stone was rolled across the entrance and three Temple guards were left on watch.

I went home in despair. My conscience was far from clear and all sorts of questions were churning round in my mind. Was Jesus who he said he was? If so, why hadn't angels come and rescued him? What was the point of the Son of God coming to earth? I spent two days and nights going over all that had happened and thinking about what Jesus had said to me. Nothing had occurred that was not in line with the prophecies that I studied so diligently. I gradually convinced myself that Jesus was the Messiah and by the morning I knew that I had to tell the Council what I thought. However all changed when it became known that the body had disappeared. The Temple Guards and Roman soldiers searched the whole of Jerusalem and the surrounding villages but the corpse wasn't found. Messages were sent to surrounding towns in case the body had been smuggled out of the city. I remembered the prophecies about the Messiah dying and rising again and my conviction that Jesus was the Christ became stronger. I realised what we had done.

Caiaphas was incandescent with rage, particularly when the search for the body proved unsuccessful. Inevitably rumours that Jesus had risen from the dead circulated and the tension in the city was clear to all. All the authorities could say was that the body had been stolen. Pilate blamed Caiaphas who had been responsible for guarding the tomb and would not allow Roman soldiers to help in the search. The guards themselves had mysteriously vanished. Various schemes seeking to prove that the body had been recovered were considered but none of them was feasible. Both the Ruling Council and the Romans became a laughing stock and there was a real possibility that Caiaphas himself would be removed from office or even imprisoned by Pilate.

I am deeply ashamed of what happened next. I was frightened and I ran away from Jerusalem because I knew that, if I said what I really believed, I would be killed. Caiaphas and his friends would never forgive someone who they felt had betrayed them so badly. I went and lived in the country and told no one who I was or what had happened. From my hiding place I heard the stories of his appearances to his disciples and his ascension. I learned of the courage of the disciples, uneducated men facing the might of the priests. I marvelled at what they achieved but it was only after nearly four years that I plucked up the courage to acknowledge openly that I believed Jesus to be the promised Messiah and went back to the city. May he forgive me?

The Samaritan Woman

He was sitting by the well looking very relaxed. It was not a normal sight for two reasons. Firstly I could tell by his robes that he was a Jew, not a Samaritan and Jews did not talk to Samaritans. Secondly he was a man and only women went to the well. I approached therefore with some trepidation. He was no longer in the first flush of youth but he looked fit and healthy. He had long wavy brown hair, a dark complexion and wonderful deep brown eyes that looked at you with great sympathy and understanding. He watched me coming, not lustfully but as one who was interested in his fellow people.

As I came to the well I didn't expect to speak to the man. Normally Samaritans and Jews did not have anything to do with each other but these were not normal circum-stances. We occasionally saw travellers using the short cut from Galilee to Judea but even these rushed through our country as if we would infect them on contact. To see one waiting like this was by any standards unusual. Sychar was off the beaten track, a real backwater. It was traditionally the site of Jacob's well. My difficulty was solved when he asked me to give him a drink. He had a soft and pleasant voice with a strong Galilean accent. I was still not at ease and replied aggressively.

"You are a Jew and I am a Samaritan and Jews never have anything to do with Samaritans, certainly not Samaritan women. Why are you asking me for a drink?"

"If you knew the gift God wants to give you and who I am, you would ask me and I would give you living water."

I didn't understand what he was saying but I could see he meant me no harm. Not many of the villagers would talk to me and I welcomed the chance for a chat. I decided to humour him. "Sir, you have no rope or bucket to draw with and the well is deep. How do you get this living water? Are you greater than our ancestor Jacob, who gave us this well and drank from it himself? How can you offer better water than that enjoyed by his sons and his sheep and his cattle?" He seemed pleased with my answer.

"Everyone who drinks water from this well will be thirsty again, but whoever drinks the water I will give him will never be thirsty again. Indeed the water I provide for him will become a continual spring of water giving eternal life."

By now I was highly confused but the idea of never being thirsty again (and never having to come to the well to fetch water again) had decided attractions, so I replied "Sir, give me some of this water so that I will never be thirsty again. Then I won't have to come back here again."

His next words seemed completely off the subject. "Go and get your husband and come back."

This was rather difficult. I had been married very young but my husband turned out to be a bit of a bore who bullied me and was jealous the whole time. If I am honest, I loved flirting and leading other men on. Being faithful to just one was not very exciting. I had therefore left him and, since then, had had a series of live-in lovers. The women in the town all felt threatened by me, as two of these lovers had left their own marriages to come to me. This was why I came to the well at midday – I didn't want to meet the other women. I seemed incapable of sustaining a long-term relationship. I was quite prepared to be faithful but as soon as a man started living with me, he became possessive. If he had trusted me I would have been content. But when he began to tell me what I could and what I could not do, I became annoyed.

"I have no husband."

"You are right. You do not have a husband. Actually you have had five husbands and you are not married to the man you are living with now. What you have just said is quite true." Strangely I didn't think he was judging me – only accepting the truth about what kind of person I was.

The conversation was taking an unpleasant turn. I didn't like the fact this man I hardly knew was putting the truth about me so brutally. Yet he was right. After the first marriage I hadn't bothered with any formal arrangements. If I didn't have somebody with whom to share my house, I felt lonely and bored. I was attractive and had no difficulty finding a man to come and live with me and I was certainly good at satisfying them in bed. I was surprised and delighted that I had not yet become pregnant. I thought children were nasty, messy little creatures who used up too much time and took over your life. But the man was right. I had no husband. I was mystified how he knew. Had he been talking to others in the village? I didn't think so as I would have heard about it. Was he himself going to make a pass at me? Again I didn't think so – he didn't seem the type. So where was this conversation going. It was certainly interesting and I was learning a lot about myself. I decided to play along with him and find out where we went next.

"Sir, I can tell you are a prophet." Well he must be to know as much as he did about me. It was very flattering to have a one-on-one conversation with such a man. I changed the subject.

"Tell me why is it that the Jews insist that Jerusalem is the only place to worship whereas we Samaritans claim that here on Mount Gerizim, where our ancestors worshipped, is the proper place." I don't know why I chose this topic; I suppose I was a bit flustered and this seemed safe.

He looked directly at me. "Believe me, the time is coming when it will not matter whether you worship the Father here on this mountain or in Jerusalem. You Samaritans know little about who you worship; we Jews know all about him, for salvation will come through the Jews." Another miss! The last thing I needed was a theological discussion. Having said that I was fascinated to know where all this was leading. I had never before talked to anyone like this.

He went on. "A time is shortly coming when true worshippers will worship the Father in spirit and in truth. They are the kind of worshippers the Father wants. God is spirit, and his worshippers must worship in spirit and with true belief."

I was now totally muddled. I sat and pondered what he had said. There was quite a long pause while I tried to marshal my thoughts but it was in no way uncomfortable. He was watching me closely, not critically but as one who knew what I was thinking and hoped that at least I would begin to understand I didn't feel condemned but cleansed. He seemed to be saying that neither the Samaritans nor the Jews had got it right. His comments on worship were a confusion. What was all this talk about worshipping in the Spirit? I had been brought up to believe that the scriptures only included the five books of Moses. We worshipped and sacrificed in our own Holy Place on Mount Gerizim. How could we praise God away from there? The only way I could continue the conversation was to make a big leap into the dark.

"I know that the Messiah (called Christ} is coming. When he comes, I expect he will explain everything to us."

"I am the Messiah."

I sat there amazed. I may even have had my mouth hanging open. The way our discussion had developed had completely thrown me. How could he make such claims about himself? I went back over what had been said. Certainly he knew more about me than any normal person should. He not only knew about me but he knew my thoughts. This was no ordinary man. What if he was telling the truth? I had to make my mind up. I had got it into my head that this was a life changing conversation and would not be repeated. I glanced at him and saw him looking at me with a slight smile on his face. A group of men approached. They obviously knew him and he welcomed them. I expected one of them to say, "Why are you talking with *her*?" but no one spoke. They were accustomed to his unusual behaviour.

I was by now so excited that I ran down the hill, even leaving my water jar behind. I said to everyone I saw "Come, see a man who knew everything I ever did. Could this be the Christ?" At first they ignored me thinking it was just another ploy by this awful woman whom they had to put up with. Who has she got her hooks into this time? But as I went on running through the village, they began to follow me. When we got back to the well, he was still there with his friends. They were eating their lunch that they had been to the town to fetch but he ate nothing.

They tried to make him eat.

"I have food to eat which you know nothing about." They looked bewildered as well they might. I was reassured because he was the same with everybody, not just me. It was comforting to know that I was not alone in finding it difficult to understand him. I could hear his friends talking among themselves. "Could someone have brought him food without us knowing?"

"My sense of achievement comes from obeying the one who sent me and completing his work. Do you think that the harvest will only begin four months from now? Wake up, open your eyes and look at the fields! They are ripe for harvest. The harvesters are paid good wages and the crop they harvest is individuals brought to eternal life. What joy that brings for both the planter and the reaper? You know the saying 'One man sows and another reaps.' It is true. I sent you to reap where you neither prepared the ground nor sowed the seed. Others have done the hard work but you will reap the benefits of their labour."

I thought his friends might be upset by this implied criticism but they didn't take any offence. They went on talking among themselves while we from the village discussed what we had just heard. To my great surprise many of them believed in Jesus because of my account of our conversation. I was not their favourite person and maybe this helped them to believe. "He knew everything I had ever done." In a way this was a sort of confession to them and they could see that I was deeply affected by what I had heard. Our leaders approached him and asked him to stay a short while more and he remained two more days. He again told us who he was and why he had come to earth and a number more grew to believe in him. Others told me, much to my relief "We no longer believe in him because of what you said; now we have heard for ourselves, and we know that this man is the Saviour of the world."

Eventually Jesus and his friends moved on and I waited for the village to return to normal. None of us actually went to follow Jesus because we would not have been welcome in Galilee but we were kept informed of his doings. We heard of his final trip to Jerusalem and of his cruel death and then the increasing number of reports of his resurrection. Because of what he had told us, this did not come as a total surprise. We had asked him why, if he was the Son of God, he had come to earth and he had said to die so that the people might be reconciled with God. The idea of the Son of God remaining dead seemed as odd as that of his coming to life again. We met together frequently to remind ourselves of what he had said to us and to discuss the latest news of his doings. We were particularly excited by what his friends did following his death.

That meeting changed my life forever. I invited my current lover to leave and I think he was glad to do so. In the end I got back together with my real husband when he realised that I no longer fancied every man in town. We have a beautiful girl named Sarah who is the apple of her father's eye. But for her I might have been tempted to go to Jerusalem to work with his followers.

In Acts 8, Philip is reported as fleeing to Samaria when the early church was scattered. People were healed, demons were cast out and many people accepted the gospel of Jesus. Maybe this was because they had been prepared by the words of the woman at the well

The Leper

Life was good. My career was going well and soon I would be able to set up as a butcher on my own. I had recently become betrothed to Lydia, a beautiful dark haired girl, kind and with a very lively personality, and we were shortly to be married. We were building ourselves a house in a lovely village in Samaria and it would soon be ready. I was becoming known locally and this did no harm at all to my prospects in business. In fact my world was pretty good and I could think of no reason why it should not remain that way.

As many troubles do, this one started in a small way. I seemed to be losing feeling in the fingers of my right hand. This did not at first worry me but it didn't get better. I told Lydia about it but she did not think it was anything serious. Nobody would notice anything wrong unless I told him. However the problem got worse. The skin where my fingers were numb started to go white and die. I took to wearing gloves but the time came when I could hide the situation no longer. I was very frightened that I had leprosy.

This illness was taken very seriously, especially with someone handling food. The term covered any skin disease. If a person had such a disease he was required by the Law to go to the priest who would decide if it was to be diagnosed as leprosy. The standard he used was whether the damage to the skin was more than skin deep. If it was, there was only one remedy, immediate expulsion from society. With good cause the authorities were terrified of an epidemic. The person with the illness had to leave the town and live as an outcast. Whenever he approached another person he had to ring a bell and call out 'Leper'. No provision was made for feeding or looking after those with the illness, which was regarded as a punishment from God. There were many different versions of it. Some forms cured themselves over a period of time and then there was an elaborate procedure before the person could be received back into society. This naturally involved the payment of substantial sums of money, unaffordable by most lepers and so it was quite common for those who had been cured to continue to live as outcasts. When women were diagnosed as leprous, this represented a death sentence, as they were unable to survive away from civilization.

In the end I could hide my problem no longer. I had to go to the priest. Lydia begged me not to but I was frightened of infecting her and those I loved and also those who ate the food I sold. The priest met me and, although he was very kind, decreed that I must become outcast from society. I noticed that he was very careful to keep his distance from me. I was escorted from the town and left to my own devices. Lydia had offered to come with me to look after me but I could not let her pay the price for my problem. She did arrange to leave me food each week in a place we both knew. We met there from time to time but I would not let her near me. The last thing I wanted was for her to be in the same state as I was.

Fairly quickly I realised that staying near the place where all my hopes had rested was not helping Lydia or me. I had to move away and so I headed for the hills along the Galilee/Samaria border. Hardly anyone went there other than those seeking to make a quick journey from Galilee to Judea. I was lucky enough to meet up with a group of other people in the same condition as me. When they saw that I could help them in catching and preparing animals for food and finding edible wild plants, they invited me to join them. We were an odd mixture. The only things we had in common were our illness and our sense of loss. Many of our group had young children they would never see again. We were truly the living dead – nobody cared if we were alive or not.

It quickly became clear that it did not matter if we were Judeans or Samaritans. Under normal circumstances I would never even speak to a Judean but now we were all members of a more exclusive tribe called 'Lepers' We came from all parts of society; from the previously rich to former beggars and to us it made no difference. We were accepted by each other only so long as we could contribute to the group. As soon as anyone was unable to do so, he was driven out of the cave and we never saw him again. There was never any trust between us. In some cases the marks from the disease cleared up and the person went off to try to rejoin society. Our saddest moments were probably when they came back having been rejected as unclean by the priest. Often this meant nothing more than an inability to pay his fees. We lived without hope as a sort of living dead. In winter we froze and starved and in summer we sweltered.

Life developed its own pattern. In spite of ourselves we did form close relationships if only to protect ourselves from others who tried to bully us. We agreed that we would share our food but there were still those who thought they were entitled to more than the others. We discussed why this terrible curse had fallen on us with no very clear answers. I was obsessed with what I must have done to be punished so. Inevitably I could think of the small dishonesties I had perpetrated but these didn't seem to be worse than those of anybody else. It was not a fair world and, if this was the case, there was no God. Yet as I looked round on the summer mornings I saw the rugged beauty of the area in which we lived. This was not an accident. Some supernatural being had designed it. Against my better judgment I began to call on this creative force. I didn't see him to be the vindictive God I had been taught about. He was a just God who loved me as much as those who lived comfortable lives in the towns and villages. He didn't want me to be an outcast any more than I did. I think it was these ideas that kept me sane. I did not believe for one moment that I would be cured. The disease had not spread although my right hand was now white and useless. I had seen some of the others in our group lose fingers or grow hideous disfigurations on their face. It was odd that these no longer defined the person. In my village the person would have been known as the man with no nose and would have become an object of ridicule. Here he was just another person like I was.

I was with that group for about ten years. We had no means of measuring time long term – all we could recognise was summer or winter and the seasons as they passed. There was nothing to look forward to but a slow, lingering passage to death. All the time the disease would spread causing increasing pain and debility. I considered whether to end things and it wasn't hope that prevented me from doing so. I just did not have the courage. Sometimes we saw people passing by in the distance. Usually we left them alone but, if we were going through a particularly bad time, we used to beg from them. Most of them were terrified as they saw us and moved on quickly. Just occasionally they left some food but not often. As far as they were concerned we had ceased to exist and they did not want to be reminded that we were still alive.

We heard no news of the outside world except when someone new joined our band. Not much changed. The priests were still in charge and the Romans still controlled our country. One man came in telling us of a new teacher who was able to heal the sick and drive out demons. This didn't mean anything to us, as we would never come into contact with him. There was no reputation to be gained by healing us.

We had just endured an especially harsh winter and were enjoying the feel of the sun on our backs and we decided to go on a hunting trip together. There were ten of us and we went up towards the path along the border. We hoped to trap hare and other small animals. As we watched the path we saw a party of travellers, men and women, coming down the track towards Judea. They were drawing near to a village and, as we watched, a leper who had just joined us recognised the one leading them. He cried out in excitement that this was the healer he had told us about. He started screaming at him calling out "Jesus, Master, have mercy on us." We all followed his example. We did not go near the road as I think we all dreaded the renewed rejection we would experience. To my surprise the party stopped. A man moved off the path towards us. He was about 30, with long brown hair and wearing a white robe. There was something particularly attractive about him, not just because of his looks but a kindness. He came right up close to us and spoke quietly. It was the first time I had been near to anyone from outside our band for many years.

He spoke quietly. "Go show yourselves to the priest." We felt compelled to go and somehow none of us doubted his authority. We all obeyed him without question. As we went along I noticed that the hands of the man in front of me were changing. His skin was clean and healthy like that of a newborn child. I looked at my hands and for the first time for years they were fresh and unblemished. We started jumping around screaming with joy and ran as fast as we could towards the village and the synagogue. The priest was there and we shouted out what had happened. He kept his distance and I compared him with this Jesus who had been prepared to come near us and who I was sure would not have hesitated to touch us. He asked us to strip and examined us. In the end he pronounced us fit to return into society. He even forgave us the fees he was entitled to for declaring us clean. I was overcome by a feeling of unreality.

My comrades ran off shouting and screaming. I suppose they were going to their own villages but what sort of welcome they would find there I could not imagine. I turned back to find the person who had healed me. He was just entering the village. I was shouting out praising God although I had no idea what words I was using. I threw myself at his feet to kiss them.

He looked down at me. I shouted 'Praise God, I'm healed. Thank you, thank you, Master'. He spoke. "Didn't I heal ten men? Where are the other nine? Is this Foreigner (I was a Samaritan) the only one who has returned to give praise to God?" He stretched out his arm to help me up and said "Rise and go; your faith has made you well." His expression was one I will never forget. Joy and sorrow were mixed in a way I had never seen before.

I turned and left him. Looking back I could see Jesus talking to those following him. I went back to my village and went to my parents' house. It was empty. I asked a passer-by what had happened to the people who had lived there and he told me that they had never recovered from the tragedy of their son having leprosy.

174

Their neighbours had shunned them as if they too might be infectious and both had died shortly after. I walked round the village but no one recognised me. I thought I knew some of the people but I didn't speak to them. My disgust at the way they had treated my parents was too great. I asked what had happened to Lydia and found out that she had married and lived in the next village. She had three children. I went along to the village and stood and watched. She came out with a baby in her arms and she was as beautiful as ever. However she looked sad as if her experience with me had taken its toll. I didn't approach her, as that would only have made things worse. She would have been torn between her husband and me and there had already been enough heartache. At the moment she didn't even know if I was still alive. I turned and left.

I decided to go and find Jesus the teacher. I hurried down the road towards Jerusalem and quickly caught up. I stayed with his band of followers for many months. There was never any mention of the fact that I was a Samaritan and Jews and Samaritans didn't usually talk. I learned to live in normal society again and to become comfortable in the company of women. It had been many years since I had seen, let alone talked to, a woman. They were so kind to me. I saw Jesus heal many people. I remember him going up to a leper who came and knelt before him asking to be made clean and touching him. Immediately the man was cured. I was astonished that Jesus took the risk of touching the man when he might have been infectious and when it was so against the Law. I listened to his teaching which concentrated on loving God and loving one's neighbour.

This was just like my thoughts when I had been in the cave in the hills. I began to recognise that this man Jesus was truly sent from God and to try to follow his teaching. I knew that I had to go and put what he said into practice rather than stay with him.

I left and went back to the hills. I met up with another group of lepers and joined them. I used to go down into the villages and buy food and ointments. The villagers found out what I was doing and for a time would not come near me. Gradually their attitude changed. They used to give me food and medicine. I told them what had happened to me and they asked me to tell them of Jesus and his teaching. Many of them decided to follow his ways and some even came to talk to the men I was helping. The priest was horrified but this didn't stop them. Even some of the women used to come out into the hills. I no longer think of my life as one wasted but as one used in the service of others. I believe my master would have been pleased.

The Woman with a Haemorrhage

I first noticed something was wrong when I was about 18. My monthly periods had started some years before but now, instead of being four weekly, they seemed to be constant. I didn't feel ill but my problem affected every part of my life. I was too embarrassed to tell anyone, even my own Mother. I was still a virgin although I had been meeting a boy for some time and we were planning to get engaged. I had to break off with Jacob and I couldn't tell him the reason for doing so. It nearly broke my heart and he could not understand. He moved away from the area and I never saw him again. His parents who lived nearby rightly blamed me and would not speak to me. I went to our doctor but he could do nothing to help. Eventually I plucked up courage and told Mother. She told Father and, to my great relief, they were entirely sympathetic. They didn't throw me out as so many parents would have done but allowed me to go on living at home. I hope I became helpful to them, as they grew older. There were from time to time other boys that I fancied but I never dared go out with them.

Mother fell ill and grew steadily weaker and I was able to look after her until, about four years after my illness began, she died. I was an only child as Mother had never been that strong and I was able to keep house for Father. He was a lovely man, gentle and kind and had his own business as a builder. He employed a team of about 20 workmen and from time to time one of them noticed me and tried to form a relationship. There was one in particular to whom I was drawn but it was no good. I was too embarrassed to grow close to anyone because if we did get together I would have to tell him what was wrong with me.

My father died when I was 25. He was at work and the first I knew of anything wrong was when a messenger arrived saying that he had had a heart attack and was very poorly. I rushed to the place where he was working but I was too late. He died before I arrived. I must say the workmen were good to me. After the funeral three of them including the one who I thought was keen on me, came to see me and asked to buy the business. They had no need to do so because I was unable to run it by myself. However they offered to buy the equipment and they paid over the odds as they said Father had always treated them fairly and with respect. What with that and the house I was a bit of an heiress. Much good it did to me because, with my ailment, I didn't dare make any close relationships, especially with men. I was very keen to have a family but, until I was cured, I could not even think about it. In fact I was desperately lonely.

My parents had been my life and I had no other close friends.

When my first grief was over, I took stock of my position. Without a cure my life was pointless. I could not go near the synagogue as, to the Rabbis, I was permanently unclean. Any one who came into physical contact with me or even sat on a seat I had used, had to go through a process of ritual cleansing which lasted a whole week. I might just as well have been a leper. However I believed I was reasonably attractive and quite intelligent. Therefore I needed to find someone who could help me. I began to visit doctors and healers, initially with considerable hope. Time went on and none of the suggested remedies were successful. The cost of these treatments was huge and I began to run short of money. I still had the small house by the lake that I had bought after Father died but otherwise I had virtually no funds. I found someone to come and live with me and share the costs but she ran off after a few weeks without paying me. I was becoming desperate. I became less able to care for myself as the illness took its toll. I could not work as it was as much as I could do to look after myself. The future looked bleak.

I was in Capernaum one day when I first heard of Jesus. It was about 12 years after my illness had started. Some people were talking in a shop of this young teacher who had such an amazing gift of healing. He didn't use it for money but gave his services free. He would help anyone who came to him. He was different from other healers who all charged as much as they could. I suppose they were worried that they would be seen as the charlatans they were and needed to make money while they were able. I found out as much as I could about him and there were always people ready to tell me the latest stories. Apparently he spent much of his time teaching and used to tell marvellous stories to illustrate his point. I have to admit that I was only really interested in being healed. He went each week to the Synagogue and many of the cures took place there, even on the Sabbath. The teachers and Pharisees took great exception to this. However I had not been since my illness as I was considered unclean. I convinced myself that he could make me better.

The great plan began to grow in my mind. There were stories of him healing really ill men and women just with a touch. It surely wouldn't make any difference whether he reached out to me or I touched him. I didn't want to talk to him as I was too shy and in any event my illness was too embarrassing to discuss in public. I was too weak to follow him around but somehow I could get near to him. I had totally convinced myself that he could help me and I decided that I would try to touch him while he was busy doing something else. That was all that seemed to be needed for his healing power to operate. Surely he wouldn't notice as he was always being jostled anyway.

My opportunity came when he passed in front of my house. When I first saw him, he was trying to move through a dense mass of people waiting to see what he would do or say next or to profit from the mob he attracted. I pushed to get near him but the crowds were too thick. I grew desperate. I was completely certain that, if I only touched the edge of his cloak, I would be healed. I managed to get into the mob around him but, try as I might, I could not get close. Then I noticed a man surrounded by a group of servants pushing his way through. I recognised him as Jairus, the Ruler of the synagogue, who I had met when I tried to get read-mitted. He was big, burly and normally very correct in his dress. On this day however he was dishevelled and red faced, sweaty and out of breath. For a person like him to come and seek Jesus rather than summon him to the synagogue was unheard of and showed that he was in a panic about something. I wondered if I would be able to go ahead with my plan I attached myself to the group and gradually we got near to the teacher. The noise was deafening and all the pushing and shouting was frightening. There was an overwhelming smell of hot humanity that was most unpleasant. Fortunately I could not turn back as getting out of the crowd was as difficult as getting in.

We drew near to Jesus and Jairus called out "My little daughter is dying. Please come and put your hands on her so that she will be healed and live." Jesus heard him and turned to go with him. I saw my chance. While everyone was looking at either Jesus or Jairus, I pushed in behind the teacher and touched the rabbi's robe which Jesus was wearing. It was as if a shock passed through my body. I knew instantly that I was healed; how I knew I don't know but I was absolutely sure that I was. I tried to edge my way out of the crowd when I heard a voice ask "Who touched me?"

There was a sudden silence. One of his friends said, "Master, How are you going to know? You are in the middle of a crowd and everyone is pushing up against you."

"Someone deliberately touched me; I know that healing power has gone out from me." He turned and looked around and his eyes rested on me. I knew there was no escape. I was trembling all over but I pushed forward and fell at his feet. I was blushing and unable to speak. I looked up at him and he was watching me. I have never seen such a face. The look he gave me showed such kindness and understanding. He wasn't annoyed. He just wanted to see who I was. In front of that entire crowd I stammered out why I had touched him. I waited and he spoke. "Daughter your faith has healed you. Go in peace."

As Jesus finished talking to me I could feel the impatience of Jairus. He was jumping up and down and swearing under his breath and the looks he was giving me would have killed an ox at ten paces. Jesus turned back to him and, as he did so, I saw a servant push his way through to the official and say 'Your daughter is dead. Don't bother the teacher any more'. Jesus overheard him and, turning to Jairus, said 'Don't be afraid. Trust me and she will be all right'.

He set off towards the official's house and I followed. I had little option really as I was in the middle of a crowd but in any event I wanted to see what happened. I heard from those around me that she was 12 years old, an only child and the apple of her father's eye. We arrived at

Jairus' house where more people were gathered outside, wailing and mourning and musicians were playing sad music. Jesus turned to them and spoke "Stop wailing. She is not dead but asleep." He and three of his friends and the parents of the dead child went in.

The crowd started to laugh at him knowing that the child was dead but I knew what he had done for me. He could do anything. We could not see inside the house but one of his friends told me later what happened. Jesus went up to the girl and took her hand. He commanded "Little girl, get up!" Immediately she stood up. Jesus turned to her parents and told them that, like any healthy child, she was hungry and needed something to eat. They were completely overwhelmed. It was too soon even for gratitude. Jesus turned and left telling them to keep what had happened to themselves although how he thought they could do this I have no idea.

The crowd began to melt away. I went home feeling that I had a new life just as much as that little girl. I began to think what to do with it. I was no longer in the first flush of youth and the chances of my marrying and having a family were slim. This man Jesus was the most remarkable person I had ever come across and I wanted to know more about him. I decided to follow him around for a few weeks to learn what I could from him. I never had any return of the illness that had dogged me for so long and Jesus had, in truth, given me back my life. I got to know many of those who followed the Teacher. They were from all sorts of backgrounds and many of them, like me, owed him a huge debt. We watched as Jesus taught and healed and were astonished not only by what he did but by the patience and love he showed. I became very friendly with some of the women who accompanied him and we used to cook and look after the clothes for Jesus and his close friends.

I didn't go when Jesus went to Jerusalem for the last time. I had met a man among his followers and we had become very friendly. By coincidence he too was a builder although he had not known Father. We were both lonely people and, in the end, we decided to settle down together. We used our home to look after people like us who had nowhere else to go. We had received so much by way of love and, in my case physically, that we felt we had to give some thing back to others who were in the same sort of situation as we had been. Unfortunately we did not have our own children but looking after other those of other people was some sort of substitute. We both felt that we were following the example set by Jesus and doing a special task given to us by him. We heard of his death followed shortly by, at first, the rumours and later the certainty of Jesus' resurrection. This confirmed to us that we should go on helping others as he had helped me and made us more keen to tell others about my meeting with him.

The Woman Taken in Adultery

I am not a bad person. In spite of all that has been said about me, I believe in right and wrong as much as my neighbour. But I have this reputation and now is the time for me to defend myself.

I had a happy childhood. Father worked as a notary and earned enough for Mother to live in a comfortable house and be looked after by a host of servants. I was the fourth oldest of her children but the first girl. After me there were two more boys and another girl. I was spoilt and almost everything I asked for I got. Other girls envied me and my friends were all from the same sort of background as me. I didn't have any formal education but my brothers taught me to read and write. As I got older I also learnt housekeeping and cooking ready for the time when I would have a home of my own. As the oldest girl much was expected of me. I would have to make a good marriage and, in order to protect my reputation, I was never allowed out without a chaperone. Mother kept on telling me that they would find someone really suitable for me to marry and I, in my innocence, believed that this would be someone of my own age.

When I was thirteen and had become a woman, I was expected to attend the dinners which Mother and Father used to have at home, and eventually I was included when my parents were invited to other people's houses. At first it was exciting but it quickly became a bore. All the other guests were much older than me and the conversation was mainly about money and belongings. It did not take me very long to realise that I was just another possession and that I would be used to enhance my family's social position. Still I was not concerned, as I could not believe that my parents would pick someone with whom I could not be happy.

I first met David at one of these dinners. He was 40 years old, bald, fat and gross. Gradually I found that wherever I went I was placed next to him. He had little conversation other than his business and, what was worse, he started to grope me under the table. I told Mother what had happened and she told me to grow up. That was what happened and I must learn to cope with it. Next time he tried I kicked him hard.

David had been married before but his wife had died in childbirth, an event he described as a wasted invest-ment. I kept telling Mother why I no longer wanted to go to these parties but she said I would never meet anyone unless I did. I was grown up now and must learn to cope with these situations. Still wherever I went, I found that he was seated next to me. I thought of him as a dirty old man who liked to be next to young girls.

I was fifteen when Father called me in and said that David had asked for my hand in marriage. He had offered an exceptional dowry and Father, who was going through what he called a period of financial instability, had decided to accept. I would be married next month. I screamed at him that I would rather be dead than marry David but he told me to grow up. It was time for me to repay some of the money he had spent on me. Nothing I said or did made any difference and Mother pointed out to me the advantages of such an arrangement. I would have a nice home with servants and a secure place in society. She told me to stop making a fuss and get on with it. I thought of running away but I had nowhere to go and was far too closely watched.

The day of my wedding came inexorably closer. I was dressed up in the traditional fashion and all the usual festivities took place. I felt like a sacrificial lamb. The only person present not enjoying herself was me, the bride. Some of my friends even came up to me and congratulated me on how well I had done for myself. Eventually I was taken home by David and had to go through the humiliation of the wedding night. He was sweaty and smelt but what was worse was that he was unable to consummate the marriage. He of course blamed me for not encouraging him but I am afraid that in my innocence I did not understand what he was talking about.

Right from the start he was very possessive. I was not allowed to leave the house without his permission. As for there being plenty of servants, I found that he was something of a miser. Unless we were entertaining I was expected to do most of the cleaning and cooking myself with the help of an elderly woman who had worked with David's family forever. For a long time I was not even allowed to visit my old home. When I did go I told Mother how things were and asked if I could get a divorce. She said that was out of the question as they would have to repay the dowry and they could not afford to do so. I knew then that I would get no help from that quarter.

Over the next year David began to believe that I had settled down and accepted my situation. We even had a few dinner parties at home so that he could show off his trophy wife. It did much for his image among his old cronies when I, suitably dressed up, made an appearance. As a result I was allowed to go to the market provided the old retainer, Naomi, accompanied me. It gradually began to dawn on me that she detested David as much as I did. We began to talk and I found that she blamed David and his family for her wasted and futile life. She was prepared to turn a blind eye to what I was doing so long as she didn't get into trouble.

I first met Gideon at the market. He was helping his father at the tanner's stall that they ran. He was dark and handsome with long curly hair and I felt an immediate attraction. We began to talk and found that we enjoyed each other's company. Slowly our relationship began to deepen and I felt a strong attraction for him. We started to seek each other out each time I went to the market. If he wasn't there, I felt deprived. We began to go into the room at the back of his stall. At first all we did was talk but gradually we began to hug and kiss. His father must have known about the situation but he decided to ignore it. He and Naomi spent much time talking and reminiscing. The feelings between Gideon and me grew stronger and eventually we made love together. It was the first time I had ever been with a man properly and this made it even more exciting. I suppose I didn't even think of the risk I was taking.

David must have realised something was going on and he questioned Naomi about what was happening. Of course she told him of my visits to the tanner's stall and next time we went out, he had me followed. He could not have missed the length of time we disappeared into the back room. Naomi was too afraid to warn me and the inevitable happened. The Temple officers caught Gideon and me. Because he was unmarried, he was sent on his way while I was taken directly to the Temple. I did wonder why I was the only one being accused. It takes two to commit adultery. I wasn't even given time to dress properly and was wearing just my outer robe I was brought before a court of Elders, convicted of adultery and sentenced to be stoned. They stared at me as if I was an animal and I felt raped by the way they looked at me. My only hope was that my parents would pay for my release and I knew that would not happen as, as well as a hefty fine, they would have to repay my dowry to David. It suited them that, because I had let them down, I should suffer the ultimate punishment.

I was led to a small courtyard outside the Temple. A group of elders who had been meeting there made their appearance and I prepared for the worst. I was too shocked to take in what was going to happen. They started to pick up stones that were lying round the edge of the courtyard. Normally my husband would have been entitled to throw the first stone. I never saw either him or Gideon again.

A man who had come out of the Temple with the elders was standing to one side. He didn't seem to be one of them and yet they were all paying him attention. I was made to stand up and one of the main group said to him, "Teacher, this woman was caught in the act of adultery. In the Law Moses commanded us to stone such women. What do you say?" They seemed to want to trap him.

The man turned and looked at me. I felt he could see right through me. He knew my story and he was full of compassion for me. He could not forget what I had done but he didn't want me harmed. For the first time in my life I thought this was a person who was totally on my side. We all waited for him wondering what he would say. For some inexplicable reason he had given me new hope. I did not know what he could do for I was certainly guilty. As a teacher he could not act against the Law. Slowly he turned round and bent down. He started to doodle on the ground with his finger. They kept on questioning him and eventually he replied.

"If any of you has never done anything wrong, he should throw the first stone."

Again he stooped down and wrote on the ground. I waited expecting one of them to hurl the piece of rock he was holding at me but no one moved. One of them, the oldest, turned and began to move slowly away. The others followed, the older ones first and then the rest, one at a time, until only the one man who I later found was called Jesus was left. I sank back to the ground. He looked at me again, came across and put his arms around me and held me tight. I felt safer than at any time in my life. It was as if I had been reborn. He spoke.

"Woman, where are your accusers? Did none of them condemn you?"

I found myself replying "No one, sir".

Again he spoke "Then neither do I condemn you. Go now and change your way of life".

The man left but I didn't even notice him go. I sat where I was unable to take in what had happened and unable to move. All that I could understand was that I was not dead. Gradually I began to think of what came next. I was alive and for this I was truly grateful. I knew some sort of miracle had happened in that courtyard. But what was I to do now. I had absolutely nowhere to go. My husband would certainly not be prepared to help as I had made him look a fool. My parents had made it clear that they were finished with me. Gideon was by now miles away having been scared out of his young life. I was really on my own with no money, no clothes, and no home. Had I been saved from stoning so that I might die of hunger?

I wanted to move from that place in case they changed their minds but I hadn't got the strength. So I hunched down waiting for my wits to return. I thought of the words that had been said to me. "Go now and change your way of life". I must have stayed there for a long time before I realised that there was a woman slightly older than me sitting next to me. She was making no attempt to talk to me – she was just sitting close waiting. She put her hand over mine. I turned and looked at her. She wasn't condemning; she was looking at me with tenderness as if she cared. I had no idea how long she had been there or what she wanted. She put her arm round me.

"Come with me" she said. She helped me up and took my arm. She led me away from the Temple into the maze of narrow streets in the inner city. We went into one of the small houses that lined the streets. There was a delicious smell of cooking. I realised I hadn't eaten the morning. Was it only then that I had gone out for my fateful meeting with Gideon? We went into an inner room and she beckoned me to sit on one of the cushions on the floor.

"Did he send you?" I asked.

"No but he told me where you were. It was up to me if I did anything about it. He teaches us that we must care for our neighbours".

"Who is he?"

"He is a teacher from Galilee. When I met him I was crippled and could not walk. He came and touched me and I was healed. Like you I had nowhere to go and no one to look after me. But Salome came and looked after me. After a time I felt strong enough to live on my own and now I try to do for others what Salome did for me".

"How often do you see him?"

"Not very often. There is a group of women who follow him round wherever he goes, looking after his needs and listening to his teaching but I prefer to stay here and help those I come across in whatever way I can".

"Can I stay here?"

"Of course- as long as you like".

"What do I do about paying? I have no money and only the clothes I stand up in".

"If I am doing his work, the money seems to come. People who have met him give me funds and we always get by".

A woman brought me a steaming plate of stew and handed it to me. I realised just how hungry I was and how tired. I stayed in that house for three months while I came to terms with what had happened. There were three women who lived there permanently and a number like me who came for a period and then left. I asked if I could stay and help them with the work but they said no. It was up to me to find my own course through life. If I wanted to help others as they had helped me, I must start on my own. During my time with them they told me of the strange teaching of the man Jesus. 'Love your neighbours and love God.' I left there with deep gratitude for their kindness and determined to follow their example. I knew that Jesus had taught them, and through them me, lessons which would guide me for the rest of my life. It was as if I had been born again. My life stretched before me, mine to do what I liked with. Somehow I knew it was going to be very different from what had gone before.

The choice that the Elders gave Jesus was between letting the woman escape without punishment which would have broken the religious laws or stoning her which would have been against Roman law as only they had the right to inflict capital punishment. Either way would have had serious consequences for Jesus. If he broke the religious law he would be liable to arrest and imprisonment by the Jews and would possibly have had an accident while in their custody. If he had broken Roman law, the Jews would have informed the Romans and Jesus would have been imprisoned by them or even executed. It is an interesting question whether the Jews would have defied Rome and stoned the woman if left to themselves. We will never know the answer.

The Man Born Blind

In some ways being blind makes you invisible. Other men and women pass by and define you entirely by your physical problem. Some might wonder where you live or who looks after you but most only think of your inability to see. They can have no idea of what it is like to have to imagine what exists around you. However well someone described what he saw to me, I had no way of picturing what it really looked like. For example what shape is a horse? I have had one described to me many times, a creature some four feet. high with legs at each corner and lovely soft, smooth skin; I have even stroked one but to imagine what it really looks like is beyond me. Or what colour is the sky? People say that it is a beautiful blue but what is blue? I have no idea. Those I love have allowed me to touch them and feel the shape of their faces. My sister who is so good to me has a velvety touch to me like the material she wears for best but, apart from this, there is no way in which I can picture her.

I was born blind. My parents were always good to me and gave me all they could. Father was a tailor and made clothes for many of the most important people in Jerusalem. Mother stayed at home and looked after my younger sister Ruth and me. I remember Ruth's birth. Mother was very ill for some weeks after. Grandma, her mother, came to look after me but there was not the kindness I was used to. Even at 2 years old I could tell the difference; it was as if she was doing her duty – there were none of the kisses and cuddles I so much valued. When Mother was better, she used to let me hold Ruth on my knee and she was adorable. She chuckled and gurgled and cuddled right up to me. We developed a close, loving relationship and, all the time she was growing up, my sister tried to include me as much as she could in her games. But she did grow up and she met Isaac and went off to have her own home and family. She was still very kind to me but I was no longer so important in her life. When her children came along, she was too busy to spend much time with me. Mother and Father grew old and were unable to have me living with them any more but they helped as much as they could. I was on my own then.

Ruth suggested I should come to live with them but Isaac rightly refused to go along with the idea. He didn't do it out of spite but he was worried that she, with a growing family, would take too much upon herself. I liked Isaac. He was always good-natured and we had some really good conversations. He tried to keep me interested in what was happening in the world. It was he who made the arrangements for me to go each day and sit in the sun with Joshua in the corner next to the market. Joshua had been lamed when he fell off a roof on which he had been working. He was a brave man as he was in constant pain but he never complained. You could tell when things were worse than usual because his breathing got louder and more rapid. He sat in a chair that someone had made for him and each morning and evening friends helped him to and from his lodgings. Between us we made almost a whole man. I lived in a hut that had been built for me near Ruth's house and was taken to the market and fetched back each day by her or, as they got older, one of her children. I could manage there as I knew where everything was and Ruth provided meals and did the cleaning.

And so Joshua and I let the world go by. I was able to help him a little with tasks he could not manage and he tried to describe to me what he could see. We developed a circle of men and women who used to come and talk to us. Some brought us money though we never asked for it. We shared it equally. Life was as pleasant as it could be for someone with my disability but I could never say it wasn't frustrating. However, much as I loved Ruth and Isaac, there was no one who saw me as the most important person in his or her life. I was aware that people were being kind. I longed for a woman who I could call my own and who loved me for myself and would tell me what she really thought. I wanted to be able to go and walk in the hills or by the lake but this was not possible unless someone could take me. Life was passing me by and there was nothing I could do about it.

When I was thirty-eight, two things happened which changed my life. The first was that Joshua died. He just passed away in his sleep. From his point of view I was not sorry. His pain had been getting steadily worse and it had become so bad that on occasions he groaned aloud. Right to the end he put a brave face on things but life for him was becoming unbearable. His friends were very good and told me what had happened but I did miss him. There was no one to describe to me what was going on or to talk to me when I felt the need. I was very lonely and, although people were still good to me, I dreaded going to my place by the market. There was nothing else to do however so I got on with life. I never contemplated ending it – I suppose I was too much of a coward.

The second thing was that I began to hear of a teacher named Jesus. He was travelling round Galilee teaching and he had a wonderful ability to heal the sick. The lame were able to walk, the deaf to hear, the dumb to speak and, yes, the blind to see. I began to hope that I might meet this man and I became almost obsessive about seeing him. For the first time in my life I felt there was someone who might be able to help me. I kept on hearing about him and what he was doing but he never came to where I was. Eventually I was told that he had come to Jerusalem for the feast of the Tabernacles. I considered asking one of my friends to take me to him but I lacked the courage to put things to the test in this way. How would I cope if he could not help me? Then one day it happened.

I was sitting in my normal place when I heard the sound of a large group of people approaching. As they went along I heard a voice say "Teacher, why was this man born blind? Was it his sin or that of his parents?" As usual it was as if, because I was blind, I didn't exist. If only people knew how much I resented this. I wondered what sin I was supposed to have committed before I was born.

Another voice softer than the first one but speaking with complete certainty. "It was not because of any sin by him or his parents. He was born blind so that God's power could be seen in him." I was pretty angry about this. Was I just a plaything who had been born blind so that God could show his power? It was an honour I could have done without. The voice went on "We must all do the work given to us by the one who sent me as quickly as possible. The time is coming soon when night will fall and work will come to an end. While I am still here, I am the light of the world".

I heard the sound of someone spitting and then, after a pause, some wet mud being put on my eyes. I don't know why I didn't reach up and wipe it away. The voice again – "Go and wash in the pool of Siloam." Of course I could not get there by myself but I felt strong arms raise me to my feet and lead me off. We went into a building. I could feel that I was in a courtyard as the sun was beating down on me and they led me into some water. I walked in and washed myself in it. And there was light. It wasn't a slow change from darkness through grey to full brightness. There was colour and movement all around. The sky was a glorious blue with a few small clouds scattered around. I could see people and for the first time really understood their shape. It was too much for me. I put my hands over my eyes and then moved them slowly away. I could still see. They led me out into the street. There was so much going on, so many things to watch and wonder at. Often I could not understand what people were doing as I watched them. The brightness was beyond anything I could imagine. I could not have dreamed of anything as vivid as the blue of the sky. The constant movement and changes of colour were almost terrifying – I did not know if I would be able to come to terms with them. And the buildings were so immense. I had no concept of the scale of everything – the Temple was truly enormous.

I asked to be taken home and they led me there. I went in and saw the reality of where I had been living for so many years. My sister, hearing the noise of all the people who had followed me, rushed across to my hut. I knew it was her because of her voice but she looked lined and tired. We hugged and cried together. The children were scared and didn't know what to do. They were as I expected Ruth to be, bright and full of movement. A man came up to me and I knew it must be Isaac. He was white haired and stooped. They were full of questions and I did my best to answer them. They took me to my parents' home and again I was shocked to see how bent and grey they looked.

I realised that I had not thanked Jesus for healing me but I didn't know where to find him. Tomorrow would have to do. Meanwhile that evening there were constant knocks at the door as neighbours and those who had seen me sitting by the market came to see if what they had heard was true. There were those who actually asked "Isn't this the man who used to sit and beg?" Some believed I was while others said, "No, he only looks like him." I just said, "I am the man".

"How were your eyes opened?"

"The man called Jesus made some mud and put it on my eyes. He told me to go to Siloam and wash. So I went and washed and then I could see."

"Where is this man?"

And all I could say was "I don't know."

Next morning there was a loud knocking ay my door. When I opened it there were men dressed in uniform. They demanded that I go with them and took me to a large room in which some men dressed in rich clothes were sitting. Later I learned they were Pharisees who had been told what had happened. I was stood up in front of them and no one offered me a seat. They asked me how I had received my sight.

"He put mud on my eyes and I washed, and now I can see."

"This man Jesus is not sent from God, for he does not keep the Sabbath." This was the first time I realised that I had been given my sight on the Sabbath. One of them asked, "How can a sinner perform such miracles?" They seemed to be arguing among themselves and they completely ignored me. Eventually one spoke.

"What do you have to say about him? It was your eyes he opened."

"I think he must be a prophet." I replied. This was evidently not the right answer and they still did not believe that I had been blind and could now see. They sent for my parents. I was annoyed as I knew how frightened they would be and how difficult it would be for them to come but nothing I said would stop them. They came.

"Is this your son? Is this the one you say was born blind? How is it that now he can see?"

"We know he is our son and we know he was born blind. But how he received his sight or who healed him we don't know. Ask him. He is old enough; he will speak for himself." I could see Father in particular was terrified and the whole occasion was too much for him. He just wanted to keep out of trouble. They had heard that anyone who acknowledged that Jesus was the Christ would be put out of the synagogue and so they had answered as they did.

They called me back and spoke to me. "Give glory to God by telling the truth because we know Jesus is a sinner."

I was getting annoyed. "I don't know whether he is a sinner or not. One thing I do know for certain. Yesterday I was blind and today I can see."

They went back to the original question. "What did he do to you? How did he give you your sight?"

I lost my temper. "I have told you already and you will not listen. Why do you want to hear again? Do you want to become his disciples too?"

At that they started yelling and screaming and throwing insults at me. "You are this fellow's disciple! We are disciples of Moses! We know that God spoke to Moses but, as for this man, we don't know anything about him."

I replied. "Now that is very strange! He gave me my sight and you still say you know nothing about him. Well God doesn't listen to sinners; he will listen to people who do his will and worship him. Never since the world began has anyone been able to open the eyes of a man born blind. If this man was not from God, he couldn't do it either."

They were spitting with rage and, as I took the hands of my parents and prepared to go, they yelled "You were born in sin; how dare you lecture us?" And they pushed us out.

Next morning there was a knock at my door. When I opened it Jesus was there. I recognised him by his voice. He was on his own but quickly news of his visit spread around.

He asked, "Do you believe in the Son of Man?"

"Who is he, sir? Tell me because I would like to."

"You have seen him and he is now speaking with you."

There was no need for hesitation. I fell on my knees. "Lord, I believe" I said and I worshipped him.

Jesus spoke again. "I have come to judge the world. I will give sight to the blind and show those who think they can see that they are blind." I didn't understand what he was saying but some Pharisees who had joined the crowd interrupted.

"What? Are we blind then?"

"If you were blind you would not be guilty of sin; but because you claim that you can see, your guilt remains." With this he turned and left.

For some days people came banging on my door just to look at me but eventually my new life could begin. I moved in with my parents to look after them but this was not a total success. I hadn't realised how much I had to learn from the simplest thing like boiling water to going to the market where I could not recognise what was what. It was amazing how quickly some of the skills that I had learned as a blind man vanished now that I could see. Fortunately I was a quick learner and I like to think that I made their last days happier. They died shortly after I got my sight back, both at around the same time. I spent my time trying to help those in the same plight as I had been. Some were grateful but many were very unpleasant both because they resented being handicapped and because I had been healed.

It was about a year later that I learned that Jesus was coming back to Jerusalem. I saw him enter the city greeted by a huge crowd and heard of how he upset the moneychanger's tables at the Temple. He obviously hadn't changed and I knew the risks he was taking. I was not surprised when he was captured and executed. I could not reconcile this with his claim to be the Son of Man and was very sad about the news. It was only when the stories of his resurrection began that I realised that what he had said was true. When the disciples returned to Jerusalem, I went to join them and help with their work. I was there on the day they came back and told us that Jesus had ascended to heaven. A particular joy to me was to help a man who named Bartimaeus who had been born blind and had been a beggar like me. He used to sit by the roadside in Jericho and had been cured by Jesus on his last journey to Jerusalem. I knew what he was going through. I still try to help people in difficulty although, as I get older, there is less that I can do. One of my great joys is that Ruth and Isaac and their children have all come to believe in Jesus as I do.

The Rich Young Man

I was born rich. I can never remember a time when there wasn't plenty of food on the table or enough servants available to allow me to do what I wanted. This didn't mean life was easy because, from an early age, it was made clear to me that, since I had been brought up with so many advantages, it was my responsibility to use them to help those less fortunate than myself. I had to treat everyone with respect and do all I could to help them. The only times I remember Mum or Father being really cross with me were when I forgot this basic rule. It became a sort of fetish with me which to a large extent shaped my life.

Ours was a happy home. Father was a merchant who, right from when he was very young, had a knack of making money. He was the son of a carpenter but quickly discovered that he had no ability with his hands. He had to find something else to do and discovered his talent for trading. When I grew older I found that I didn't share his talent. Father was a man who took life seriously and the only person who could make him relax was Mum. Marrying her was the only extravagance that he ever allowed himself.

She was very pretty with bright red hair and always cheerful. From when I first thought about these things she was the most beautiful woman I ever saw. When I grew up, I never saw anyone as attractive as her and was never therefore tempted to marry. She was fifteen years younger than Father and was only fourteen when they met. Her father was a labourer who worked on anything that came to hand. Often, particularly in winter, there was no work available and life was hard but somehow they managed. Mum was the oldest of five children and I never remember her being in low spirits. This didn't mean she was always trying to cheer you up but when she there, laughter wasn't far away. There was never much money in her home but this didn't seem to worry any of them. They were a close knit family and even when her parents both died while Mum was still young, they remained close to each other. My aunts used to tell me how Father had helped them when they were growing up.

Mum used to tell me about how she and Father met. She first saw him when she went to work in one of his stores. She was there to keep the place clean and act as a general helper. Father noticed her one day and they started to talk. From that day on Father was at that shop for some time each day and always made time to talk with Mum. What she saw in him I don't know but eventually Father saw her parents and arranged to marry her. At first her parents were very opposed to the match. He was much older than her and with no obvious attractions. The only thing going for him was that he had plenty of money but, to their credit, Mum's parents wanted her to be happy rather than rich. Mum saw something in him which nobody else saw and it was only when she insisted that Father was the only man for her that they gave permission for the wedding. They were devoted to each other and very happy together. Neither my sister Ruth, who is five years younger than me, nor I understood how lucky we were to grow up in a happy home such as ours. It was only when we started visiting our friends' homes that we saw the truth.

Because of his money Father became a senior member of the synagogue and I was encouraged to help there. Many of the families who came were very poor. I was expected to treat them as my equal and, to my surprise, I found that they all had some qualities I could admire. I grew close to some of them and was able to help them because they were at their wits ends. This gave me great satisfaction. I was proud of what I was able to do but every evening I went back to my comfortable home.

We lived in a backwater on the East side of the River Jordan down by the Dead Sea. There were rarely any visitors to our area but there was a constant flow of people going to and from Jerusalem and they kept us aware of what was happening outside. We began to hear stories of a man named Jesus who came from Galilee and was able to heal people from incurable diseases. There were even stories that he had raised people from the dead. He was also a great teacher and, when he spoke, huge crowds gathered to hear him. He was hated by the Pharisees and Priests because he told them off for their hypocrisy and greed. There was enormous excitement when we were told that he had come into our area.

I was nineteen when I met Jesus. I wanted to see him because he was helping people in the same way that I hoped to. He was changing their whole lives rather than giving them the cost of their next meal. Perhaps he could teach me to be more like him. I went to where he was staying and was lucky enough to find him alone except for two or three of his closest friends. I had decided on my approach to him before I went on my visit. I didn't want to seem presumptuous and I knew that he often talked about eternal life. This wasn't what I really wanted to discuss as I was more interested in how I could help people in the same way as he did but it seemed a good opening to our talk. I fell on my knees in front of him and asked "Good teacher, what must I do to inherit eternal life?"

His answer was a surprise. "Why do you call me good? Only God himself is good." I was impressed by his modesty. From what I had heard he had every right to call himself good. He went on. "But in response to your question, you know the commandments. Do not murder, do not commit adultery, do not give false testimony, do not cheat, treat your father and mother with respect."

I was able to reply in all honesty "I have done all these things since I was a boy." He turned and looked at me astonished at my answer. He seemed to be smiling at me and there was real love in his expression. He turned and spoke again. "Go and sell everything you have and give it to the poor and you will earn for yourself treasure in heaven. Then come back and follow me."

I was totally taken aback by this. How could I help people if I had no money? I didn't want to leave home and I wanted to go on living as I was. Jesus seemed to know what I was thinking. I heard him say to his friends "How hard it is for rich people to enter the kingdom of God. It is easier for a camel to go through the eye of a needle than for a rich man to enter the kingdom of God."

The friends replied "If that's so, who in the world can be saved." Jesus looked directly at them. "Humanly speaking no one can be saved but, with God, all things are possible."

I slunk away feeling sad and very discouraged. What was the point of trying to help people if this was the response that I received? I think I was hoping that Jesus would call me back but nothing happened. When I got home I told Mum of our conversation. As usual she was very positive and said that I should go on doing what I thought was right. However this meeting with Jesus was a watershed in my life. I began to question what I was doing and why. There was no doubt I was providing short term help for people but this was only curing the symptoms. Jesus was healing the disease. Those to whom I gave money would use it and want more. I was in a sense making them dependant on me. I had no idea how I could change this as I had nothing else with which to work. I could see that what Jesus was doing was of long term benefit to the people he helped. Because I could find no alternative I went on doing what I had been doing but there was no satisfaction in it. I was terribly hurt by the way Jesus had treated me.

The year after my meeting with Jesus was the worst in my life. Mum became ill and, although she never complained, it was obvious that unless there was a miracle, she would not survive very long. Right to the end she was cheerful but it was awful to see the pain she was in. She died in her sleep and both Father and I were glad that her suffering was over. Without her our home was a desolate place. Father rarely talked and communication between us ceased. It was not long before he too became ill and followed Mum to the grave. It was as if he didn't want to go living without Mum. Ruth had already married and lived in Jerusalem so I saw little of her.

With Father gone my life changed completely. I had to take over his business and was quickly aware that I had no gift for it. Several of the deals I negotiated went very wrong and eventually I sold the business for far less than it was worth to Father's assistant. This meant that I had no source of income and had to live on the money I received from the sale. I moved out of what had been our home and was no longer able to continue with my charity. I became very lonely. The people who had flocked around me when I could help them no longer took any notice of me. I began to see myself for what I was – of no use to man or beast. There were times when I was tempted to take my own life but I didn't have the courage.

The thought of what Jesus had said to me continued to haunt me. He had seen through the shell and how empty the space beneath was. What he had told me was right but it was too late to do anything about it. I became almost a recluse having nothing to go out for. I continued to hear about Jesus and what he was doing from returning travellers. I was shocked when I learned that Jesus had been crucified by the Romans under pressure from the High Priest and his council. Whatever Jesus had done, he hadn't deserved that. It wasn't until about a week later that I heard the rumours about Jesus' resurrection. At first I didn't believe the stories but, when the body was not produced, I began to wonder. The High Priest said that the body had been stolen but this seemed unlikely. I knew that the tomb would have been guarded and in any event it would have been extremely difficult to dispose of a body in a city as tight packed as Jerusalem.

I spent much of my time pondering what had occurred in my life and in particular what had happened to Jesus. He had been a good man who had been able to do things which were beyond normal humans. In the end I had to go to Jerusalem and find out more for myself. I knew Ruth would put me up and so I set out for the city about three months after I first heard about the resurrection of Jesus. I found where my sister lived and she gave me the welcome I hoped for. She had two beautiful children, a boy and a girl. That night I sat down to talk with Ruth and her husband Joel. We started by telling each other what had been happening in our lives but I was soon able to ask about Jesus. She said that there was a rapidly growing group of people who believed that Jesus was the Messiah. They were becoming increasingly daring in opposing the High Priest and his followers. Their leaders were the friends who had been with Jesus when he visited our part of Judea. Only one of them had deserted Jesus and it was he who had betrayed Jesus into the hands of the High Priest. There had recently been a healing of one of the beggars, a cripple who sat outside the Temple every day begging. Two of the leading followers of Jesus had been arrested for claiming that they were acting in his name but, instead of backing down, they had defended themselves so strongly that a number of people had been converted to their cause. I asked Ruth and Joel what they thought. They said they were beginning to believe that Jesus had been the Messiah but they were scared to do anything about it. They wanted to be able to bring up their children in peace.

I decided that I must try and meet some of Jesus' friends. There was no difficulty in finding them and I was welcomed to the house where they lived. When I said why I had come I was invited in and one of the people who had been with Jesus before came to talk to me. His name was Andrew. I told him about when I had met Jesus and he remembered the incident. I said how upset I had been about what had happened. He explained to me that I couldn't serve Jesus if I was seeking glory for myself. They could only do the things they did if the glory was given to God. If they relied on themselves they failed. I said that I had been trying to help people in the best way I could. Andrew looked me straight in the eyes and replied that I had actually been trying to build up my own importance. The real reason I had been doing what I did was pride. I had been trying to buy friendship rather than form real relationships. Jesus was the Son of God and he had come to earth, lived as a normal human and died to pay the price for the evil that each one of us had done. If we accepted this, our misdeeds would be forgiven.

This was hard for me to take but Andrew went on to say that, if I wanted to serve Jesus, I must accept that he was the Messiah and act in his name. I went away and thought hard about what I had been told and, in spite of the anger I felt about what Andrew had said, realised that it made sense. I went back and told Andrew that I wanted to become a follower of Jesus and he invited me to join the community living in the house.

I have never regretted making this decision. I have seen the most wonderful miracles done in the name of Jesus and I have seen men gladly die rather than renounce their belief in the Saviour. In a small way I have been privileged to serve Jesus and I have got more satisfaction from this than I did in all my days on the other side of Jordan. The main reason is I believe that I have something real to offer. I thank God for his patience with me.

Zacchaeus

It is no great benefit to be short. Apart from the physical things you cannot do, there is a psychological disadvantage. Constantly having other people look down on you gives you an inferiority complex that affects everything you attempt. Being short is a state of mind. I even look up to most women which might explain my failure with the fairer sex. On the other hand it may be that I do a job that makes me universally loathed. In any event I am a very lonely man.

I was born into a family of masons. I had three strapping elder brothers and a sister. We lived in Jericho and Father was one of the leading businessmen in the town. It quickly became clear that I was going to be physically unable to join the business. I was not able to lift the big blocks of stone around. This doesn't mean I was weak; I was wiry and agile and very fit. Part of the problem was that my brothers didn't really want me to join them. Splitting the business three ways was bad enough. Otherwise I am sure they could have found me a job in the office or preparing estimates. So, as soon as I was able, I left home to make my own way in the world.

I went to Jerusalem. At the back of my mind was the idea that I might train as a scribe. I was interested in history and it might be possible to get a position helping in research into this subject. However things didn't work out like that. I had no money and had to get a job straightaway. Having no experience I could not afford to be choosy. The result was that I ended up doing repetitive and badly paid work for some rather shady outfits. To cap it all, I was lonelier in Jerusalem than I had ever been in Jericho. There at least I had a home to go to. Here my lodgings were unpleasant and there was no one to talk to. I took to going to a nearby tavern. I became expert at making one drink last the whole evening.

Some of the men at the Tavern were hoping to become tax collectors gathering money on behalf of the Romans. They worked as Publicans helping established collectors and they suggested that I should join them. My initial reaction was to refuse, as I knew how tax collectors were regarded. No one of any reputation spoke to them as they were regarded as traitors to their people.

The way that a tax collector worked was that he purchased an area in which he was allowed to operate and negotiated a target that he was required to pay to the Romans. There were rules as to individual liability for tax but, so long as the target was met, the Romans didn't care much how. The collector could retain any amounts collected in excess of the target. It was possible to become exceedingly rich very quickly but the cost was complete exclusion from respectable society. Not without justification, tax collectors were classed with prostitutes and beggars as the dregs of society. I knew the cost but I was starving and in the end I became a publican.

I decided I knew how to do the job and borrowed money to purchase the right to gather taxes in my hometown of Jericho. Naively I believed that in a familiar environment, it would be easier to identify those who could afford to pay tax. In the event my family would have nothing to do with me and again I was reduced to living in lodgings. Former friends passed me in the street when they learned what I was doing. It was not unusual to have people spit in my face and I was not even allowed to enter the synagogue. This was a big problem for me as I had enjoyed going there and meeting all sorts of different people. In my new role I was considered too wicked to be able to worship God.

I began work. The first task was to identify a list of those who might be able to pay and to contact them. My predecessor had left virtually no records so I had to start again from scratch. The job took me some time and meanwhile I had no income and a large debt. The results were not surprising. Those I approached explained that they were down to their last shekel, the business was in terminal decline and they could not possibly afford to make any payment. There were only two remedies. The first was to ask the Romans who might be persuaded to act to help if I threatened to report them to the Procurator. However they were loath to get involved. They had to live in the towns like us and they didn't want the bother and unpleasantness of chasing after people who had not paid what I claimed was due. The second remedy was the ability to seize property for which purpose I used a band of hoodlums who were of course paid by results. Once I had possession, there was no way that those whose property I had seized could get it back. Eventually I worked out a method of operating. I demanded an impossibly high sum. There was great wailing and gnashing of teeth and eventually a sum was agreed. On the whole traders and professional people did not want to be in trouble with the authorities. We used a whole series of bribes (20% off if you paid within 7 days etc.). I began to make money but the inevitable result of meeting the target one year was a much higher demand the next. The Romans were nothing if not greedy.

In time, when I had paid off my debt, I became rich. I had a big house and servants but no on of any repute would speak to me. I could find a woman to come in and satisfy my needs but there was no one who I could treat as a friend. I had never learned to love other people or to accept love from them or think of anyone's needs but my own. I thought of giving up my position but this would not have helped. Once a tax collector, always a tax collector. Retirement did not bring respectability. Loneliness was a constant problem and mostly I got little satisfaction from my work. There was the occasional case where someone had been particularly insulting and I was able to force them to make an excessive payment but even this soon palled.

I began to hear stories of a new teacher in Galilee, Jesus by name, who was creating quite a stir there. What intrigued me was that he would associate with the low end of society. He even had as one of his close friends Levi, a former tax collector. I longed for an opportunity to meet Jesus but for a long time it didn't seem as if it was going to happen. One of the problems of the tax collector's job is that he always has to be there. As he deals with other people, so other people deal with him. It was by accident that I heard that Jesus was passing through Jericho. I rushed to the main street but many other people had the same idea. No one was going to let me through to see him and I certainly could not see over their heads. I looked down the road and saw a lone sycamore tree that hung over the road and climbed up it. I must have been an extraordinary sight lying along a branch but I could see who was coming and he would be able to see me. I didn't know whether I wanted him to spot me or not - perhaps I was too far gone even for him. I saw him coming along the dusty track. People were standing staring at him but there was a strange silence as if they did not know how to behave. He moved along greeting them and smiling. He reached the end of the village nearing where I was and he looked up. A broad smile spread across his face.

He called out "Zacchaeus, come down immediately. I am going to stay at your house tonight." He knew my name. He knew my need and he had recognised me. I almost fell out of the tree in my hurry, scraping the skin off my hands as I slid down. I could hear a background of murmuring and discontent. " What is he doing talking to this sort of scum?" I didn't care. He was coming to my house to stay. I went up to him, welcomed him and led him to my home. I could hear the whispers again. "He has gone to be the guest of a 'sinner'."

The moment was too much for me and I blurted out "Look, Lord! Here and now I give half of my wealth to the poor and if I have overcharged anybody on their taxes, I will pay back four times the amount". It was almost as if someone else was speaking through me. I was as surprised as everybody else at what I was saying. To call him Lord somehow seemed natural and in the face of his obvious honesty, I could do no less than I had said.

He replied, "Today salvation has come to this house because this man has shown himself to be a son of Abraham. The Son of Man came to seek and to save people like this man who are lost." He recognised my humanity and treated me as a person. He went on to tell a story to those who had gathered at my house. I don't think there was ever a more attentive audience.

"A nobleman was called away to a different city to be crowned king and then to return. Before he left he called ten of his servants and gave them each ten pounds of silver to invest while he was away. 'Put this money to work until I come back' he said. But his subjects hated him and sent a delegation after him to say that they didn't want this man to be their king'. He was crowned in the other city however and returned home. Then he sent for his servants to whom he had given money to invest to find out what profit they had made with it.

The first man reported a tremendous profit; he now had ten times as much as he was originally given. 'Well done' the king replied. 'Because you have been trustworthy in a very small matter, you will be appointed governor of ten cities.'

The second came. 'Sir, your silver is now worth five times as much.' His master answered 'You will be appointed governor of five cities.'

Another servant came and said 'Sir, here is your silver; I have kept it hidden away in a piece of cloth. I was afraid of you because you are a hard man. You steal and take the benefit of other people's work.' His master replied 'You idiot! If you knew how unscrupulous I am, you could at least have put the money on deposit in a bank so that it would earn interest for me. '

Then he said to those standing by, 'Take the money away from him and give it to the one who has increased his tenfold.'

'But master,' they said, 'He has enough already!'

He replied, 'Those who make good use of what they are given will be trusted with more but those who cannot be trusted with even a little will lose even that. Now bring in those men who didn't want me to be king and have them executed immediately'".

It was not until later that I grasped the meaning of this story. Jesus was about to leave his people. When he had gone, they must continue to work faithfully for him. He was telling me there was no going back. I had been given my task and I must carry on with it.

The first thing was to pay back the money I had stolen. Fortunately I had been scrupulous in my record keeping and could identify the amounts I had amounts fairly easily. When I started visiting people to give back what I had wrongly collected, the reactions I got were almost comical. I could almost hear them asking 'what is the catch?' Some were reluctant to accept any refund. There were of course those who accused me of over charging them although I had not done so. They got very irritated when I was able to show them the truth. I also, as I had promised, gave half my fortune to the poor.

I thought long and hard about what I should do with my life. In the end I thought that Jesus had hinted through his story that I should go on as I was but do the job honestly. I wanted people to see that my ways had changed forever. I charged what was due and no more and, because I was honest, most of them were honest too. The amount I collected actually went up.

It would be good to be able to say that I was received back into society but this didn't happen. However my house was always full of the needy and the lonely and I was able to use it for them. I told them of what had caused me to change my way of life and it was my great delight if, as happened occasionally, one of them said he wanted to follow the teaching of Jesus. I found real friendship in that group. We had our loneliness in common and were able to help each other. For the first time in my life I felt needed. I could see and accept people as they were and value them. Because I loved them, they returned my love.

When I heard that Jesus had been executed I was devastated but when the stories of him rising again began to circulate, I began to understand that he really was the Son of God. Everything I did, I did in memory of him and his love for me.

Death and
Resurrection

Mary

Luke:- So in spite of your warnings Jesus went to Jerusalem. Did you go with him?

Mary:- No. He only made up his mind when to go at the last minute. As usual I went up with my friends from the synagogue in Nazareth. The first I heard of his arrival was when I was told of the welcome the people had given him as he entered the city. While I was naturally proud of him, I was worried because I knew how this would antagonise the Jewish leaders still more. I met up with some of the women who followed Jesus including Mary Magdalene and Salome, my sister and I spent my time with them. It was an odd atmosphere in Jerusalem that year, heavy and ominous as if everyone was expecting something unusual.

Luke:- Did you meet Jesus in Jerusalem?

Mary:- He used to stay with Martha in Bethany and I met him there when he came back one night. He was as loving as ever to me and I asked him if he had to risk his life as he was doing. He replied that whatever must be must be.

Luke:- When did you hear that he had been taken prisoner?

Mary:- Soon after it happened. Some of his close friends came running from the Garden of Gethsemane where he had been and told us what had happened. I knew then that there was no hope for him. My friends were as upset as I was. We went back to where we were staying in despair. Early next morning, after a sleepless night, someone told us that Jesus was to be crucified that day at Golgotha, the execution ground. However much we wanted, we couldn't stay away. I didn't want to be there but he had to know that some of those he loved were there and that not everyone had deserted him. The only one of the apostles there was John.

John:- I am afraid my colleagues were too frightened to be there.

Luke:- Were you there the whole time?

Mary:- Yes. We arrived just as the crosses were being hoisted into the vertical. The sight of my son then will haunt me for evermore. He was offered wine mixed with myrrh to dull the pain but he wouldn't even accept this. His body was a mass of lash marks and his face was bruised and scarred. I wanted to go and cuddle him as I had done when he was a little boy. I could not understand why the people who had greeted him so enthusiastically and worshipped him earlier in the week had turned against him. He had healed the sick and done absolutely nothing to harm them. On the cross was a notice saying "Jesus of Nazareth, the King of the Jews". There were a few Pharisees mocking and calling out "He saved others; himself he cannot save". For a time the High Priest and his acolytes were on one side watching what went on. Jesus looked down at them and said "Father, forgive them for they do not know what they are doing". Soon after I saw them move off.

Two others were being crucified with him – one on each side. One of them even joined in the mockery saying, "Aren't you the Christ? Why don't you save yourself – and us too while you are at it". The other could be heard telling him off. "Don't you fear God even while you are dying? We deserve to die for our crimes but this man has done nothing wrong." Then he said, "Jesus, remember me when you reach your kingdom". Jesus answered "You can be certain that today you will be with me in paradise". There was a strange silence in the crowd so that all could hear the words Jesus spoke.

How could they be doing this to my son? He had never deliberately harmed any one in his life. How could he hang there in agony and still consider others? I could tell by watching the crowd that this execution was different. I could feel his agony hanging there, the constant struggle to breathe, the nagging pain of the rough cross rubbing on his whipped back. I had tears streaming down my face and wanted to look away but I couldn't. In a strange way I would be deserting him if I did so. Jesus looked at me and said "Mother, this is your son" and to John "Here is your mother". How he could think of me when he was in such torment I will never know.

As time passed it grew dark - darker than most nights as there was neither moon nor stars. Black clouds covered the sun and it teemed with rain. I was soaked to the skin. Suddenly Jesus called out "My God, My God, why have you forsaken me?" I think this was the first time I had heard him address his prayers to anyone but 'Father'. Had even the Father who he loved so much deserted him?

A pause and then he called out "I am thirsty." His body convulsed in mortal agony. I couldn't help thinking of that perfect baby I had loved so much. I had taken such pride in his beauty and in the joy of cuddling him and now it was come to this. I was sobbing uncontrollably and collapsed into John's arms. One of the watchers ran and got a sponge. He filled it with wine vinegar, put it on a stick and offered it to Jesus to drink. Others said, "Now leave him alone. Let's see if Elijah comes to save him".

The darkness deepened broken only by sudden vivid flashes of lightning and the wind grew stronger. It was as if the world itself was complaining at what was being done. Jesus called out "It is finished" and then later "Father into your hands I commit my spirit". And he was gone. His agony was over. The ground shook and there was a deafening bang. I stood there unable to move. John kept his arm around me. The soldiers came and broke the legs of the two men crucified with Jesus.

I was frightened they would do the same to Jesus but when they came they saw he was already dead. Instead they thrust a spear into his side. I was horrified as blood and water spurted out. I saw them draw lots for his clothes and looked on as they took his body down from the cross and gave it to Joseph of Arimathea for burial. I followed as they laid him to rest in a new tomb and rolled a huge stone across the entrance. Guards from the Temple were posted to ensure that the body wasn't stolen. And then John took me back to his lodgings, numb and in total despair.

That night and throughout the next day, the feast of the Passover, I thought back over the life of Jesus. He was my son born of my flesh and his pain was my pain. The Son of God had come to this. How could it be? I remembered the happy times in Nazareth, the strange events surrounding his birth. What would the shepherds have made of all this? Would the wise men have possibly been able to anticipate what had happened? Was this what Simeon and Anna expected? Where was the sense in it? Why had someone so good suffered so much? However much I tried, I couldn't get to the bottom of it. If this had happened to the Son of God, what hope was there for the rest of us? Life seemed too difficult to understand and there was no one to give me help.

Time after time I went over the events of the day. Were the darkness and the eerie silence, broken only by the sobbing wind, natural or was God mourning over the suffering of his son? It was as if some great play that I didn't understand was being played out in front of me.

In a way I felt sorry for Pilate and Herod and Caiaphas. They were men caught up in a chain of events over which they had no control. Yet I did hate them. They did not need to do what they did to my Jesus. I could see no meaning in his death and I blamed those who caused it.

Strangely I wasn't ashamed of how Jesus had died although he had been crucified with two criminals and had himself been treated as if he was one. No one but me knew the circumstances of his birth and I had no idea how something which had begun with so much hope had ended like this. That there was a reason I had no doubt but what it was I could not begin to guess.

I thought about why Jesus had put me under John's protection rather than expecting my family to look after me. That would have been the natural thing and it was what was laid down in the Law. James and my other children had been very upset when Jesus left Nazareth and started out as a teacher, particularly as he had earned the family living through the carpentry business. I had never told them of the circumstances of Jesus' birth. When Jesus was expelled from the synagogue at home, they had been the ones who were teased because they were related to him. Since then there had been a slightly strained relationship between them. They saw the close relationship Jesus had with his disciples as a sign that he had deserted his family. They had seen little of him over the last three years while he was away teaching and they didn't believe he was interested in them any longer. I knew this was untrue and how much

Jesus had been hurt by their attitude but to have their responsibility taken away in this way would be a bitter blow to them. However John was a lonely man who needed someone to look after him and we were related. I didn't really understand but I knew I had to do what Jesus had said.

Luke:- John, what did you think when Jesus said this?

John:- I was taken completely by surprise. It had never entered my head that Jesus would do such a thing. I had enough on my mind thinking that all my dreams had come to nothing without this. James and his brothers were my cousins and I could see no reason why they should not look after their mother. I dreaded telling them what Jesus had said. However if this was Jesus' dying wish, of course I would do what he wanted.

Luke: - The Passover must have been a time of great sorrow. What were you thinking?

Mary:- My mind was churning and I just did not understand what had happened. How could the Son of God be executed and in such a barbarous fashion? Why had I been put through this? There seemed no point in the Son of God coming to earth just to be killed. I thought I was the victim of some cruel joke. How could God have built me up as the mother of the 'Chosen One' only to allow my son to be put to death as a common criminal. It was difficult to believe that I had not been totally misled. Was what Simeon and Anna said just sentimental nonsense? Up to now I had had no doubt that they were telling the truth as they had heard it.

One thing at least was true. Simeon was right when he said Jesus would cause me as much suffering "as if a sword had pierced my heart".

Luke:- Why did you stay in Jerusalem?

Mary:- I didn't want to be away from him. Before dawn on the morning after the feast Salome, Joanna, Mary Magdalene and I got up to go and anoint Jesus' body with spices. When we got there, we found the entrance open and the stone rolled away. Mary went ahead to see what was happening and, when she returned, told us that the tomb was empty. She ran back to find Simon and John while Salome and I remained standing nearby. Suddenly two men in white clothes which shone like lightning appeared and spoke to us.

"Why do you look for the living among the dead? He is not here, he has risen. Think back to what he told you when you were all still in Galilee. The Son of Man will be captured by sinful men and crucified. On the third day he will be raised from the dead." The angels disappeared just before Mary arrived back with Simon and John.

John:- I was younger and thinner than Simon and got there first but didn't have the courage to enter. Simon came puffing noisily, pushed past me and went in and I followed him. I could see the burial clothes lying neatly folded where the body had been laid. The body was not there. We were completely dumbstruck. Over the feast day we had remembered the times that Jesus had told us that he must die and rise again and

I couldn't get this thought out of my head. I knew that all he had told us was true. We went back to the other followers and told them what we had seen and we began to discuss exactly what Our Lord had said. Later that morning Mary Magdalene, who had stayed by the tomb, rushed in to tell us that she had seen the risen Jesus. Simon was in despair. How was he going to face the Lord when he had let him down so disastrously? We sat and talked all that day and recalled events in his life that had slipped our memory or had been insignificant at the time. In the evening two of the disciples who lived in Emmaus came back to us in great excitement. They had been on their way home when a stranger had come and walked with them. They told him of Jesus' death and he explained to them from scripture exactly what had been foretold about himself. It was only as they reached their home that they recognised him. At this point he vanished from their sight. Later that evening he appeared among us. I mean just appeared. He didn't come through the door – he was suddenly there. We were startled and frightened thinking him to be a ghost. He showed us his wounds and invited us to touch him and to show us that he was real, he asked us to prepare some fish for him. He was the same but different. His body was merely a cover for his spiritual presence and no longer seemed subject to the laws of nature.

He reminded us again of the times when he had said he must die and rise again after three days as foretold in the scriptures and he explained them to us. Finally he told us to return to Galilee where he would meet with us again and then he vanished.

Mary:- I needed to be on my own. Yet again I went over all the things I had heard Jesus say and which I had only partially understood. It began to be clear to me why he had come to earth. He had died and come alive again. Of his death there was no doubt. Too many people had seen it. And now many people who I trusted had seen him and I was certain he was alive. But what was the purpose of his sacrifice? He had been perfect. He didn't need to die. I went back to Nazareth.

Luke:- Did you see him again?

Mary:- Yes. He came to our house one day. Some of the children were there and were astonished to see him. There seemed no change in his outward appearance except for the hideous nail marks on his hands and his feet. He talked to us as if he was still living with us and then beckoned me aside. He was as gentle and kind as ever. He explained why he had come to earth, how he had been born and why he had had to die. He came of his own free will and out of love for humanity. God, his father was a just God and could not associate with evil. Men and women were evil and constantly broke God's laws. Therefore there was a chasm between God and man and someone had to bridge it. That person had to be perfect, completely without fault. Jesus, the Son of God was the only person who matched this description. Out of love he came down from heaven and was born as a human. He lived a life without wrongdoing and then allowed himself to be captured, tortured and executed. At any time he could have saved himself but, still from love, he went on to the bitter end. Now those who believed in him would be forgiven their wrongdoing and go to be with their creator God because they were perfect in his sight. I could see understanding dawning in my children's eyes and, from then on, they believed fully that Jesus was the Son of God. This caused me great happiness.

I asked him why he didn't just replace humanity with another group of people who obeyed God's will and he explained to me the covenant God had made. He had given men and women freewill and, when they used it to disobey him, he had to provide a means of reconciliation. This was only available to those who would accept the sacrifice he had made on their behalf. At last I began to understand why he had come to earth. He had come not to live but to die. The three years before his death were to show people who he was. Only the Son of God could control the elements and heal the sick as he did but his real purpose was to die for us. When he had done so, he could come back to life again as a further demonstration of his divinity. He could have gone straight back to heaven but he had unfinished business with his apostles on earth. They too had to understand.

We went back inside and he said farewell to his brothers and sisters. He hugged and kissed me and then he was gone. About eight weeks later I returned to Jerusalem hoping to see Jesus again. His brothers came with me. When we met John, he told us that Jesus had been taken up into heaven a few days earlier. He had eaten with the apostles the night before and the next morning, after he had instructed them not to leave Jerusalem, they had set out along the road to Bethany. Suddenly he started rising into the sky and was quickly hidden from them by a cloud. Two men dressed in shining white appeared and told them "Men of Galilee why do you stand here looking into the sky? This same Jesus who has been taken from you into heaven will come back in the same way you have seen him go into heaven."

John took us to a room where many of the disciples were staying and Simon (who was now called Peter) stood up and said that it was necessary to replace Judas Iscariot who had betrayed Jesus. Two candidates, both of whom had followed Jesus around since he had started preaching in Galilee, were selected and, after prayer, lots were drawn and Matthias was chosen. It was an odd feeling to see Simon, who had let Jesus down so badly, acting as leader. There was an aura about him as if he knew he was the right person for the job. Anyway there was no one present who hadn't failed Jesus in one way or another. I know that Jesus had forgiven Simon when they met in Galilee. I left reassured because I knew Jesus would not be forgotten. However I would remember him as a baby, dependant on me for everything and in those happy years in Nazareth where he was just a normal, mischievous, happy child.

A few days later the same group of us were meeting for companionship and prayer when suddenly there was a noise like a violent gale which filled the whole building. It didn't hurt my ears but there was no escaping it. I looked around and saw what looked like small tongues of fire coming from the forehead of each person there. I could feel that the same thing was happening to me. I felt elated and full of love and care for other people. Some of those who had been in the room went outside and were talking to the crowd that had gathered as a result of the noise we had heard. Everyone there heard what was said in the language they normally spoke. I knew that Peter and the others had never spoken in any tongue but their own. I was so glad that my other children had received the same gift as I had. From that day I began to tell others about my wonderful son.

Luke:- Where did you go then?

Mary:- I stayed with John in Jerusalem. From time to time I went back to Nazareth to visit my children but my home was now with John. I saw the number of followers increase and thanked God as people came to accept the sacrifice made out of love for them. I was able to talk to them and hear of the changes Jesus had made in their lives. At last I understood the huge importance of the honour of being Jesus' mother. I was humbled that this had been my role. Even now it is difficult for me to believe that those strange events happened to me. I am happy in my new life but I do miss seeing my grandchildren grow up.

John:- It took time for us to realise that out of love, God had sent his only Jesus so that the world might be saved through him. Even when he came, people, including those from his own land, didn't recognise him. However those who did accept him were given the right to become the 'Children of God'. That is what I have spent my life telling anyone who will listen and I praise God that so many have heard.

Andrew

I told you before about what happened when I was with Jesus in Galilee. Now I want to tell you what happened on that last trip to Jerusalem.

As planned we set out for Jerusalem some time before the Passover. We stopped for a while with Jesus' friends in Bethany and then went on to the city. We went down from the Mount of Olives into the city where news of our arrival had preceded us. A crowd had gathered and they took Jesus, mounted him on a donkey and led him in procession into the City. The way was strewn with palm branches and the people greeted him as King of the Jews. Jesus made no effort not to upset the authorities. He went into the Temple and immediately created an uproar. He made himself a whip from some ropes and chased all the money changers from the premises. He upset their tables scattering coins all over the ground and released the cattle and sheep held for sale to those wanting to sacrifice. He ordered those selling doves to leave the Temple because they were turning it into a market place. The resulting confusion was fun, with the lambs running round the Temple getting between people's feet and everyone trying to pick up the coins. Jesus ended up by driving the moneychangers out of the Temple. The Jewish leaders asked him what right he had to do these things and demanded that if he had this authority from God, he should perform a miracle to prove it. Jesus replied, "Destroy this Temple and I will rebuild it in three days."

The leaders were astonished. "What" they said "it took 46 years to build this Temple and you could rebuild it in three days." We realised later that Jesus was referring to his body rather than the building. We remembered these words and understood them after he was raised from the dead.

Jesus went back to the Temple each day, teaching large crowds made up equally of his followers and visitors to Jerusalem for the feast. Some of the names he called the Pharisees and religious leaders were deeply insulting and it was as if he was trying to get himself arrested. You could see the anger on their faces as they listened. The only safety he had was in the large crowds which surrounded him. At night we went to Bethany to stay and at least there was no threat there. I was surprised at the violence of Jesus' attacks on the religious leaders. I knew he despised them but I could not see any point in upsetting them in the way that he was.

He began to tell us that it was his fate to be captured and executed but I don't think any of us registered what he was saying. The night before Passover we all gathered to have supper together in an upper room. Simon and John had been asked to prepare the meal and I remember thinking how odd this was. Cooking was woman's work and there were plenty of women who would have been only too willing to help. After the meal Jesus got up from the table, took off his outer clothing and wrapped a towel round his waist. He poured some water into a basin and began to wash our feet. When he came to Simon, my brother was affronted.

"Lord, are you going to wash my feet".

Jesus replied, "You do not realise now what I am doing, but later you will understand."

Simon, being Simon continued to argue. "You will never wash my feet."

Very quietly Jesus replied, "If I don't wash them you will not belong to me."

"Then Lord, wash my hands and my head as well as my feet."

Jesus answered "A person who has recently had a bath only needs to wash his feet when he arrives somewhere; the rest of his body is clean. You are clean, though not every one here". Looking back it was clear that he already knew of Judas' plans to betray him. When he had finished, he explained what he had done. Although he was our teacher and lord, he was also our servant. We should wash one another's feet as a sign of our willingness to serve one another. No servant is greater than his master and no messenger greater than the one who sent him. We understood that we were to serve one another and those with whom we came in contact. I found it difficult to accept that someone I admired as being superior to all of us could stoop to perform this service for me. It should have been me doing the washing. It was not until years later that I really understood what he had done.

He then took bread, gave thanks and broke it and gave it to us saying "Take and eat; this is my body given for you. Do this in order to remember me". After our meal he took a cup of wine, gave thanks and offered it to us saying, "Drink from this, all of you. This wine represents my blood which I am going to shed for you; it is the sign of God's new covenant through which he will save you from your sins." He went on to tell us that the man who would betray him was sitting at the table with us. "I, the Son of Man, must die since that is God's plan but the fate of my betrayer is truly terrible." We were all wondering which of us would do such a thing and began questioning Jesus. He showed clearly that it was Judas Iscariot but somehow this didn't sink in at the time and Judas just got up and left. When I think back I am amazed that Jesus allowed Judas, who he knew was going to betray him, to have his feet washed and join with us in the Passover meal.

Later we went out to the Mount of Olives. Jesus warned us that this very night we would desert him. Simon vigorously denied it in words which would come back to haunt him saying that he was prepared to go to prison or even to die for him. Jesus told Simon that he would betray him three times before the cock crowed. We all joined Simon in saying we would never betray the Master.

We went into the Garden of Gethsemane in the valley between the city and the Mount of Olives and Jerusalem. Jesus went off to pray with Simon, James and John asking the rest of us to keep him company but we were all too sleepy. We heard later from Mark, a young lad who followed us around, what happened. The Master went off by himself to pray asking his father that he would not have to go through what was planned. Peter and the others fell asleep. Twice Jesus came back to them but each time they were asleep. Once he woke them and once let them lie. Jesus was covered in sweat and deeply distressed. He came back again, woke them and told them that the hour of his betrayal had come.

Around two in the morning we were woken up by the sound of drums and a bright splash of light from torches held by people coming towards us. They turned out to be Temple guards led by Judas Iscariot and they had come to arrest Jesus and take him to the High Priest. As the soldiers drew near to Jesus he stepped forward and asked who they were looking for. "Jesus of Nazareth" they said. "I am he." The soldiers stepped back in surprise and some of them even fell to the ground. Again he asked them "Who are you looking for?" "I told you that I am he. Since it is me you want, let the others go." Judas stepped forward and kissed Jesus and the guards took hold of Jesus. Simon lost his head completely and drew a sword that, for some reason, he was carrying. He cut off the ear of one of the guards. Jesus saw what had happened and called out to Simon to stop. He then reached out and touched the guard's ear and he was immediately healed. Jesus then spoke to the guards. "Am I such a dangerous criminal that you need to come to arrest me equipped with swords and clubs? Every day I taught in the courts of the Temple, and you did not lay a hand on me. But this is the time you choose – when the prince of darkness reigns." Jesus made no effort at all to protect himself although, with the number of guards who had come, he didn't stand much chance anyway. Mark tried to follow Jesus at a distance but he was noticed. They chased him and caught hold of his robe but he managed to slip out of it and run, stark naked, to his home.

I don't want to talk about the next few hours. All of us, including Simon, deserted Jesus and most of us went back to where we were staying on the Mount of Olives to hide. Simon and John did go with Jesus as far as the courtyard outside the guardroom where he was being held. John who was known by the High Priest's household went inside and managed to persuade the doorkeeper to let Simon in. He went and stood by a fire to keep warm and, while he was there, he was asked three times by people standing nearby whether he had been a follower of Jesus. Each time he denied that he was anything to do with him, swearing and cursing as he betrayed his teacher and friend. Eventually he took fright and ran off to join the rest of us. As he left he heard the cock crow.

As dawn broke John and some of the women, including his mother, went to watch the crucifixion returning to join us later. I think all of us felt despair and complete desolation. Jesus, above all else, had been our friend and for him to be killed in this way was unthinkable. However we had also believed in him as someone who was going to change the world and our trust had been misplaced. We had wasted three years and given up our livelihoods. None of us knew what we were going to do next.

On the day following the Feast Mary, with Mary Magdalene and Salome, went to the tomb to anoint Jesus' body. They arrived at the tomb to find the stone rolled away and the tomb empty. The women were terrified and Mary Magdalene came rushing back to fetch Simon and John. Later they all returned bewildered to our lodgings and told us what they had found. Mary Magdalene remained at the tomb and she came to us a little later and told us that she had met Jesus and that he had spoken to her. "Go to my brothers and tell them, I am going back to my father and your father, to my God and your God". I remembered Jesus telling us "My kingdom is not in this world."

All of us began thinking back and discussing what Jesus had said about himself. The air of excitement was tangible. We were on fire with expectation. And that evening Jesus came. He greeted us in the way to which we were used. "Peace be with you." The scars on his hands were a vivid, raw red. We were amazed and overjoyed. To us he was the same but different. He no longer seemed confined by the dictates of time and space. Thomas, forever practical, wasn't with us and when we told him of our Lord's appearance, he said he could never believe unless he could see the wounds in his hands and his feet and put his hand in the hole in his side. When the Lord next came, he invited Thomas to see and touch the wounds and he acknowledged who Jesus was. I felt sorry for Thomas. He didn't know whether to cry with shame or to shout for joy. He stood there red faced and shaking. Jesus told him "Stop doubting and believe. Because you have seen me you have believed; how much better it will be for those who do not see me but still believe."

We saw Jesus many times before he was taken up to heaven. We went back to Galilee and soon after we arrived, Jesus nearly caused the boat from which Peter, John, James and I were fishing to sink. We had caught nothing but then a stranger appeared on the shore and told us to throw our net over the right side of the boat. When we did so we were unable to pull it in because it was so full and we nearly capsized. We had not recognised Jesus who would have found what happened very funny. Simon, with his great strength, had to go into the sea and pull the net in. We landed 153 fish and, even with this load, the net was not broken. When we saw Jesus he was laughing at what had happened. Later Simon was able to make his peace with Jesus. He had been in a dreadful state but Jesus spoke to him on his own and after this he seemed to be a different person – Peter not Simon. Jesus spent many hours talking to us and telling us what was going to happen. He said that he was going to be taken up to heaven and told us what we were to do. "I have been given full authority in heaven and on earth" he said. "Go and make disciples from all the nations, baptising them in the name of the Father, the Son and the Holy Spirit. Teach these new disciples to do all the things I have taught you to do. And be sure of this; I will always be with you, right until the end of this age."

We, all eleven of us, were there when Jesus went to heaven. He seemed to rise gently from the ground and disappeared from our sight into a cloud. We stood there staring into the sky when suddenly two men dressed in white appeared. "Men of Galilee" they said, "Why are you standing here looking up into the sky? Jesus who you have just seen taken up into heaven, will someday return in exactly the same way as you have seen him go."

We had been warned by Jesus to wait in Jerusalem until the Father sent us the gift that Jesus had promised. Ten days later, as we were meeting with many other believers, we suddenly heard a sound like a mighty wind and what appeared to be tongues of fire came and rested on each of us. All of us were filled with the Spirit of Jesus and began to speak in different languages so that everyone could understand us. It was as if Jesus himself was working through us. We found later that we were all now able to read and write.

We stayed in Jerusalem gathering more and more believers and teaching them what the Master had taught us. We shared all our possessions and it was as if the kingdom of heaven had come to earth. This went on until the persecution started and Herod had James, John's brother, beheaded. We were driven out of Jerusalem and began to spread our gospel throughout the world. God has indeed blessed a young fisherman from Bethsaida and to him be the glory.

Malchus

There was no doubt about it – Annas was a real case. He was as sharp as a handful of nails and as slippery as eels in a barrel of oil. To work for him and his son-in-law Caiaphas was no great honour but it gave a regular income and, whatever else, it was interesting. Their role seemed more political than spiritual and they had the Jewish Council, the Sanhedrin eating out of their hand. Well it would be more true to say that Annas did. He was the one who got things done. My function was to act as 'Fixer'. If either of them wanted to deal with someone without making direct contact, I was the man. Usually I had to tell people of the error of their ways. I seldom had to resort to violence as most people recognised that the enmity of the High Priest would make their life a misery. A nod was as good as a wink.

I had reached this position by accident. I suppose it is not the sort of job one deliberately seeks. I joined Annas' household as a junior servant. I was a Jew from a family that had recently fallen on hard times. Once it had been fairly influential but Father soon remedied that. He had been working for a leading member of the Sanhedrin in a confidential capacity and he had spilt the beans about a sensitive matter while drunk. A major scandal erupted in which several members of the Council became involved. It was something to do with selling contracts to supply the Temple. The result was that Father lost his job and was reduced to earning his living as a letter writer. Our standard of living dropped like a stone and Mother was not pleased. She made Father's life a misery and he spent more and more time at the bar. His health gave way and he died when I was about 11 years old. Mother had a close friend who worked for Annas and he got me a job as messenger boy/dogsbody for the great man. This didn't mean I ever met him but his officials used me to run their errands. These could range from shopping to giving out party invitations.

It was while giving out invitations that my moment came. I happened to notice that a group of thugs was gathering near the stall of one of the moneychangers in the Temple. I rushed back to Annas' quarters and told them what was happening. The Temple guards were sent to investigate and the robbers were caught in the act. Of course the guards claimed all the credit but, when Annas found out what had happened, he asked how they had got the tip off. I was called to see the great man and he invited me to be his personal odd job man.

My new position was not that different from the old one except I took my orders direct from the Boss. I got to know him as well as anyone did and a more unpleasant specimen it would be difficult to find. The only person he trusted was his daughter Sarah who was married to the High Priest, Caiaphas. He was greedy, vicious and had to get his own way. If he didn't, he was absolutely ruthless in getting his own back. He had been High Priest but had been sacked after he had been caught trying to bribe Roman officials to release one of my predecessors who happened to have some information that Annas urgently needed. But for this, he would have been left to rot. The man had been shopped to the Procurator by one of the Temple officials. As a result Annas had to work through a third party but there was no doubt where the power really lay and he still remained treasurer of the Temple. Caiaphas, a weak but self-important man, did what he was told. I knew only too well that, if I got into trouble, I needn't look to Annas for help.

I had been in my new position for about 5 years when we first started to hear of Jesus of Nazareth. We had a network of informers who kept us up to date with what was happening throughout Judea and Galilee. We heard from Galilee of this teacher who was stirring up trouble in the synagogues. He had proclaimed himself the Christ and many people claimed that he had healed them from illness or disease. While he remained in Galilee he was no real threat to us and indeed came under the jurisdiction of King Herod. However it was best to know of potential sources of trouble. These reports went on for about three years. Jesus actually came to Jerusalem for one of the festivals and taught in the Temple. He also helped many people including a blind man who used to sit begging by the gates. This guy was known by sight by many of the Council members. We were unable to do anything about capturing Jesus. His supporters always surrounded him and harming him would have started a riot. Many in the crowd were prepared to follow Jesus. Because we couldn't act against him, they believed that the High Priest had nothing against him. Annas was very disturbed when our most senior teacher, Nicodemus had a secret meeting with Jesus. After this I was asked to watch him and keep him out of mischief.

One of our informers went with Jesus when he left Jerusalem. He was with him when Jesus performed an apparent miracle in Bethany by raising a man named Lazarus from the dead. The man had been in his tomb for four days and how he contrived this trick I still don't know. The informer stayed with Jesus and told us that Jesus was intending to come to the Feast of the Passover. He was still with him when Jesus arrived in Jerusalem a week before the celebration. I think by this time my spy believed that Jesus was the Messiah but he still needed money and so told us what was going on. Jesus certainly didn't attempt to conceal his presence. His disciples arranged a procession to welcome him and then, as if that was not enough, he came into the Temple, upset the moneychangers' tables and chased them away. If it hadn't been so serious it would have been very funny. They had it coming to them as they always ripped off the visitors to the Temple who were forced to come to them. Jesus went on to insult the High Priest and the Teachers and the Scribes. It was as if he was trying to upset them and some of the things he called them were not only funny but very much to the point. We could not imagine why he was doing what he did.

Annas could still not think of any way of capturing Jesus without a major riot because he was always in the middle of a crowd of his supporters. However we had to find a chance to take him out of circulation. Luck was on our side when one of Jesus' close followers, a man named Judas Iscariot, contacted me and asked to talk with Annas I arranged to meet him and he was not a very impressive character. His great ambition was to see Galilee and Judea freed from Roman control. He thought Jesus might be the leader to achieve this. However Jesus had let him down by taking no steps to start an uprising. Judas believed he might provoke Jesus into action by betraying him and having him taken prisoner. Jesus would then have to use his miraculous powers to release himself. I did not in any way trust Judas but since the price he was asking was only 30 pieces of silver, we hadn't much to lose. I arranged that he would contact me when a suitable chance to capture Jesus arose.

Later in the week Judas got in touch and said that Jesus would be in the valley of Kidron at around midnight on the night before the feast. He asked me to meet him with a squad of temple guards just before the time. To show them which was Jesus he would go up to him and kiss him. Events turned out as planned except that one of Jesus' followers, a huge fisherman named Simon, drew a short sword he was wearing and cut off my ear. The pain was excruciating and I reeled away.

Blood was flooding down the side of my face. Jesus was watching and shouted at Simon "Put your sword away! I have to do what my father has asked of me." He then stretched out his hand and touched my ear and it was healed. It was as if I had never been hurt and the whole episode had been a bad dream. There were no aches or bruises, it might never have happened except that later I found bloodstains on my tunic. I have never seen a look like that which he gave me as he touched me. It wasn't scared, it wasn't angry but it was full of sorrow. I thought he could see right into my inner soul. The thought rushed through my mind 'What sort of man will go out of his way to help someone who is doing his best to harm him? How can he do it anyway?' but I was so absorbed in what I was doing that the moment passed. Jesus then went on to say something even odder. He asked why it was necessary for us to come and take him at night with an armed guard. After all he had been teaching openly in the Temple for the last few days. Why couldn't we have taken him there? He must have known that would spark off a riot. It was only later, when the pressure was off that the magnitude of what he had done struck me. I would have been left an unemployable beggar but for him. Certainly I would have expected no help from Annas.

We took Jesus, tied his hands and led him off to the boss's house. When we arrived I took Jesus straight in to see Annas. I think the plan was to scare Jesus so that he would slink off and lose himself in the country. Annas blustered and threatened and even had us knock Jesus about a bit. The prisoner would not say a word until Annas began to question him about his followers and what he was teaching them. Jesus replied "You already know because I have preached openly in the Synagogue and the Temple. Many people have heard me and I have said nothing in private that I have not said openly. Why are you asking me this? Ask those who have heard me." I was enraged and stepped forward and slapped his face saying "This is no way to talk to the High Priest." Jesus, in no way cowed, stood calmly and said "You have to prove that I have said anything wrong. Should you hit a man for telling the truth?" In the end there was nothing for it but to take him over to Caiaphas for a more formal hearing.

As I was setting off to go with Jesus to the High Priest's palace, Annas called me back. He had found a number of people who, for payment, were prepared to bear false witness against Jesus. Some would say that Jesus had insulted the Emperor and others that he had claimed that he would destroy the Temple in three days and rebuild it. I was required to rehearse them but there was just not enough time. I took them into Pilate's court but the evidence they gave was useless. They got their stories wrong, contradicted each other and were totally unbelievable. Fortunately we still had the charge of blasphemy. Caiaphas happened to mention rather stupidly that Jesus' ministry had started in Galilee and Pilate sent him to Herod for judgment but he was returned shortly without any verdict being reached. Annas asked me to collect together some messengers who we could use to influence the crowds gathered in the courtyard outside Pilate's palace. It was clear that Pilate was seeking to release Jesus but we were determined that this wouldn't happen.

It was the Procurator's custom each year to release a condemned prisoner to mark the Passover. Only two were available, Barabbas, a notorious robber rightly feared by the wealthier citizens, and Jesus. I sent my messengers scurrying round telling people to ask for Barabbas to be released in spite of the fear in which he was held. I was surprised how easily people were persuaded. Pilate said that neither he nor Herod could find cause to condemn Jesus. My messengers rushed round telling those present to call for him to be crucified and to keep doing this whatever happened. We knew that what Pilate feared above all else was civil unrest and in the end he gave in. He had Jesus flogged and sent him to be crucified.

I didn't go to the crucifixion. I was tired having had no sleep the previous night and executions were not my favourite entertainment. In any event I had no wish to see Jesus killed. I had seen others who had claimed to be the Messiah and how they had reacted when the consequences were spelt out. Jesus was very different. He had had no need to heal me but he had not hesitated to do so in spite of knowing that I was seeking to harm him. He maintained his dignity throughout his various trials and was very clever in the way he replied to the questioning. He was flogged and then beaten up by the Roman soldiers. He accepted what happened and looked as if he expected his fate. He was not going to go back on the claims he had made. I began to wonder if he was truly the Messiah. He had made no effort to save himself from condemnation. What sort of man was he and what did he hope to achieve? More to the point, what sort of man was I?

He had, for whatever reason, healed a serious wound for me when he himself was about to face inevitable execution. He must have known his fate if we ever caught him. And all I could do in response was slap him round the face. I could say it was in the heat of the moment but I knew that wasn't true. I had just given no thought to what I was doing. What sort of animal was I becoming?

During the day I heard a rumpus outside the door of my lodgings. I had met Judas there on one previous occasion. I went to the door and found him there distraught. He was screaming and carrying on like one out of his mind. When he saw me he threw the money back at me and shouted that our agreement was over. He said that he was responsible for the greatest sin ever committed and demanded that Jesus be released. When I told him this was not possible, he rushed off cursing like a mad man. I gave the money back to the priests rather than pocket it as I would have done normally as, even to me, it seemed tainted. The priests would not accept it into the treasury, as it was blood money. They used it to buy a field for the burial of strangers. Later I heard Judas had hanged himself.

There was one other unusual event. On the night Jesus was captured, my cousin was sitting by the fire in the courtyard of Caiaphas' palace. He had seen Simon earlier at the arrest of Jesus. He recognised him when he came to sit by the fire but, when the Galilean was challenged, he got into a terrible state swearing that he had nothing to do with Jesus. Not much difference there then.

I was woken very early on the day after the feast and told to go and see Annas immediately. When I got there, he was spitting blood. The stone guarding the tomb had been rolled away and the body had disappeared. The three guards posted by Caiaphas had no idea what had happened and were in a state of complete bewilderment. They had been watching as instructed and suddenly the stone was gone. At first I assumed they had been asleep but I quickly realised that, if they had been, they would have concocted a far better story. Annas told me to instruct them to tell any enquirers that Jesus' followers had come during the night and stolen the body while they were asleep and I gave each of them a substantial sum of money to persuade them to comply. It was a pretty thin story as, if they had been asleep on duty, they would have been severely punished but it was the best we could come up with. We started a search for the body but of course it was too late; no trace was ever found.

The rumours of the resurrection started three days later. We took no notice because we believed they would fade away but they grew stronger. The body had disappeared and no amount of searching found it. Within three months there was a sizable group claiming Jesus had risen from the dead and was the Messiah. Simon, now known for some reason as Peter, was the leader. I happened to meet him one day as he was going to the Temple. He didn't recognise me; there was no reason why he should. It had been dark in the Kidron valley. I told him who I was and he was deeply embarrassed. I then repeated what my cousin had said. Instead of denying it as I expected, he said without hesitation that this was the most shaming moment of his life. I thought I saw tears in his eyes. He had denied his Master but when Jesus met him after his resurrection, he had apparently forgiven Peter. The resurrection was taken as an acknowledged fact. I have met Peter several times since and he has almost persuaded me that Jesus was the Christ. There is a huge difference between the terrified Simon immediately before Jesus' death and the confident aggressive Peter now leading the Christian movement. Yet there is still a humility about him as if he is dependant on someone else for his power. I have stopped working for Annas, as I can no longer go along with his method of operation. I am spending my time studying to see if Jesus fulfils the prophecies concerning the Messiah and so far the evidence seems to be in his favour. I grow increasingly ashamed of my part in his death.

Judas Iscariot

It was not long after the crucifixion that a stranger came to see John. He came at night when there were few people around and he introduced himself as Benjamin, the brother of Judas Iscariot. He came because he was annoyed that it was being rumoured that the only reason that his brother had betrayed Jesus was for money. If that were the case Judas would certainly not have settled for a paltry sum of just 30 pieces of silver. Benjamin wanted the truth about his brother to be heard. John let Benjamin tell his story not even interrupting when he himself was criticised. Immediately afterwards he wrote down Benjamin's words while they were still fresh in his memory and they are what is reproduced here.

I think the first thing I have to say is that Judas loved Jesus as much as he was able. My brother was not the sort of man who wore his heart on his sleeve. He had suffered too many disappointments in his life to accept people at face value and had become deeply cynical. He approached everything from a rational rather than an emotional point of view. To understand why it is necessary to go back to his roots.

Father was a carpenter who lived in a small house just below the Temple on the steps leading to the Beautiful Gate. His family came from Kerioth, a village in Southern Judea. He earned a very good living carving mementos for pilgrims. I still have some of them and they were good value for money. He married Mother when he was still young and Judas came along quite quickly. To their regret it seemed for a long time as if there would be no more children. However the small family were, apart from this, happy and contented and lived in this house until Judas was about seven years old. It was then that Mother learned that she was pregnant again.

Their happiness was shattered when one day one of the High Priest's officers came round and told them that their house was needed by the Temple authorities and that they would have to find other accommodation. In spite of Father going to see everybody who he thought might be able to influence the decision, he was unable to get it changed. With Mother only three months from giving birth, Father was jobless and the family homeless. It was impossible to find other housing near the Temple and eventually they were forced to move to the outskirts of the city. Father became a jobbing carpenter, far worse off than he had been previously. I was born in our new home shortly after the move.

These events had a huge effect on Judas. From then on he was full of hatred for the Priests and the Temple officials. They had made him move from the home he loved and caused his parents great unhappiness. I was never affected in the same way because I had never known anything different from our new house which I loved. Judas grew to hate all authority; to him the Romans were just as bad as the others because they allowed the Temple authorities to do as they liked and didn't stop them abusing their power. His heroes were Gideon and Samson who had freed the Jews from foreign invaders many years earlier.

As Judas got older he became a loner. He was never much interested in women and he had no close friends. He worked on his own as a carver and carpenter. He was highly political and had few other interests. He was looking for a new leader who would free his people from both the High Priest and his officials and the Romans. Being on his own, Judas was able to go and hear any speaker expressing new or radical views. Later he would come home and tell me what he thought of them.

For some reason I was the only person he would really talk to. When he first started I couldn't fully understand what he was telling me but as I grew older, he began to make sense. What he wanted was an independent Jewish state free of what he regarded as the evil influence of the priests and of Roman domination. He had no time for the modern interpretation of the Jewish faith and could not stand the obsessive obedience to the Law that orthodox Jews insisted upon. To him it was nonsense that no work could be done on the Sabbath and that there were all the precise dietary rules. He was scathing about many of the people he heard. As he grew older, he became more disillusioned – he did not think the person he was waiting for existed. Judas never saw himself as top man; he imagined his role as dedicated supporter – maybe even the power behind the throne.

There came a time when Jerusalem was full of rumours about a man named John the Baptist who was attracting large crowds to the River Jordan in the North of Judea. He was baptising all who were willing as a sign of their repentance for their misdoings. Inevitably Judas went off to see what all the fuss was about. Although he was greatly impressed by John, the message was not what he was looking for. However he decided to stay for a few days to see what effect John's words would have on the large crowds who gathered to hear him. A few days later something happened which really caught Judas' attention. A man came and started talking to the Baptist. There was a discussion during which John seemed to be trying to deter him but eventually it was agreed that the baptism should go ahead. When it was over and the man was coming out of the water, they all heard a voice from heaven saying "This is my beloved son: I am delighted with everything he has done." At the same time a figure like a dove came and landed on the man's shoulder.

Judas stayed by the Jordan interested in the crowds coming each day to hear the Baptist. The man John had been so reluctant to baptise disappeared. There was no sign of him for about six weeks when, as suddenly as he had gone, the man reappeared. Judas discovered that his name was Jesus and that he was a carpenter from Nazareth in Galilee. He preached to large crowds each day and his followers baptised those who believed in him in the same way as John baptised those who came to him. As time went on Judas noticed that the number coming to Jesus increased and those to John decreased. He managed to stay near to Jesus and even got to talk to him on a one-on-one basis. Jesus seemed to be as against the established order as Judas was and to be the sort of leader he was waiting for. Nevertheless when Jesus asked Judas to travel round with him as one of his closest followers, he faced a big decision. He had two major questions. Firstly was Jesus a man who might inspire an uprising that would overthrow the current ruling clique; secondly was he prepared to give up his current way of life to follow Jesus. Eventually my brother decided that he would be false to himself if he didn't take the plunge. He closed down his business and went with Jesus. Quickly he found himself among those baptising people on Jesus' behalf. His feelings about this were of surprise and satisfaction. He felt no embarrassment at what he was doing.

Judas found that there were eleven others who Jesus had asked to follow him as his close disciples. The others were Galileans, mostly younger than himself. Five of them were fishermen from the Sea of Galilee and, right from the beginning, he had difficulty getting on with them. The others were of mixed backgrounds, even including a tax collector. The twelve were with Jesus the whole time. He spent many hours training them and his teaching was different from anything that Judas had heard before. He preached humility and how, in order to lead, it was necessary to serve. I am not sure how Judas dealt with this. He thought that a leader had to be a figurehead, respected and maybe held in awe by his followers. Jesus seemed to want to form a personal relationship with those he met. He was putting forward a message of love. Men should love God with all their might and love their neighbour as themselves. Only those who were humble could find God. They were not to judge others as they themselves were far from perfect. Nobody would be excluded from the kingdom of God, however poor or disadvantaged.

As well as teaching, Jesus performed many miracles, healing people from illness, curing the blind, the lame and the mentally deranged and seeming to control the elements. Judas told me how Jesus had come to the disciples walking on the water when they were in a boat. The disciples were even sent out in pairs to do the same work as Jesus was doing and Judas found that, by calling on the name of Jesus, he was able to heal the sick. He found this role very difficult as he was not used to close contact with other people but, if he was to follow Jesus, he had no option but to do as he was asked.

During his travels Jesus often fell foul of the Teachers and Pharisees. They were always snooping round trying to find ways of trapping him into saying something that would allow them to imprison him. Jesus stood up to them and the teachers were never clever enough to catch him out. They constantly accused him of breaking the Sabbath rules and associating with those who were

considered outcasts. Jesus' response was that he had
come to save those who knew they were not perfect,
not those who thought they were already good enough.
Jesus went on to tell them that he was the Son of God.
Every time he said this, the Pharisees were beside themselves with fury. They literally frothed at the mouth.
One of the things Jesus said was that he must be lifted
up and Judas took this to mean that he would become
a ruler.

I did not see Judas that often at this time as he was
mostly in Galilee but when I did, he was impatient to
tell me what he had been doing. Jesus, in his view, had
the ability to lead a movement to overthrow the existing
government. He disliked the Temple officials and the
Pharisees as much as Judas did. However he seemed to
be making no moves to start an uprising. He wouldn't
even let those he healed go and tell people about what
had happened. Judas just could not understand this.
Surely publicity was good but Jesus was content to go
round doing his good works and having his arguments
with the authorities. Judas was impressed by the strange
powers Jesus constantly used to cure the sick and to
look after the crowds who followed him. There were
two occasions when Jesus fed them all although there
was virtually no food available. However this was not
enough. Judas longed for the day when these powers
would be used to start a revolution. He was always
impatient and it was at about this time that he began
to doubt whether Jesus was worthy of his support. He
liked and admired him as a person but was disappointed
that Jesus repeatedly denied any intention to set up
an earthly kingdom. Although large crowds followed

him around, Jesus made no attempt to use them for his purposes. Arguing with the Pharisees and Teachers was all right but it did not get Judas any nearer to what he wanted. If Jesus was not going to bring down the authorities, there was no point in deliberately winding up the people who surrounded him.

Judas told me that he had been asked to look after the small amounts of money given to Jesus to support his ministry. My brother had given up everything to follow Jesus and, because he was unsure if Jesus was the man he had thought him to be, he had started taking small amounts of money to enable him to set up in business again if he needed to. Some of the other disciples suspected what was going on and there was an ugly scene when Mary, a woman well known to Jesus and the sister of Lazarus whom he raised from the dead, poured a very expensive bottle of perfume over Jesus' feet. Judas was outraged and asked why the perfume hadn't been sold and the proceeds given to the poor but Jesus told him to leave the woman alone saying "There will always be poor people but I will only be with you for a short time." I thought Judas was wrong to do what he had done and I told him so in no uncertain terms. The incident had a lasting effect on Judas; He couldn't believe that someone who he hoped would become a king could welcome the attentions that Mary gave him.

Jesus said that he was going up to Jerusalem for the Passover and Judas decided that he would take a final decision whether to continue with Jesus after that. Things started off as Judas hoped. Jesus was welcomed into the city by a large crowd and the idea of riding into the city on a donkey to show his humility was a publicity masterpiece. He then went to the Temple and caused a sensation by upsetting the desks of the money-changers and throwing them off the premises. This was more like what Judas wanted but, instead of continuing to create problems for the authorities, Jesus went back to his previous tactics of deliberately antagonizing the Pharisees and not following up by firm action. Judas could not understand why he hesitated. He was shocked when Jesus didn't say clearly that it was wrong for the Jews to pay taxes to the Romans. It was then that the idea of artificially creating a situation where Jesus was forced to assert himself came to him. He had seen enough of the extraordinary powers used by Jesus to know that, if he wanted, Jesus could avoid capture. It was even possible that Jesus, working with the High Priest, could lead an uprising against the Romans.

During his time in Jerusalem Judas came to see me several times. He told me what he was thinking but didn't really listen to anything I said. I was there as a sounding block, someone who would listen while Judas put his thoughts in order and my ideas were not even considered. Judas was still a great admirer of Jesus and valued his friendship enormously. He believed totally that what he was planning would help Jesus achieve his destiny. I tried to tell him that the chances of the High Priest allying himself with Jesus were nil but I didn't get anywhere. I thought it much more likely that the authorities would arrange to have Jesus killed rather than cooperate with him but by this time Judas was beyond rational argument. He was convinced that what he was planning would achieve what he wanted, a great uprising against the Romans. I began to fear greatly for my brother's safety. It seemed to me that he had moved outside the bounds of reason.

To put his plan into action Judas went to see the High Priest's officers and offered to betray Jesus into their hands. The amount of money he would get was unimportant and this was why the paltry sum of thirty pieces of silver was agreed. Judas then went back to Jesus and accompanied him in the normal way. He had arranged with the High Priest's assistant that he would lead him and his men to Jesus at a time when his arrest would not cause a major commotion and for a long time he did not think a suitable time would come but eventually it did. Jesus arranged to share a meal with his disciples on the evening of the feast. At this he said that he wanted to go and pray as usual in the Garden of Gethsemane before going into the city. The garden was just outside the city and ideal for Judas' purpose. It was secluded and there would be no one there late at night.

The meal itself for Judas was an unnerving experience. It began with Jesus washing the feet of his disciples to show his humility. He told his friends that they also must wash each other's feet to show that they were ready to serve their fellows. As he reached Simon he said that as a result of the washing of their feet the disciples, all except one, would be clean. Judas knew that it was him that Jesus referred to. Later, during the meal, Jesus again said that he was going to be betrayed by one of them. The other disciples pestered Jesus to find out who was to be the guilty party and Judas asked directly if it was him. "Surely not I Rabbi." Unlike the other disciples Judas would never call Jesus 'Master'. He would not accept that anyone was superior to him. I couldn't understand how Judas could ask such a question as he had already agreed to betray Jesus.

Jesus replied "Yes it is you." Judas still thought that, by creating a situation where Jesus could demonstrate his power, he was serving him and was encouraged by this response. He was greatly upset when Jesus went on to say "How terrible it will be for the man who betrays me. It would have been better for him if he had never been born." The others were still not clear who would betray Jesus and he told them it was the one to whom he gave a piece of bread which he had dipped in the sauce. He handed the bread to Judas and told him to hurry and do what he had to do. My brother left the others as he hoped without being noticed and went to fetch the Temple Guards to Gethsemane. Even then he was tempted to call off the arrangement with the High Priest but he knew that, if he did, the people paying him would have him killed.

The capture of Jesus went as planned and afterwards Judas came to me. He told me how he had gone up to Jesus and greeted him. Jesus spoke to him "Friend, do what you have to do." Judas kissed him and the men stepped forward and arrested him. Judas was disappointed that Jesus had not resisted arrest but thought that he was waiting until a time when more people would be present before setting himself free. He stayed with me all night growing more and more restless. He expected to hear that Jesus had freed himself and was leading a rebellion. He was full of hope right to the end. I have never seen anyone more devastated than Judas when he learned that Jesus had been crucified and had died. My brother looked as if all the cares of the world had been placed on his shoulders. He had betrayed his friend who was about to be crucified. His face was a mask of misery and tears were running down his cheeks. His whole body was convulsed. He kept on saying "What have I done? What have I done?" He rushed out of my house.

I was told later that he ran back to the office of the High Priest's secretary and threw the thirty pieces of silver at his feet. Hoping for sympathy he told the secretary that he had betrayed an innocent man and was told that that was his problem. Faced with a situation that had become a nightmare, he went and hanged himself.

I mourn for my brother. He was a man obsessed with the idea of freedom for his people and he had interfered in matters that were too difficult for him. As a result he had been instrumental in the death of someone who he had loved and respected. If he had known what he had done and that he would go down in history as a byword for treachery, he would have been appalled. Anyway he deeply regretted what he had done and Jesus taught that all who repent will be forgiven, so that will be true for him, won't it?

Barabbas

Freedom for Judea! This was the slogan I used and everyone thought I was a genuine patriot seeking freedom for my people. I was happy for them to think this and did believe that all of us Judeans would be better off without the Romans lording it over us. However, if I am honest – a slightly doubtful idea, my main purpose in what I did was to earn an easy living. I had collected together a group of down and outs and we spent our time robbing and terrorizing the city. We lived in caves in the hills just outside Jerusalem and we lived well. There was always plenty of money and, if one wasn't caught, life was exciting. Unfortunately I got caught.

I got into this life by accident. I came from a loving home and I had been taught to read and write. Father however was insistent that I should become a candle maker like him. For a few months I worked in his shop but then I began to suffer from terminal boredom. He would not hear of my changing career, so I ran away.

There was a girl involved of course but, when I had spent all my money, she was soon gone. I couldn't find other work and fell in with a group of ruffians who 'earned' their living by small-scale robbery and theft. When their leader grew careless, I was the natural choice to take his place. At first not all the gang shared my conviction about this but I was a strong lad and this helped them to accept my point of view.

We became more daring as time went on and began to operate on quite a big scale. Indeed we became quite notorious. The authorities began to take us seriously and made some effort to catch us. This was when we had the idea of posing as freedom fighters. We put up notices in public places and distributed inflammatory leaflets about the injustice of Roman rule. It is better to know your enemies and we made sure we did. Surprisingly we received considerable support from the ordinary people and were regarded as folk heroes. When we got into trouble there were always those who would hide us. Life was good. More recruits came to join us and we gradually expanded our operations. However we became careless and one of the recruits was a plant from the Romans. We planned our largest operation yet and were caught in the act. Many of us, me included, were captured and taken to the Roman prison.

Most of my mates were executed without further delay. I was held back for a show trial to be held after the feast of Passover which was coming shortly. Pontius Pilate, the Roman procurator, was in Jerusalem at that time as it was traditionally a period of great unrest. I was taken to see him and it was made very clear to me that my fate was to be crucified. Meanwhile I was kept in close confinement chained to the wall in an inner cell with no light. I was sometimes fed but there was no reason to waste good food on someone about to be crucified. This was just about all the care I received except for the odd blow from a passing guard. They had no reason to love me, as I had been responsible for the death of a number of their fellows. I lay in my own filth waiting for my execution. I was in quite a state as I couldn't help remembering being told about the Day of Judgment and I didn't think I could ever be forgiven.

On the day before Passover, there was a considerable rumpus in the jail as a new and important prisoner was brought in. I didn't see him of course but I heard the warders talking. He was some sort of religious nut from Galilee called Jesus. He was taken prisoner by the High Priest's guards and accused of blasphemy. I had no idea of the truth of their allegations. The men who captured Jesus had beaten him up before the High Priest and his Council examined him. Since one of the accusations was that he claimed to be King of the Jews, they did not take long before sending him to Pilate accused of treason against Rome. The Governor, in an attempt to avoid responsibility, passed him on to be tried by King Herod of Galilee. After all that was where the prisoner came from. Jesus refused to answer Herod's questions and the king had no option but to send him back to Pilate for judgment.

There was a tradition that, at the feast of the Passover, the Roman governor released a condemned prisoner as a gesture of goodwill to the Jews. Apparently there were only two prisoners who qualified, Jesus and myself. Pilate was keen that Jesus should be chosen but the Priests sent agitators to stir up the crowd and demand my release. I had no idea why they should do so as I had been a considerable problem to them. In the end Pilate, who was something of a timeserver, gave in to the pressure and agreed to release me rather than Jesus. He had Jesus flogged and then handed over to the High Priest to be crucified. I was set free by the guards who left me in no doubt that, as soon as the feast was over, they would be out looking for me again.

Much of what I have said I learned later but even then I was aware that Jesus was the victim of a frame up and I could not understand why the priests were so against him. The guards were upset at being expected to crucify a man they regarded as innocent if a bit mad.

It was still early in the morning, the events I have described having taken place during the night. I passed Jesus as I was released. He had been dressed in a scarlet robe and was wearing a crown of thorns that was pressed down into his head. The guards were mocking him and knocking him around. Nevertheless he looked directly at me as I passed him. There was no condemnation in his glance, just a look of understanding. This was not what I had expected. I thought he would be in the same line of business as me but immediately realised this was not the case. For some reason the Jews wanted him crucified before Passover so he was taken out almost immediately to the place of execution.

I followed the crowds as they went to watch. This could so easily have been me. I heard people say that three people were due to be crucified, Jesus and two robbers. I half expected the other two to be my old partners in crime but fortunately they weren't. We arrived at Golgotha after the three men had been hung on the crosses. I stayed at the back of the crowd so that I would not be recognised. I had no idea why I had come to watch. Looking back it seems ghoulish but I could not get out of my mind that it should have been me hanging on the cross. I heard Jesus speak "Father forgive them; they don't know what they are doing". People, including the High Priest and some of his colleagues, were mocking – 'he saved others, himself he can not save'. My mind was in complete confusion. The man on the cross was no threat to anyone. He should not have taken my place. I heard one of the robbers join in the mocking and the other tell him to be quiet. "We are punished fairly because we have done things which deserve punishment. But this man has done no wrong. Jesus, remember me when you come into your kingdom". And Jesus replied "I tell you the truth; today you will be with me in heaven".

I knew how that robber felt. I too deserved to be killed but this man had died in my place. I thought of all the members of my gang who, in my pride, I had led to their death and of the victims. In my heart I begged for forgiveness for all my wrongdoing. Who could forgive me now? I could not get those words 'Forgive them father' out of my mind. I remembered the innocent people I had harmed, the ones I had killed and those who I had robbed and scared half to death. For the first time I began to think of what I had done. Some had begged for mercy, others had been proud and accepted what was happening to them. What right had I to kill them or maim them or make them frightened to walk in the streets? A great feeling of guilt overwhelmed me.

It began to get dark although it was only midday. The winds rose and the gloom became overwhelming. I crept away unable to watch any longer. There was nowhere else to go so I made my way to the cave where I used to live. It was empty, no fire and nothing left. I went in on my own and had time to think. One idea overrode all the others. He had quite literally died in my place. Nothing could undo the things I had done. They were with me for life. But "Forgive them father". I spent the next two days there. I had no food or bedding but I had to be on my own.

I came out on the day after Passover. The sun was shining again. I made my way back to the execution ground but the crosses had gone. I remembered that they would not be allowed to stay up over the feast. I moved on with no idea what I was going to do. I had no money and no food and I had this vast guilt. I knew that I could not go back to my old way of life. Quite apart from the fact that I was well known to the authorities, the evil that I had done overwhelmed me. My only hope was in those words that I had heard from the cross. "Forgive them father for they know not what they do". I knew he was referring to those who were crucifying him but could they apply to me as well.

"This day you will be with me in paradise". But what I had done was so wicked.

There were some women there talking among themselves and highly excited. They were saying he had come back to life. Somehow I was not surprised. I never doubted the truth of what these women were saying. He was not a man like other men. I knew I hadn't the courage to see him face to face but I had to seek his forgiveness for all the evil I had done. This was the only thought in my mind. "Forgive them father for they know not what they do." These words still drummed in my head and I knew they applied to me. Relief flooded through me but also the knowledge that I had harmed many, many people. His forgiveness would mean nothing unless I tried to give my life to serve others. He had died in my place and I had a debt to repay. It was too late to help those I had hurt and led into trouble but there were many who had problems which they could not deal with themselves. I personally could not solve them but there might be something I could do. I committed myself to finding out what this was.

Mary Magdalene

We couldn't persuade him not to go and so I went to Jerusalem with Mary and her friends. We followed Jesus as the people surrounded him, mounted him on a donkey and led him towards the city praising him and waving palm branches. There was nothing quiet about his arrival. We heard of him upsetting the money-changers' tables and we began to be frightened. Surely the Temple authorities would not allow such behaviour to go unpunished. It came as no surprise to us to hear that on the night before the feast he was betrayed and taken prisoner. Next morning we heard he was to be crucified that very day so that everything was over before the Passover feast.

I went with Mary and some other women to the place of execution. The only one of his close men friends who came with us was John. We arrived as the cross was pulled upright. The suffering Jesus had already endured was all too obvious and I never want to see another crucifixion. The agony that he went through hanging there could be clearly seen. I was too overcome to watch closely. Was the new life I so much prized to be taken from me? Why did such a good man have to suffer so? I wondered if I should just disappear quietly but I couldn't bring myself to desert him or his mother. I noticed the wind get stronger and the clouds darken. There were all sorts of cracks and noises and sudden blasts of thunder. The rain was bucketing down and I was soaked to the skin. Mary leaned on me in her agony and I tried to support her. We watched until Jesus' body was taken down from the cross and then John took Mary back to his lodgings. We saw two men, one dressed in the elaborate clothes of a Pharisee, approach the centurion. We had no idea who they were. They handed him a message and he looked at it and nodded. The two stepped back. We wondered if this was a plot by the High Priest to ensure that the body wasn't stolen. The other bodies were taken down from the crosses and thrown on to a pile of bones next to the execution ground. They would be mauled by the jackals and other scavengers. I knew that Mary had been terrified that this was what would happen to Jesus' body but this was placed carefully on a sheet provided by the two men. The men called up some servants and they lifted the sheet by its corners and carried it towards some new tombs standing just behind the place where Jesus had been crucified. We followed and watched what happened. The body was laid on the ground and lovingly washed by the two men themselves. When they had finished they bound it in grave clothes and lifted it into one of the empty tombs. They then started to anoint it with spices which they must have placed in the tomb earlier. It began to get dark and they had to leave before they had finished in order to get back into the city before the gates were locked. Two Temple Guards had been watching what was happening just as closely as we were.

Salome and her friend went back to the city but I couldn't bear to leave Jesus and stayed thinking about all that had happened   I felt as if the light had gone out of my world. I loved him so much and he had completely changed my life. At first I thought that I would have to go back to my former existence but, as I considered this, I remembered the times that he had told us that he would be killed by crucifixion and would rise from the dead on the third day. He had made no attempt to avoid what happened to him although I was sure he could have done if he so wanted. What he had said so far was true so why shouldn't the rest of it be. It was as if a light had dawned and, from then on, I knew that he would rise from the dead. I hugged this thought to myself and decided that I would not speak to the others about what I believed. I couldn't have borne being laughed at. I went back over the time I had spent with Jesus and remembered with joy all the things he had done and the words he had spoken. So many people had been helped by him. This was what God should be like, loving and forgiving. I decided I would hang around nearby to see if anything happened. I was there until the Temple guards marched out to see that the body wasn't stolen and chased me away.

Next day was the worst day of my life. I met with his close friends and they were in a state of black despair as not only was he dead but they, all but John, had deserted him in his hour of need. John seemed to be the only one who had listened to what Jesus had said. Their hopes were gone and their future was more than uncertain. What were they to do now? I was reminded of the words Jesus had spoken to me when we had first talked. He had told me that hard times are coming when my courage would be tested to the utmost. In the end Mary, his mother, and I went out and sat in the hills, far enough away not to attract the attention of the guards but in a place where we had a clear view of the entrance to the tomb. We didn't talk much, both of us being taken up with our own thoughts. I had told Mary about what had happened to the body and she was so relieved. I also told her that the anointing had not been completed and she asked Salome and I to go with her at dawn next day to finish the job. We were worried about how we were going to move the stone at the tomb's entrance.

At dawn the next day the three of us with Joanna were waiting at the gate before dawn. When we arrived at the tomb, I was amazed to see that the huge stone that had been placed across its entrance had been rolled away and that the Temple guards who had been standing watch had disappeared. My heart gave a great leap as I wondered what could have happened. I ran ahead and found that an angel, dressed in glowing white, was sitting on the stone. He was swinging his legs over the edge and grinning so that his face was almost split in two. He said to me "Don't be afraid. I know you are looking for Jesus who was crucified. He told you what would happen and he has been raised from the dead." It was happening and I wanted to be near the action. I knew then that I had not been mistaken in my beliefs but I still wondered if and how I would see Jesus again

I ran back to fetch Simon and John leaving the others at the tomb. When the two men arrived Simon (now called Peter) went in and found the funeral clothes carefully folded with the cloth that had been used to wrap around Jesus' head lying separate from the others. There was now no sign of the angel. Mary and her friends with the two disciples went back to tell the others what had happened but I stayed nearby weeping. I plucked up courage to go and look in the tomb and saw that two angels in white were now sitting where Jesus' body had been, one at the head and the other at the foot.

"Woman, why are you crying?" one of them said.

"They have taken my Lord away and I don't know where they have put him." I turned round and saw a man standing there but I didn't recognise him.

"Woman" he said, "Why are you crying? Who are you looking for?"

Thinking he was the gardener, I said, "Sir, if you took him away, tell me where you have laid him and I will go and get him."

I heard the one word "Mary" and I knew it was him. His voice was unmistakable but there was something different about his appearance, a radiance that had not been there before. I cried out 'Teacher' and rushed to hug him. He put up his hand and spoke again. The mark of the nail was clear on his hand.

"Don't cling to me, for I have not yet returned to the Father. Go and find my brothers. Tell them 'I am about to return to my father and your father, to my God and your God'." I swear that he had a twinkle in his eye as he spoke to me. I was thrilled to be the first to see him after he came back to life. At first I was upset that he refused to allow me to touch him but, when a man has risen from the dead, you would expect him to be rather different.

I rushed back to his friends, skipping like a young girl. I burst in shouting "I have seen the Lord" and told them everything that had happened. As we talked Peter and the others began to remember how Jesus had often said to them how he was going to die and rise again after three days but they were still full of doubt, unable to accept what had happened.

That evening Jesus appeared; he was suddenly there; he didn't come through the door. Mary and I and some of the other women and the eleven disciples had locked ourselves in because we feared the Jews. We couldn't believe what we were seeing. "Peace be with you" he said and showed us his hands and his feet. We were all amazed and overcome with joy. I don't think any of us could quite take in what was happening in front of us.

"Do you have anything to eat?" he asked and we gave him some broiled fish that he ate. I think he did this to show us we were not dreaming. He then explained to us all that had been written about him in scripture and how it had now come to pass. As he left us he told us to go back to Galilee. I travelled there with Mary.

I saw him once more before he ascended when I was with all his followers in Jerusalem. Here was the man who had saved my life and who I loved and admired more than anyone else on earth. He was going to be taken from me and yet he would still be with me in my memory and in those of my friends. And more! He had promised that his spirit would come and live in us. If I looked back to what I was before I met him, he had performed a miracle. The incredible thing was that, by respecting me as a person and considering my needs, he had restored my self worth. I was myself again.

I was there when, after the ascension, all his followers met the disciples. This was the first time we saw the man Simon, now Peter, had become. He took the lead with complete confidence. They appointed Matthias to replace Judas Iscariot as an apostle. Mary and her four other sons were there. We spent the days praying and remembering his teaching. Ten days after his Ascension; we were gathered together when the Holy Spirit came. I cannot really describe my feelings as the tongues of flame danced round from person to person but I knew that, from then on, I could do wonderful things in his strength. I stayed in Jerusalem for a time while I considered how to use this gift. Before I decided that I would go back to Galilee and try to help others as he had helped me. I would befriend girls who like me had been forced to live on the streets and, after meeting their physical needs, show them that there was someone who cared about them. He would save them as he had saved me. To him be the glory!

Caiaphas

Another day, another Messiah! Each year the Pass-over feast seems to spawn another claimant to the title. Usually it is enough to warn them of the consequences of continuing with the pretence and they disappear into the dirt from which they came. But this one was different. We had been hearing rumours about him for some time now, of the 'miracles' he had been performing and of the following he was building up in Galilee. Some of the strange stories told about him had been well substantiated and there had been cases when he was said to have raised men from the dead. He had even been to Jerusalem and healed people while in the city.

There are many examples of what we were up against. On one occasion, when he was in Jerusalem Jesus cured a cripple who, for 38 years, had sat by the pool of Bethesda, just outside the Temple, begging. There was a legend that an angel used to come and stir the water in the pool and that the first one into it after this would be cured. Of course this man had no one to help him and was never first in but hope springs eternal. I was told that Jesus saw him and asked him if he wanted to get well. The man said that, with no one to help him, he could never be first into the pool. Jesus healed the man and to make matters worse, it was the Sabbath. He rose and carried his mat away. Some watchers told the man that it was illegal to carry his mat on that day but he said this was what he had been told to do. He was asked who it was that had healed him but genuinely didn't know. Only later did he find out that it was Jesus. There was no way we could hide what had happened, as so many people had been witnesses. Events such as this did us immense harm as people began to believe Jesus was the Messiah and the man who had been healed would not keep quiet. I had no idea how Jesus got his magic powers but I am certain that it was not from God.

There were far too many cases like this for them all to be false. There did not seem to be any political purpose behind him but that didn't matter. If he built up a band of supporters, that would come to the notice of the Roman procurator and he would feel threatened and blame us. Above all else Pilate wanted a quiet life. This man, Jesus of Nazareth had to be stopped. The problem was that in Galilee we had less influence than around Jerusalem and so we had to wait till he came to us. We had tried to trick him into saying something which would enable us to accuse him of insulting the emperor or of blasphemy but he had a knack of evading our traps.

Much to my surprise, I had been High Priest for some years now. I was not from one of the main priestly families but, as a young priest, I had come into contact with Annas who had been High Priest and remained the treasurer of the Temple and the dominant force in the Sanhedrin. I was invited to his home and there met his daughter, Sarah. She was an attractive girl and there was considerable surprise that she hadn't married earlier but the thought of Annas as Father-in-Law was enough to put most men off. It didn't take very long for me to realise that behind Sarah's pretty face there was a hardness which would not tolerate any opposition. Anyway she seemed keen and Annas encouraged me to get to know her so eventually we married. I soon realised that, while I was her husband, I was not the most important man in her life. In any matter of consequence she talked to Annas although she kept up a pretence of consulting me. We had one child Matthias and Sarah took great care to ensure that he was brought up to follow in Annas' footsteps. About two years after we were married the High Priest died and Annas suggested that I should take his place. He himself was not able to fill the post because of some earlier falling out with the Romans with who the high priest had to work closely. I had no doubt that he would still want to exercise the power but, after some consideration and having talked the matter through with Sarah, I agreed to take the job. I hoped that this might alter my wife's opinion of me but of course I was wrong. She had been brought up in the High Priest's home and to her Annas would always be the High Priest.

When I took up the job I was not quite as naïve as Annas assumed. I knew that he and his sidekick Malchus, a very unpleasant character who could barely bring himself to be civil to me, would look after day to day matters as they arose. My concern was in safeguarding the faith and I would do anything necessary, however unsavoury, to preserve the Law and protect the Temple. In the end this would bring me into conflict with Annas and his cronies as their interest was purely political. Annas liked power and money (the same thing to him) and he would do anything necessary to get them. Some of the things he did filled me with despair but there was nothing I could do about them. I wanted to be remembered as someone who had kept the faith.

I had been in office for about ten years when I first heard about a man called John who came out of the desert and started baptising people. It was reported to me that he was preaching that men needed to repent of their sins and seek forgiveness. As a sign of this they should be baptised. The promised Messiah would come soon and John believed he was preparing the way for him. There was a lot of other stuff about how we should help the poor and behave honestly but none of it was terribly harmful and I decided I did not need to take any action. He did make some unpleasant remarks about the significance of the Jews being descended from Abraham but they were not important. He took great care to deny that he was the Messiah and this was the most important thing as far as I was concerned.

His ministry had been going on for a little while when things took on a more sinister turn. A man named Jesus, a carpenter from Nazareth, appeared and John greeted him as soon as he saw him by saying that this was the man who would take away the sins of the world. This was of course seriously blasphemous. I was told that John was totally in awe of this Jesus even going so far as to say that Jesus should baptise him rather than the other way round. In the end he was persuaded to baptise Jesus and, as the teacher came out of the water, a voice was heard from heaven saying, "This is my beloved son; I am highly pleased with all he has done." When I learned what was going on, all was quiet again. I hoped we had heard the last of Jesus.

It was a few months later that I got news of him again. He had been travelling round the Lake, preaching and healing people. He had been in to some of the local synagogues and, in his home town of Nazareth, he had caused a riot by claiming to be the Messiah. The men there had tried to push him off a cliff but he had slipped through their fingers. He was also reported as having worked on the Sabbath. I would have liked to bring Jesus in for questioning but unfortunately Galilee was under the jurisdiction of Herod Antipas and I could not interfere. I wrote to the king asking him to take action but, as usual, I got no reply. I knew that the Messiah must come from Bethlehem and would be a great leader rather than a local tradesman.

The stories kept coming in and I was becoming considerably worried by what was happening. The local leaders were complaining about the new teacher and I suggested they take action into their own hands. John had disappeared from the scene by this time as he had upset Herod by telling him his relationship with his brother's wife was sinful. I must say I agreed with John. Then I heard that Jesus was proposing to visit Jerusalem for the feast of the Tabernacles. This was our chance and I even discussed with Annas what we should do. My major concern was that we should not upset the Romans. Some of the things Jesus said seemed designed to create social unrest. It does not help anyone to make them discontented with their lot. People should accept their place in society. The procurator, Pontius Pilate, was a weak man who, above all else, wanted a quiet life. On previous occasions we had made him see our point of view by threatening to riot and to withhold taxes if he did not do what we asked but, as with most weak men, if you pushed him too far, he would suddenly take up an entrenched position and then nothing could move him. In these circumstances he might clamp down on our religion.

We had hoped Jesus would come at the start of the feast but he didn't turn up to half way through. When he did arrive he was always surrounded by a large supportive crowd and to try to arrest him then would have caused a riot. He rapidly became the talk of the city. As I have said earlier he did some very public healings including that of the man by the pool of Bethesda. What was worse this was on the Sabbath. He attracted large crowds when he spoke and openly claimed to be the Son of God. I discussed the matter with the Sanhedrin, our council, and we were all frustrated by our inability to do anything about what was going on. What was worse I was told that one of the Council members, Nicodemus had gone to see Jesus secretly. Of course I didn't let him know I had this information but his disloyalty was worrying. He was not important in himself but it was a sign of the way things were going.

Some of the members of the Sanhedrin complained that, if we did nothing, everybody would follow Jesus. To the people listening to Jesus we appeared powerless and they might even have thought that, because we did nothing, we had no problem with what the Galilean was doing. It could not be denied that he was carrying out many miracles and making a big impact. The Romans would be upset if there was major unrest and they would take control of the Temple and Judea. Pilate had already tried to force us to place statues of Tiberius, the Emperor, in the innermost parts of the Temple. For once in my life I had the courage of my convictions. I told them not to be so stupid. Here was the perfect scapegoat. If there were any problems with the Romans, we could blame him. Better by far that one die for us all than that we all suffer. I sent some of the Temple guards to arrest Jesus but they failed to do so. When I asked them why, they replied "No one has ever spoken like this man?" I told them that they also had been deceived. None of the Rulers or the Pharisees believed in him and the mob was suffering from a curse.

On his way home Jesus stopped with some friends in Bethany about six miles out of the city. The son of the house, Lazarus, had died and been laid in a tomb. When Jesus arrived on the scene it was about four days after his death. Jesus went to the tomb and called to Lazarus who walked out. I had no explanation for what had happened but it never occurred to me that it was from God. When the Messiah came he would arrive with great glory, not in a small backwater which nobody had ever heard of. It was prophesised that the place of his birth would be Bethlehem.

This incident convinced me that we must stop Jesus once and for all. I was not going to allow him to destroy everything I had spent my life working for. I gave instructions that he be captured dead or alive. This was meat and drink to Annas and he concocted all sorts of ingenious schemes to take Jesus which naturally all failed. Moreover Jesus was back in Galilee and seemingly untouchable. It was some time later that we heard he was coming to Jerusalem for the Passover and we began to plan. During the feast the city seethed with visitors and this time, for no good reason, there was a feeling that something momentous was going to happen. Passover was always a difficult time when everyone was over excited and there were all sorts of unpleasant incidents. It was the one time in the year when Pilate came to Jerusalem. I knew that, whatever else happened, we had to solve the 'Jesus' problem once and for all.

Jesus arrived about a week before the feast. He was greeted outside the city by large crowds, mostly visitors. At the time of the Passover the population of Jerusalem increased to six times the normal. They welcomed him as a king although he was in fact riding on a donkey. A funny sort of king that was. The demonstration didn't worry me as it was made mainly by visitors from outside the city. The next day he went to the Temple and made a scene by driving out the moneychangers from the Outer Courts where the general public could go. They may not have been very attractive but the money they contributed was extremely important to us. The coins in general use had the image of Caesar on them and therefore could not be accepted in the Temple as that would have broken the Law. We introduced Temple coins and, even if they were worth less than standard coins, we had to pay for the administration.

He came to the Temple each day to preach and attracted large audiences. Many of the poor came to hear him and claimed he had healed them from illnesses of all sorts. I had no problem with that as it would do no harm to the Temple. However Jesus took to insulting the Pharisees and Teachers of the Law as well as me personally. He called us 'hypocrites', 'whitewashed tombs', 'blind guides', 'snakes' and 'sons of vipers'. He accused us of attempting to impress people by our strict observance of the Law so that they thought how pious we were. This really hurt as we were all trying to obey what was written in the scriptures and what had been handed down to us as required behaviour by our ancestors. When I made all the sacrifices I did to be holy, I didn't appreciate some country yokel telling me that I had got it all wrong. I did it to obey God's Law. I was angry and I had good reason to be so. The way to God is through obeying the Law and Jesus certainly didn't do that. However I knew how cunning he was, always able to avoid our traps, and I told our followers to approach him with great care.

One of the Teachers managed to get near enough to him to ask by what authority he taught and performed his miracles. However Jesus would not give a straight reply. He answered the question with another question and he still managed to keep the crowd on his side. We had the same problem as before in that we could never catch him on his own to arrest him. However we were lucky. One of his closest followers, an unpleasant specimen named Judas, had become disillusioned and offered to betray him for an insignificant sum of money. Not only did he offer but he performed and we were able to arrest Jesus on the night before the feast.

He was taken first to Annas who thought that, by roughing him up, he could make him recant but he failed. Jesus was then brought before me and the Sanhedrin. He refused to answer my questions until I asked him if he was the Messiah. His reply was arrogant. "If I tell you, you won't believe me. If I ask a question, you won't answer. The time is soon coming when I, the Son of Man, will sit at God's right hand in heaven." Many shouted "You are then claiming to be the Son of God." What was worse he boasted that he could destroy the Temple and rebuild it within three days. Two witnesses confirmed this, so it was acceptable evidence   It was not only blasphemy but, vitally, a clear incitement to riot so we wasted no time in sending him to Pilate. The governor had to be involved as only he could pronounce the death penalty.

We had great difficulty in persuading Pilate to do what we wanted but, by threatening to riot and to report him to Caesar, we got our own way. The crucifixion took place immediately so that it was over before the feast began and I went along to make sure there were no accidents. Pilate greatly upset me by insisting that a sign was put on the cross saying "Jesus, King of the Jews." A petty action by a small minded man. It would be ungenerous of me not to mention the courage Jesus showed throughout his ordeal. It was almost as if he wanted to die.

I was in my room later that day when one of the duty priests at the Temple came to tell me that on of the rocks on which the Temple was built had split in two, fortunately without major structural damage. He also reported that the huge curtain separating the Holy of Holies from the rest of the Temple was torn from top to bottom. This was about 30 feet high and beautifully woven in blue and crimson and purple with golden cherubim embroidered on it. Later Jesus' followers claimed that it was split to symbolise that he, by his death, had opened the way for man to communicate directly with God. I did not and can not believe that God would desecrate the Temple he had blessed. Personally I don't think the storm that had been raging outside caused the damage although at one stage there had been a terrific noise and the whole building seemed to shake. There had been other storms as bad as this and the curtain was hung inside a strong building. I think vandals must have caused the damage although how they managed to reach up that high I have no idea. The Temple was never left unattended. We spent most of the night trying to mend the curtain but the result still looked a mess.

I was told that Jesus was dead before the Passover feast began. Pilate had given permission to Joseph of Arimathea, a member of the Sanhedrin take the body and bury it. I was annoyed that a senior member of the Sanhedrin had come out openly as a follower of Jesus. I had already had suspicions about Nicodemus but what had happened meant that no one was to be trusted. The body was taken and laid in a new tomb originally intended for Joseph himself. I would have preferred that the body be treated like that of other convicted criminals and left in the open for the predators. The fact that it was an unused tomb was important because we could then be certain that the only bones in it were those of Jesus. I insisted that a large rock be rolled across the entrance to the tomb and that Temple guards protect it after Pilate, ever spiteful, had refused to let Roman soldiers undertake this duty. Much good that did! I hoped that, as had happened when others had pretended to be the Messiah, if their leader was killed his followers would disappear down the holes from which they had emerged but it soon became clear that I was to be disappointed.

On the first day of the next week I was told that the body had disappeared. To say that I was furious was an understatement. I was so angry that for once I totally lost control of myself. I was told later that I had thrown things around and that no one had dared approach me until I calmed down. I couldn't imagine what had happened. It was not in our interest or that of the Romans for the body to disappear and Jesus' followers could not have got past the guards or move the stone. I could think of no one else who would have wanted to steal the body. There was no doubt that Jesus had been killed. The Romans didn't make that sort of mistake.

An immediate search was started but with no success. Rumours began that Jesus had risen from the dead and, without the corpse; there was little we could do to disprove them. Annas circulated a story that the guards had been asleep and Jesus' followers had come and stolen the body but nobody believed this as if it had been true the guards would have been severely punished. Immediately a movement led by his closest followers and stating categorically that Jesus had risen from the dead started and grew rapidly. We heard all sorts of stories of the risen Jesus appearing and eventually of him ascending to heaven. We sent a report to the emperor Tiberius in Rome about how Pilate had failed to prevent the body being stolen but, so far as I know, no action was taken.

I continued to try to suppress the 'Jesus' movement but with limited success. Two of the leaders, fishermen called Simon and John healed a lame man who used to sit on the steps outside the 'Beautiful' gate of the Temple. I had them brought before the Sanhedrin and tried to frighten them into giving up their ministry. My efforts were doomed to failure and there was no way we could punish them because the people had seen what had happened. I did manage to have another of their leaders Stephen who had once been a leader in the Temple, stoned for blasphemy but the movement just went on growing. I was particularly distressed that a number of priests converted to follow Jesus. The balance had changed and, from now on, we would always have to take into account the followers of Jesus in reaching decisions. Where we failed was in not having him assassinated before he reached Jerusalem.

I am retired now. I did what I thought was right and tried to protect the true faith but I failed. I will go down in Jewish history as the man who allowed an impostor to claim successfully that he was the Messiah. I lost control as soon as Jesus appeared on the scene. I know that in everything I obeyed the Law but it is not enough. In spite of all my work, this blasphemous belief that Jesus was the Christ continues to spread. The Romans have begun to accept that the followers of this Christian heresy are here to stay and they are too many to be ignored. It will bring great harm to my people and I fear for their future.

Pontius Pilate

I went to Judea thinking of it as my pension! I had joined the army when I was 17 years old and spent the next 20 years fighting for and protecting Roman interests. Because I was prepared to do anything I was ordered to do, I became noticed and was promoted quickly through the ranks. Maybe my having married Claudia, a protégé of the emperor, helped this process but I prefer to think not. Progress was swift, first as a Centurion, then as commander of a Legion and eventually general of an army.

During my career at the request of Sejanus his Chief of Staff, I had been fortunate enough to be able to perform some private services concerned with his personal life for General Tiberius. When he became emperor, he remembered me. He gave me some special assignments and promised me that he would appoint me procurator of one of the provinces the next time a vacancy occurred. I had hoped that it might be in Gaul but, regrettably, it turned out to be Judea, which was probably the worst job in the empire. A procurator's job was to represent the Emperor, to be responsible for seeing that peace was maintained, to maximise tax revenue and to be the final arbitrator in legal matters. Such posts were regarded as opportunities to save money as one was entitled to keep any cash collected in excess of the demands from Rome and that, together with the patronage opportunities that existed, made it possible to plan for a luxurious retirement.

I met Claudia when with Tiberius in Rome. She was the daughter of Julia, the Emperor Augustus's child. She had had a difficult childhood being looked after by servants while her mother was enjoying a spectacular social life. If the stories were to be believed, Julia was not above disposing of her ex lovers in a rather permanent manner and interfering in politics. She died while Claudia was still a child and Tiberius took the girl under his wing. She was not like her mother in any way and we had a good marriage. When I went to Judea, she asked Tiberius if she might accompany me and, unusually, he agreed. I never heard of any other procurator being allowed to take his wife to his place of duty. I was under no illusions though that, if I failed to collect the required amount of taxes or if there were an insurrection, my life would be forfeit, whoever my wife was. Claudia was a great help to me in reaching decisions but I resented the rumours that she was in all but name the governor.

I knew little about Judea and when I arrived and I disliked it from the first. Some time ago a local man,

Herod Archelaus, had been allowed to assume office as king but he made such a mess of the job that he had to be removed and the emperor decided to appoint a procurator. My predecessor, a man of little ambition, had passed the responsibility for day-to-day law and order to the Jewish religious council, the Sanhedrin, under the control of the High Priest. I had as little as possible to do with the people and made no effort to learn the local language. If the locals wanted to talk to me they would have to speak Latin. After all we were the conquerors.

The main people I would have to deal with were Caiaphas and Annas, an effective double act. Caiaphas, the High Priest, was a difficult man. He was big and solidly built and I never saw him other than in his priestly robes. He wore his holiness like a cloak and seemed to look down on the rest of humanity. He liked a quiet life but, if his faith or his status was threatened, woe betide anyone who got in his way. He had a violent temper and could be totally ruthless. I always had the impression he was manipulating me and he probably was! Annas, his father-in-law, was the practical one of the two and a really nasty piece of work. He was a little like a veteran centurion. When he saw that something needed to be done, he went for it without much thought for the consequences or who he hurt in the process. He was the treasurer of the Temple and therefore in a position of great power. Caiaphas was reputed to be scared of Annas but I never saw any evidence of this – he just had different priorities. I never understood what Annas' motivation was other than grabbing and using power.

Judea was one of two Jewish provinces, the other being Galilee. This was still ruled by Herod Antipas, the brother of Archelaeus. Antipas had been brought up in Rome, where he was an honoured hostage for the good behaviour of his father, and therefore knew the emperor. He believed that, like his father before him, he should be ruler of Judea as well as Galilee. He watched what I did like a hawk seeking any opportunity to discredit me. He, naturally, did not speak to Caiaphas and Annas who thought him to be a traitor to the Jewish people. Although they were supposedly religious leaders, the Sanhedrin and the priests seemed more interested in their role as legal authority. They had a complex and adaptable set of laws that they could use to say that almost any action I took was illegal. If I overruled them, they could and would call mass demonstrations that brought Jerusalem to a halt. Antipas then threatened to report me to Tiberius for not keeping the peace. Instead of being a cushy number leading smoothly to retirement, the job became a nightmare. I had great difficulty keeping my temper and, indeed, often failed to do so. On one occasion I was accused of slaughtering some Galileans and having their blood mixed with the Jewish sacrifices. I have no idea if this was true but the story was told and it temporarily united Annas and Antipas against me.

I came to Judea with great ideas of helping the Jews improve their standard of living. I started off by initiating a major project that I believed would be of lasting benefit to the citizens of Jerusalem. Claudia had noticed how poor the water supply was and I decided to remedy this by building an aqueduct to bring water from outside the city. This was a huge operation and I decided to use the accumulated funds held by the High Priest to finance it. I didn't think they would mind because it was for the benefit of the people. I was wrong and it proved a struggle to force them to release the money, which they believed was for the upkeep of the Temple but eventually force prevailed. I had noticed how well the High Priest and his fellow priests lived and was in little doubt where they got the means. I didn't improve my standing with Caiaphas and the other Jewish leaders by allowing the Legions to bring their eagles into Jerusalem and inside the gates of the Temple. The Jews regarded this as idolatrous. Eventually I had to back down. Later I tried to insist that busts of the Emperor were placed in the Temple. I think Tiberius in Rome could have heard the noise emanating from Jerusalem without any trouble. Eventually we did a deal; they would pay for the aqueduct if I would drop the idea of busts of Tiberius in the Temple. The work was completed but, instead of being grateful, the priests complained that I had routed the water supply through a sacred burial ground. In the end I had to reroute it. When the aqueduct was in use, it was of great benefit to the people of Jerusalem and, of course, Caiaphas took the credit. After this I no longer tried to do anything constructive. My sole aim was to have a quiet life. My wife and I often doubted whether the job was worthwhile. However, if we decided to return to Rome before being recalled, there was a considerable risk that the Emperor would punish us for disobeying his orders.

Claudia was a great help to me and really set out to learn about the Jewish religion. She learned the language and read their sacred works. We sometimes used to discuss them in the evenings. She particularly liked the idea of a single all-powerful God and considered it much superior to the Roman system of a collection of deities. She had to be careful in this as the emperor considered himself to be a god. There was a strict code of conduct for Jews laid down in the 'Ten Commandments' supported by myriads of subsidiary rules. The Pharisees, a particular sect, had made a life's work of observing these laws and, over a period of time, legal observance became more important than serving God. The lengths to which they would go were absurd. For example they would give one tenth of their crop of herbs for personal consumption to the Temple although the gifts were totally useless. It was very obvious however that their religion did not stop them being grossly dishonest in their dealings with me.

Usually I lived in Caesarea but, once a year, I went to Jerusalem, the site of the Jewish Temple for the feast of the Passover, an event that invariably caused huge unrest. Jews from all round the country came to the city to celebrate the feast. Caiaphas and Annas never failed to use the gathering to stir up the masses in support of their pet project of the moment. I have to admit that they were very clever in doing so in such a way as to cause maximum embarrassment to me as representative of the Emperor. King Herod Antipas who had a palace next door to mine did not usually become involved but sat laughing at me. He was looked at with disdain by the Jews as his bloodline was not pure Jewish.

In the eighteenth year of Tiberius' reign, my wife and I as usual went up to Jerusalem for the Passover. It was a time of more than usual unrest. A young man had been travelling round, mostly in Galilee, teaching and performing apparent miracles of healing in a way that was contrary to their Law. He was even reputed to have raised people from the dead. Many of the poorer Judeans were beginning to believe that he was the 'Messiah', a leader who would restore the Jews to their former glory. Caiaphas, the High Priest, would have none of this. Why this should so upset him, I could not work out. I would have expected that the priests would be delighted that such wonders were being done in their God's name but this was not the case and they were determined to capture this teacher and have him put to death. He was expected in Jerusalem for the feast. Since I alone could authorise executions, I feared the worst. Sure enough, shortly after I was woken on the morning before the Jewish feast, I learned that this teacher, Jesus by name, had been arrested and was being questioned by the Sanhedrin, the Jewish Council. It would not be long before he was brought before me.

Caiaphas and his supporters believed they had enough evidence to persuade me to condemn him and the whole assembly moved over to my palace. It was still early in the morning when I received the expected call and went down to meet the High Priests and their supporters in the courtyard. When I saw Jesus I was immediately struck by his immense dignity and by how badly he had been treated. His hands were tied behind him and he had been blindfolded and beaten up. I ordered the blindfold removed and his hands freed. The High

Priest told me what the charge against the man was. He had called himself a king and opposed payment of taxes to the Romans. I asked why I needed to be involved.

"If the man isn't a criminal, we would not have been brought him before you." This was just plain arrogant and certainly not calculated to make me want to help them. I told them to go away and judge him under their own laws. They reminded me that only I could pronounce the death penalty.

I asked Jesus "Are you the King of the Jews?"

"Yes, it is as they say"

I sensed the sharp intake of breath as the priests heard what, to them, was blasphemy. They began to introduce their witnesses against Jesus who gave evidence that Jesus opposed payment of taxes to Caesar and had threatened to destroy the Temple and rebuild it in three days. Neither of these charges worried me but he also claimed to be the Christ, a long awaited king who was to lead the Jews out of captivity. This accusation had to be taken seriously as I could not overlook anything that threatened the sovereignty and complete authority of Caesar. If I did, Antipas would have a field day. However the witnesses they called to support their charges had been so badly prepared that they contradicted each other. In the end the people were laughing at the ineptitude of the accusers and I could ignore them. Caiaphas accused Jesus of blasphemy because, in front of me, he had called himself King of the Jews. He did not respond.

I asked him "Don't you hear the accusations they are making? Help me by proving your innocence." He still gave no answer. He wasn't an easy person to help. I was very keen that he should defend himself.

The priests would not come into my palace as they had been ritually cleansed in preparation for the forth-coming feast. Entering an unconsecrated building would defile them and they would then have to go through the lengthy cleansing process again. This gave me the opportunity to take Jesus into a court-yard in the palace, where I could talk to him privately away from all the noise. I asked him again "Are you the King of the Jews?" We had difficulty in commu-nicating as he spoke little Latin. I asked for an inter-preter to help. This worked well as it gave me time to think while what we said was being translated. He could also act as scribe as, even in a God forsaken hole like Judea, if a man was to be executed proper records had to be kept ready for inspection. If there weren't any and someone complained to Rome, my job would be at risk.

He immediately responded "Did you think of that ques-tion or was it suggested to you by others?"

"Am I a Jew? Your own countrymen brought you here. Why? What have you done?"

"I am not an earthly king. If I were so, my followers would have resisted when I was arrested. My kingdom is not of this world."

"You are a king then?"

"You tell me that I am a king and you are right. I was born to bring truth into the world. Anyone who loves truth recognises that what I say is true."

"What is truth?" I replied but this was not the time for a philosophical discussion.

After further questions I was clear that Jesus was no threat to me or to Rome. I went outside and told the priests I could find no basis of a charge against him under Roman law but they insisted that he would cause unrest throughout Judea by his teaching. He had already done so in Galilee.

From then on the trial was conducted with me acting as a messenger between the High Priest and his supporters outside the Palace and the prisoner inside it. Obviously the Priests were not interested in anything Jesus had to say. I found it ironic that the priests were pretending that they protecting Roman interests – usually they were doing their best to reduce our power. Anyway I had heard that Jesus lived in Galilee and I could therefore legitimately pass the matter over to Antipas. I gave the necessary order and the whole assembly, led by the prisoner and his guards, moved over to his palace.

Antipas was delighted to be able to question Jesus as he had heard much about him. He hoped to see him perform some miracle but Jesus remained mute before him even though his accusers were standing there shouting and gesturing at him. As expected Jesus was brought back before me and Antipas told me what had happened. I invited him to sit with me. This was the first time I had talked to Antipas for many years. We talked the situation over and he agreed with what I planned to do.

I was pretty sure that I had not heard the last of the matter. The priests were out for blood and would be back. I consulted my advisers and they reminded me that, as a good will gesture, it was my custom each Passover to release to them a Jewish prisoner who would otherwise be condemned to death. Apart from Jesus there was only one other possibility, a well-known brigand named Barabbas who had robbed many of the leading citizens of Jerusalem. I thought it unlikely that they would want to spare his life. . I went outside and offered to release Jesus as my Passover offering. I could see the priests going round telling the people to shout for Barabbas to be freed and knew that that idea hadn't worked. It finally made me understand just how much the priests wanted Jesus dead.

As I sat thinking what to do Claudia, who had been watching what was going on, sent me a message. She had had a dream and advised me "Don't have anything to do with this innocent man; I have had a terrible nightmare about him." This was easier said than done. My chief concern was to keep the peace. I thought that, if I had Jesus flogged, this might satisfy the Jews. When that was over the soldiers dressed Jesus in a purple robe and placed a crown of thorns on his head. I wished they hadn't done that. It made it more difficult for me to make the case that he didn't claim to be an earthly king.

I led Jesus out wearing his crown of thorns and purple robe. I tried to argue with the priests saying. "Look, I can find no basis for a charge against this man". Bearing in mind Claudia's warning I was desperate to find a way to save Jesus' life. I could see the priests running round the crowd stirring up the people to shout out "Crucify him".

I told the priests "You go and crucify him. As for me I can find no basis for charging him." They replied "We have a Law and, under that Law, he deserves to die. He claims to be the Son of God."

I took Jesus inside and talked to him again. I could not get him to retract his statement about being a king. I asked him "Where do you come from?" He refused to answer.

"Why are you refusing to speak to me? Don't you realize that I can either free you or have you executed?"

"You have no power over me unless it is given to you by my heavenly father but you are not as guilty as those who brought me before you?" This didn't really help me much. I was terrified that the situation would get completely out of control.

I sat on the judgment seat. Jesus was led out and I shouted "Here is your king." The mob responded by screaming. "Take him away! Take him away! Crucify him!" They were getting more and more excited. Someone said "If you let this man go you are no friend of Caesar's." I kept on trying to persuade the leaders that Jesus had been punished enough but they wouldn't listen.

"Shall I crucify your king?

"We have no king but Caesar."

"What crime has he committed? There are no grounds for the death penalty."

The shouting grew louder. "Crucify him! Crucify him!"

In the end, if I was to avoid a major riot, I had no option but to give in. I ordered that a bowl of water be brought out and I washed my hands in front of them. "I am innocent of the blood of this man. It is your responsibility."

They replied without hesitation "We will take the blame for this man's death – we and our children." Somehow this didn't seem to relieve me of my feelings of guilt.

The High Priest was insistent that the execution be immediate so that the bodies were taken down before Passover began. I ordered the soldiers to execute him. I nearly sparked off another riot by insisting that a notice saying "Jesus of Nazareth, King of the Jews" was hung round Jesus, neck as he was taken to the place of execution and then nailed to the cross. At least that would show them that the Romans couldn't be pushed around.

When I got back to the palace with Antipas and told my wife what had happened, she was much distressed. We sat inside and tried to find a way by which we could have saved the prisoner. In the evening, just before real nightfall, a centurion came and reported that Jesus was dead and that his body was lying in a sealed tomb. I remember being surprised at how quickly he had died.

An elderly Jew named Joseph of Arimathea, a member of the Jewish Council, had requested that he be given the body for burial and, much against the wishes of the priests, I had given permission. I was impressed by Joseph's courage as his life would certainly be in danger because of what he was doing. Jesus deserved an honourable burial.

Early next morning, the day of the feast, Caiaphas sent a messenger to ask that I send Roman troops to guard the tomb and make sure the body wasn't stolen. I was irritated that he would break his own rules about Sabbath observance in this way as usually he was so meticulous in observing them. I refused to use my troops for this purpose because of my disgust at what had happened.

The next day I heard that the body had vanished. This news shocked me. I knew how careful the High Priest would have been in having the tomb guarded. I found what had happened frightening. What if Jesus was divine as he had said? I immediately gave orders that a citywide search be mounted but with no success. The priests came and accused me of taking the body but I told them not to be stupid. The Temple guards who had been at the tomb had apparently 'disappeared' although I was sure Annas knew where they were. The body never was found even though we extended the search to Galilee and inevitably the rumours about Jesus having risen from the dead started. I still wonder how the miracle was worked and the corpse removed. As time went by the whispers grew stronger. People claimed to have seen Jesus, both in Jerusalem and in Galilee. Eventually I was told that Jesus had been taken up to heaven in a cloud. As a result of my failure to appoint Roman soldiers to guard the tomb and my insistence that the notice about Jesus, King of the Jews being put on the cross, Caiaphas wrote to the Emperor Tiberius complaining about me. Fortunately he took no action.

A few weeks later I asked that one of the teacher's followers be brought in, expecting to see someone terrified at being called to meet me. The man who came was not in any way frightened. He told me that Jesus was the Son of God and that he had been raised from the dead. Many people had seen him before he went up to heaven. The purpose of Jesus coming was to pay the price for the wrong doing of all the people on earth who would then be able to be with their master in heaven. Meanwhile those who followed him had been given special powers so that they could continue their teacher's work. The number of his disciples was growing fast. I sent the man away with my thanks.

There was much to think about here. I could understand that, if Jesus was the Son of God who had come to earth to die, he might behave in the way he had. He had certainly showed superhuman courage. Nothing I could have done would have prevented his death. This was a comfort to both Claudia and I as we discussed things together. We had all been caught up in matters too big for us.

Two years later I was recalled to Rome. This was not before one final showdown. Some Samaritans went to Mount Gerizim, their holy place, because they believed that some treasures from the original Temple were buried there. The Temple leaders claimed that, if anything was found, it belonged to them. I had some of the Samaritan ringleaders executed and complaints were made to the Governor of Syria who ordered me back to Rome to explain my conduct. Sejanus had long since fallen foul of the Emperor's ill temper and there was therefore no one in Rome to look after my interests. As Claudia and I travelled back I feared for my life as Tiberius was notorious for his vengeance on those he thought had failed him. I could feel some of the pain that Barabbas and Jesus and others I had condemned must have felt. I didn't enjoy it. Fortunately Tiberius died before I arrived in Rome and I was never required to explain the reasons for what I had done.

I don't have many happy memories of Judea, that parched land, or of Jerusalem, a city where the squalor was beyond belief and the bustle and noise level were far greater than anywhere else I had been. I am glad not to have to deal with the priests anymore but am left with an acute feeling of guilt that I had caused an innocent man to be crucified. I could never shake this off. I still cannot forget Jesus' look of patient suffering as he stood before me. Claudia still has nightmares about it. I wish I could have saved him but he would not do anything to help himself. He had decided that, for whatever reason, he must die. One thing I was clear about – he knew what he was doing.

We have retired to a lovely village just outside Rome and keep a low profile. We are not welcome at court but this bothers neither of us. We have watched with amazement the growth in the number of Jesus' supporters in Rome itself and presumably elsewhere. Perhaps he was who he said he was.

There are many stories that Pilate committed suicide, unable to live with his guilt, but there is no historical evidence to back any of these up.

The Centurion at the Cross

It was the duty we all tried to avoid. Each year a unit was chosen to go to Jerusalem with the Procurator for the Jewish feast of the Passover. We all knew that the duty was dangerous and unpleasant. We would be insulted and hassled by the locals and, more often than not, some of the detachment would be killed or seriously hurt. About 300 men were sent under the command of a senior centurion who was chosen by lot from among those who had not previously performed the duty. This year I drew the short straw.

I had been in Palestine for 5 years and this was my last posting before retirement. Caesarea where we were normally stationed was not a bad billet. The city was mainly a Roman garrison and was relatively safe for us. The people largely depended on us for their living and therefore did not seek to harm us. My wife and children liked it there and had settled well. Lucia was originally from Gaul and found the heat trying but there were plenty of people to talk to and there was education of a sort for the children.

Anyway this was my turn and there was no use moaning. We were briefed before we set out and told that Jerusalem, the centre of the Jewish religion, was more restless than normal. There were the usual number of robbers and rabble-rousers around who would miss no opportunity to make our lives unpleasant. As seemed to happen every year, a new teacher had emerged and he had gathered a considerable following. He operated mainly around the Sea of Galilee, an area which came under the jurisdiction of King Herod in Galilee rather than Pilate. Jesus was expected by the High Priest, Caiaphas, to be present in Jerusalem for the feast. Of course the Establishment were against him as he was disturbing their nice little world. So far he was of no concern to Rome as he seemed mainly intent on helping his own people in Galilee. One of my colleagues who was stationed there thought highly of this Jesus. He told us that the man taught peace and had been instrumental in healing his servant.

We set out on our three-day march to Jerusalem two weeks before the feast. It was hot and sweaty and Pontius Pilate the Procurator was in a foul mood. There were a number of factors that contributed to this. Firstly his wife had insisted on going with him and she pretty much ruled the roost when she was around. Secondly Herod Antipas was also going to be in Jerusalem. He was the local ruler in Judea but he had spent his youth in Rome and knew the Emperor Tiberius personally. He and Pilate had never got on as Herod saw Pilate as interfering with his rule. They fell out over what proportion of the taxes collected by Herod should belong to the Emperor. The king was always threatening to report Pilate to the emperor and there was real bad blood between them. Thirdly Pilate was nearing retirement and would do anything for a quiet life. Going to Jerusalem was not his idea of fun. His bad temper meant that none of us could do anything to please him. He even had his cook whipped because breakfast wasn't to his liking.

Marching through Judea was not particularly pleasant but we made good time and reached Jerusalem on schedule. We were greeted there by the local garrison commander and settled into our duties. There was much moaning among our men as their arrival meant that the accommodation was overcrowded. I talked over the situation with my opposite number in the city and we agreed how to split our duties. I was told that Jesus had not yet put in an appearance. The Jewish guards had recently captured a local villain named Barabbas, a much sought after thief who had pretended to be an independence fighter.

We expected that the Jewish leaders would ask Pilate that Barabbas be executed. Only the Procurator was allowed to pronounce the death sentence. Generally things were relatively quiet although there seemed a high level of tension among the people. Prime responsibility for keeping the peace lay with the Temple guards who reported to the High Priest. We Romans were present as a back up force and to ensure that Roman rights were not abused.

The first few days went as well as we hoped. There were a few riots but the guards were able to deal with these and were none too gentle in doing so. Caiaphas asked Pilate for the death penalty for Barabbas and he was transferred to our prison in the garrison. The first hint that we got of any possible problem was when we heard that Jesus had arrived one week before the feast. Enthusiastic crowds greeted him as he entered the city riding on a donkey. Caiaphas was apparently much put out by this but it didn't constitute a risk to security and we were not involved. In fact the crowds were astonishingly well behaved; not only was nobody injured but no property was damaged.

Things began to get worse next day when Jesus and his followers went into the Temple, the most holy place for all Jews, and upset the moneychangers' tables. These people changed normal coins into Temple coins that were the only currency that could be used to buy animals for sacrifice. This was a racket organised by the Temple authorities as the Temple currency cost more than normal coins but the price of the sacrifices was the same as in the normal market. The profit went direct to the Temple. Jesus' action caused consternation but again we were not involved as the last thing the priests wanted was for non-believers to enter the Temple and defile it. While he was surrounded by his supporters Jesus was safe. I had a lot of sympathy with Jesus when I heard what he had done as the Priests were cheating their own supporters. However Pilate told us that the matter would not end there, as the priests would want the last word. He too seemed to have some sympathy with Jesus.

For the next two days things were blessedly quiet although Caiaphas' palace remained a hive of activity. Annas, a previous High Priest who had been banned from office for trying to bribe some Roman officials, was constantly in and out of the building. He was an unscrupulous little man whose reputation preceded him. He was reputed to be the person who really held the power and Caiaphas, his son-in-law, was said to be just a figurehead. Annas made no secret of his ambition for Palestine to regain its independence but in fighting for it he had made himself a very rich man.

On the morning before the feast at around 6 o'clock in the morning I was woken up by one of the sentries and told that Caiaphas was demanding an urgent meeting with Pilate. The governor had no option but to agree to this and I was instructed to provide a guard for the occasion. I selected a squad of 20 men and we marched to the courtyard of the procurator's palace where Pilate was to meet the Jewish leaders. I had expected just a few of the Jewish leaders to be there but found a mob of about 500 people. I immediately sent for another 50 men. Jesus was escorted by the Palace guards and had already been beaten up. His hands were tied behind his back and there were the marks of blows on his face. He was in obvious pain but he retained his dignity and showed no fear. I looked carefully at him and saw an almost unnatural serenity.

Pilate asked the Jews what accusation they had against Jesus. Initially they produced witnesses who said Jesus had instructed his supporters not to pay taxes to Caesar and had claimed that he would destroy the Temple and

John Lindeck

rebuild it within three days. If it had not been so serious, the situation would have been quite funny. The priests who normally spent their time abusing the Romans were suddenly their defenders. The witnesses that they called had been insufficiently trained and could not remember what they were supposed to say. As a result they contradicted each other and eventually became a laughing stock. Throughout all this Jesus remained still and silent. Caiaphas then accused Jesus of treason. He had called himself King of the Jews and this, together with the previous allegation that his followers should refuse to pay taxes, was, according to him, enough to cause Jesus to be convicted. Pilate had to be careful, particularly with Antipas also in Jerusalem but there was no real evidence for Jesus to be condemned. The false witnesses had discredited each other.

The priests had already completed their ritual cleansing for the feast and so Pilate was able to take Jesus into the Palace away from the priests. I stayed outside watching the crowd and only four of my men went indoors. I was told that the governor asked Jesus if he was the King of the Jews and to everyone's astonishment he agreed. Jesus said nothing more although Pilate continued to question him. In the end Pilate came out to tell the Jewish leaders that he could find no cause to condemn Jesus but this caused further uproar and the priests claimed that the prisoner was causing unrest throughout the provinces of Galilee and Judea. As Pilate did not have responsibility for Galilee, this gave him the excuse to send Jesus to Antipas, who was responsible for law and order there, for judgment. I was instructed to escort Jesus to Herod's palace. The more I saw of Jesus, the more sure I was that he was not likely to pose any threat to the empire.

Followed by the entire mob, I took Jesus over to Herod's palace. Herod came to meet us and confronted Jesus. He asked him if it was true that he had been able to heal people and work miracles. Jesus gave no answer. Herod then asked Jesus to perform a miracle for him to prove his power but still Jesus remained silent. He would not respond either to Herod or to the taunting of the mob. In the end Herod gave up. He was intrigued by Jesus and wanted to hear him defend himself but Jesus refused to do so. Not knowing what to do, he ordered me to take Jesus back to Pilate and accompanied me himself. We came back to Pilate's palace and Herod explained what had happened.

Pilate reminded the High Priest that it was his custom at the feast of the Passover to release to the Jews a condemned prisoner. He said they could have either Jesus or Barabbas and I am sure he thought they would choose Jesus. Barabbas had caused great suffering to many of the Jewish leaders and his capture had been greeted with immense relief. I could see Annas in a corner of the courtyard sending out messengers into the crowd and wasn't surprised therefore when they called for the release of Barabbas. Now the decision really was down to Pilate. He consulted with Herod. This was a matter of great surprise, as the two of them had not spoken to each other in years. They took Jesus back indoors again to try to find a way of saving him and Pilate reminded him that he had power of life and death over him. Jesus reacted by saying this was only because he, Jesus, wished it to be so. Pilate went outside again with Jesus and sat down on the judgment seat. He told the crowd that neither he nor Herod could find any cause to condemn Jesus and presented the prisoner to them as their king. He asked what they wanted done with him. I noticed the messengers pushing through the crowd. "Crucify him," they yelled. He asked again "Shall I crucify your king?" The immediate response was "We have no king but Caesar." As I looked round the mob I knew that Jesus' fate was sealed. The hate and violence on their faces was like I had never seen before. And still Jesus stood silent before his accusers.

Pilate ordered that Jesus be flogged. I was not sure why he did this; surely crucifixion was punishment enough for any man. I have never heard of anyone else being scourged immediately before being crucified. A Roman flogging is no small matter - 40 strokes on the bare back with a multi-lashed whip. Only the strongest could survive it. It fell to me to oversee its administration and then take him to be crucified. As he was being tied up prior to the flogging I caught his eye. Instead of the fear I expected to see I saw pity. It was as if he was forgiving me. The flogging was administered and, apart from grunts of pain, he didn't call out. By the end his back was running with blood and he could hardly stand. I offered him drink but he refused. To my shame, while the crossbar to be used in the crucifixion was being fetched, the soldiers occupied themselves mocking Jesus. They dressed him in an old scarlet robe and placed a crown of thorns round his head. The thorns were pressed tight down and, where they punc- tured his skin, blood trickled down his face. I still do not know why I didn't prevent my men doing this and my weakness has haunted me ever since. Jesus bore all the humiliation as if in a trance. He showed no reaction to their taunts. Pilate washed his hands in front of the crowd and gave Jesus up for execution. He thought that by doing this he could absolve himself of responsibility but, if I felt dirtied by what was happening, he must have felt a thousand times worse.

The place of execution was about a quarter of a mile from the palace. Jesus was so weakened that he could hardly lift the crossbar. We started out through a dense throng lining the narrow streets and the soldiers had to push people out of the way so that we could make our way to the execution ground. A lady reached out of the crowd and wiped the prisoner's face. Twice he collapsed and had to be helped to his feet again and the third time I saw that he could not bear the weight any more. I grabbed a spectator and made him carry the cross. We reached the place of execution and two others were waiting there to be crucified with him.

Something which I have always remembered happened on the way to the place of execution. A large number of people followed Jesus, among them a group of women who were mourning and wailing. Jesus turned to them and said "Daughters of Jerusalem, do not weep for me. Weep for yourselves and for your children. For a day is coming when women will consider themselves fortunate that they have no children. People will pray that the mountains will fall on them and the hills bury them. If these things happen when the tree is still young, what will it be like when it is full grown?" How he could think of others when in his situation, I will never know.

As I watched they nailed Jesus to the cross through his hands and his feet. Still he didn't call out although tears were running down his face. He looked utterly forsaken but yet, in a strange way, he maintained his dignity. I have been unfortunate enough to witness many crucifixions and in every case the prisoner, knowing that there was no hope and no one for who to put on a show, had screamed and cursed in agony. Jesus had an inner strength that prevented him from doing so.

The crosses were lifted to the vertical and dropped into the sockets prepared for them. The jerk almost dislocated the arms of the prisoners and even Jesus called out. Pilate had ordered that a notice saying "Jesus of Nazareth, the King of the Jews" be nailed to his cross and this served to inflame the crowd more. As he hung there, the crowd including the High Priest and his cronies mocked him. "He saved others but he cannot save himself". I was watching Jesus and I swear that I still saw a look of pity on his face. I heard him say, "Forgive them father for they don't know what they are doing". Regrettably my men joined in the mockery. I was struck by the complete indifference of Caiaphas to Jesus' suffering – so long as it didn't affect his comfort he didn't seem to care. The crowd was more vicious than any I had seen previously in a fairly long experience of these things.

Soon after the crosses had been lifted upright one of the two men crucified with him started scoffing at Jesus.

"So you are the Messiah are you? Save yourself and come down from the Cross and, while you are at it, save us too." The other looked across to the man and said "We deserve to die for the evil we have done but he hasn't done anything wrong." Turning to Jesus he said "Jesus, remember me when you come into your kingdom." I heard Jesus tell him "Today you will be with me in heaven." And the man appeared to be at peace.

Because of the unrest caused by the notice on the cross I placed four guards round its base, as I was frightened of further violence from the mob. In accord with custom, the guards divided his clothes but agreed not to cut up his robe, which was made of one piece of material stretching from neck to feet in the style that rabbis wore, but to draw lots for it. They passed the time playing dice. Gradually the crowd began to drift away.

I had no interest in seeing the agonies of those being executed and normally I would have kept my distance. Crucifixion was no easy death. However in this case I felt compelled to stay. Jesus behaved like no one else I had seen. Most victims hung there in silent misery. Some swore at the watchers or pleaded their ignorance or screamed in pain. Jesus spoke little but it was what he said that was so amazing. He prayed for those who had had him condemned to death. "Forgive them Father for they know not what they do."

I continued to watch Jesus. He was weakening fast. The physical and mental ordeal of the last hours was, not surprisingly, taking its toll. Only a gathering of Pharisees in their ridiculous clothes and a small group of men and women were left. One of the women was Jesus' mother. She was standing directly under the cross. He spoke to her "Dear woman, this is your son". To one of the men he said "Here is your mother". Then a little later "My God, My God, why have you forsaken me?" He spoke twice more to say "It is finished" and "Father into your hands I commit my soul" and he was gone. The rain was pouring down and we were all soaked to the skin. There was a howling wind and a great crash and the whole earth shook. I knew that these were signs connected to the death of the man on the cross. This was not just any crucifixion. What sort of man could think of others when enduring the agony that he had been in?

I was so moved that I spoke aloud "Surely this man was the Son of God."

I had been instructed by the priests to make sure that all the prisoners were dead before sunset as it was against Jewish law to execute anyone on their holy day. I was glad of this for death by crucifixion could take up to 36 hours. The usual way to finish prisoners off was to break their legs. The shock would kill them. However I knew Jesus was dead so I drove a spear into his side to prove it. We took the bodies down and I handed that of Jesus to two members of the Sanhedrin, the Jewish Council, who had been given written authority by Pilate to entomb him. I was glad of this as I didn't want Jesus' remains left out to rot or to be savaged by wild animals. We all had to go with him to ensure that the body was not stolen and, after the corpse had been placed in the tomb, a huge stone was rolled across the entrance to protect it. I went to report to the Governor that the execution was complete. He was surprised that death had been so quick and I could see that he was highly upset. Caiaphas asked Pilate to place sentries to guard the tomb to avoid any danger of the body being stolen but, I imagine because he was annoyed that he had been manipulated as he was, refused and so three Temple guards were posted there.

There were all sorts of rumours next day. People were talking of those who had been long dead emerging from their graves. I heard these stories too many times for them to be unfounded. I had no idea what was happening but the whole city seemed to be in a state of high excitement.

Two days later I was woken up just after dawn. The stone had been moved and the body was gone. I hurried to the tomb and found that the three Temple guards on duty had vanished. To say that Pilate was furious was an understatement and the High Priest and his supporters were beside themselves with rage. Caiaphas organised an immediate search for the body but it was never found. The Temple guards who had been watching the tomb had disappeared, probably not without a little help from their friends.

My mind was racing as I went over the little that I knew about Jesus. He was like no other man I had ever met. He had certainly felt pain like any of us but he never once complained of his treatment or responded in anger to his accusers. It was as if he had decided that he had to die and was going to do so with dignity. I had to find out more about him. I told my wife exactly what had happened and we agreed that we would stay in Jerusalem to watch what developed. Pilate gave me permission. Rumours reached us that Jesus was alive again but I never saw him. I began to ask questions but people recognised me and suspected that I was a spy. Eventually Mary, his mother, spoke to me and explained how Jesus was the Son of God and had died so that men might be presented perfect before their God.

It took me many weeks to grasp her meaning but, when I did, I knew that what she was saying was true. Even I could be forgiven for what I had done to Jesus. I joined the rapidly growing ranks of his supporters and worked to tell others of what I had learnt. I have never regretted this change in my lifestyle and indeed it has proved the most rewarding decision of my life. Helping others to discover the truth about Jesus was as rewarding as learning about him for myself. These were the most fulfilling days of my life. The older I get, the more I believe in the fact that Jesus did come alive again.

Simon from Cyrene

It was my first trip to Jerusalem. Right from when I was
a little boy I had looked forward to this moment. Father
had moved away from the city when he was just 6 years
old. He was none too clear what had made his father
take the huge step of leaving his own country and going
to live many hundreds of miles away on the North
African coast. He never remembered any other home
and had no ambition to visit the country from where he
came. He met Mother at the local synagogue and they
had been very happy together. Like all couples they
had their disagreements but these never resulted in any
bitterness and things were soon back on an even keel. It
was a matter of deep regret to them that there were only
2 children, Jacob my younger brother to whom I was
very close and myself, but we were happy together as a
family. When I married Miriam, she was immediately
accepted into our little family. We had three children,
two boys, Alexander and Rufus and a daughter Sarah.
My parents were so proud of them and made a great

fuss of them. The children later told me what a happy childhood they had had. Membership of the synagogue was an essential part of their upbringing. Jacob married Esther but they had no children. We were very happy to share ours with them. Both Jacob and I went into the family's business as apothecaries.

My parents died within a few months of each other when the boys were 16 and 14 and Sarah was 10. Miriam's mother had died earlier and her father had moved away to live with her sister's family. We moved in to my parents' house but tragically Miriam discovered a lump in her breast and, in spite of the best medical care we could find, she passed away shortly after. Sarah, much assisted by Esther, took over the running of the house but things were not the same. I missed Miriam enormously and could not settle to anything. My work no longer absorbed me as it once had and I began to make mistakes. The boys started to help Jacob in his work and he and Esther looked after them and ran the home. I worked when I felt like it. I think they were all grateful when I was away.

Miriam and I had always planned to visit Jerusalem when the children were grown up and able to look after themselves. We used to look at each other as we said the old words 'Next year in Jerusalem' and dream but we never thought it would happen. The boys started urging me to make the trip on my own. I was not keen as it would not be the same without Miriam but eventually they persuaded me. I agreed to travel with a group of pilgrims visiting the city for the feast of the Passover. We sailed from Cyrene and arrived in Joppa in good time to walk over the hills to Jerusalem for the feast. We joined the thousands of other pilgrims going up to the Temple for the celebrations and we all joined together in singing the traditional Psalms. It was such joy to be caught up with others who shared our faith singing the praises of the Lord together. I cannot describe the sense of fellowship, the companionship that we enjoyed.

We arrived at Jerusalem the day before the feast and camped just outside the walls. On the eve of the feast we made our way into the city. It was seething with people, more than I had ever seen before. All were heading in one direction – up to the Temple. We passed through one narrow street after another, always heading uphill. And then we stopped. A procession was passing along the street led by Roman soldiers. They were pushing and shoving to get through the dense crowds. The troops were followed by a group of priests and then a man staggering under the weight of the cross bar to a crucifixion cross. As I looked at him, he collapsed under the weight. I could see that he had been recently flogged and blood was still running down his back. His head was bleeding where sharp thorns had been pressed down and he had been beaten round his face. The pain must have been unendurable. In spite of a lash from the whip of one of the guards, he was unable to rise.

I felt a hand grab me by the shoulder. I looked round and saw the centurion in charge of the guard. "Carry the cross for him" he said. I turned thinking why me but his grip grew tighter. My first reaction was embarrassment and annoyance at being picked out in front of all those people. I had no idea why I had been chosen.

Possibly it was the colour of my skin but, more probably, being in the wrong place at the wrong time. Then I looked down and saw the criminal. I wondered what he had done to deserve such a fate. He glanced at me and I was stunned. In spite of the pain, his eyes were full of kindness. I wanted to help him more than I have ever wanted anything else in my life. I took the cross and lifted it. It was heavy for a fit man like me let alone someone who had been treated like him. He was hauled to his feet and we moved off down the street. He was barely able to walk and lent on me for support.

It was not far to the execution ground where two other men were waiting for crucifixion. As I walked I could feel the blood from his wounds on my arms and hands. The whole length of the beam was sticky with his blood and sweat. My heart bled for the man who was suffering so much. I laid the cross bar down where I was told and stood watching. I was told I could go but I still waited. They took him and nailed him to the cross through the arms and the legs. He must have been in agony but he did not call out. The other two were tied to their crosses and they swore and cursed the whole time. The crosses were lifted and dropped into the sockets in the ground that were ready for them. I could feel in my own flesh the ripping as the cross fell and then settled. He gave out a loud groan as he hung there.

I had no idea what he had done to deserve such a punishment. I remembered his look of gratitude when I took the load for him. There were priests in their rich vestments there mocking him. "He saved others, himself he cannot save". The look he gave them was of love rather than hate. I heard him say, "Forgive them father for they do not know what they are doing". How could he think of others when himself in such pain?

The crowds drifted away as the best part of the spectacle, if that was how they regarded it, was over. Two groups were left, one mostly of women who seemed to be connected to the man on the cross. The other was of priests but not the ones who had been mocking him earlier. I went to the priests and asked who he was. They looked surprised as if everyone must know his name. One answered. "Jesus from Nazareth"

"What has he done?" I asked

"He has proclaimed himself the Messiah."

"Has he harmed anybody?"

"No. Many people have been healed through his ministry"

"Why is he being killed and why so cruelly?"

"The High Priest thought he was preaching blasphemy"

"What do you think of him?"

"He is like no one else I have ever met. I don't know what I think."

I could see that he did not want to talk any more and I moved a little distance away. I wanted to see what happened. The weather was terrible. The skies darkened and it teemed with rain. Thunder blasted and lightning shot across the sky. Still I watched the tortured figure on the cross. He spoke again but the noise was so great that I didn't hear what he said. And then he was gone. With one last sigh he breathed his last and his torment was over. The earth groaned and shook violently as if to recognise the end. They pierced his side to confirm his death. The other two were killed before sunset so that the feast was not desecrated and the bodies taken down. I followed as two of the priests took that of Jesus and laid it in a new tomb a short distance away. A huge stone was rolled over the entrance and Temple guards were left to see that the body wasn't stolen.

I returned to my tent in a state of shock. I could not accept what I had seen. There was something good about the man who had been killed. Sleep was difficult that night. In the morning I went with my party to the Temple to celebrate the Passover. We heard of how Jesus had upset the tables at which the moneychangers sat and driven them out of the building. When I saw the rates of exchange they offered, I didn't blame him. We gave our animals for sacrifice and, after staying at the Temple for some time, went back to our lodgings.

I went back to the Temple next day. All was much quieter but there was a buzz around the courts. The body of Jesus was missing and his followers were accused of stealing it. The guards watching over the tomb had disappeared, presumably because they were frightened of their fate. I could not imagine how a small group of men could possibly have rolled away the heavy stone used to seal the tomb without being noticed. The story that was going round was too cut and dried to be wholly believable. I made up my mind to stay in Jerusalem a few more days.

It was two days later that the stories started to circulate. Jesus had risen from the dead. None of the people who had watched as Jesus died were in evidence. However the crowds were talking about the dead man. There were all sorts of stories about things he had done and too many people said they had been witnesses for them all to be made up. Those who said that he had healed them told their stories. No one described him as any sort of threat and there were many complaining about how they had been tricked into demanding the death of Jesus rather than that of Barabbas, a notorious brigand. The atmosphere was growing rapidly less stable. Rumours abounded and there were those who were saying that they had met Jesus since his death. A search for the body had of course been started and, equally unsurprisingly, had been unsuccessful. If the corpse had been stolen, those who had done it were going to make very sure that it was never found. I think the strategy of the High Priest was to let the fuss blow over but it was not working. Obviously if they could have produced the body, all arguments would have been settled.

I stayed in Jerusalem about two months. It was now possible to find lodgings in the city. There was no rush for me to get back and there was much I wanted to see. The Temple itself was an ongoing fascination with the constant throng of people passing through. The atmosphere began to change. Men started to appear saying openly that Jesus was the Messiah and that he had risen from the dead. The priests were enraged and tried to drive these men out of the Temple but they persisted. I talked to one of them, a man named Andrew. He had been a fisherman in Galilee and had been accompanying Jesus for over three years. He told me of what Jesus had done, of the miraculous way in which he had healed many who were sick and, above all, of the care and compassion with which he had treated all who came to him. Everybody was equal in his sight. Jesus said that those who believed in him would go with him to be with his Father in heaven. None of his followers had understood that he must first die for this to come to pass. Only now was it clear. Andrew invited me back to a meeting and I heard others talking about Jesus. One of the statements Jesus was quoted as saying was particularly striking to me. He had said "If anyone wants to be worthy of me, he must deny himself and take up his cross daily and follow me." I had certainly taken up his cross. The speakers were ordinary men who were saying extraordinary things and I believed them. They explained how they were able to do what they were doing because the spirit of Jesus had come upon them and how they were working through his power. I asked if I could receive this power and they prayed with me before I was baptised. As I was dipped under the water I was sure that my jealousies and anger had been forgiven and that I would go to be with him. I began to tell others and stayed for a while longer but I was keen to get home.

When I got back to Cyrene, I found my family worried. They had expected me back much earlier. I told them what had occurred and my sons in particular asked many questions. I think they believed me but Alexander especially wanted to see for himself. I agreed to look after the business with Jacob and the two boys set out for Jerusalem. They stayed for three months and returned, convinced like me, that Jesus was the Son of God. We tried to get the leaders of the synagogue to let us tell our story but they refused permission. We were forced to set up a separate meeting. Others who had been with me in Jerusalem and had been at the meeting when the Holy Spirit came upon them joined with us. The meetings grew and Jews and non-Jews joined us. We were able to look after the sick and care for the widows and the needy. Some of the others knew much more about Jesus than I did and were able to talk to us about his teaching. A few even went back to Jerusalem and to other cities like Antioch to tell others of the Saviour. God seems near to us as we continue to worship him and serve him as we can.

Rufus left home fairly soon to help to spread the truth about Jesus in other countries. With some friends he moved to Antioch and became one of the elders in the church there. I missed him but I knew that he had no choice but to do what he did. Eventually he moved on to Rome. I continued to run the business with Alexander but my main interest was in seeing the truth about Jesus spread through the city.

Joseph of Arimathea

My father was a wonderful man. I was his only son and, from the earliest time I can remember, he was always there for me. I had two sisters who seemed mainly to be with my mother but, as soon as Dad came home, I followed him around like a shadow. I went to his office with him and he would never get impatient with my endless questions. I was called 'his little shadow'. He was the owner of a number of tin and copper mines, mostly near home but some further afield. His father had been employed at one of them but, when he started working, Dad decided he was going to run the business, not work for it. When I was fourteen I started working with Dad full time and earning a proper wage. I used to travel round with Dad and he grew to trust me more and give me greater responsibility. This was just as well as, when I was twenty one, Dad had an accident and died. As it was I was able to continue the business with minimum disruption.

Don't get me wrong, I loved my mother deeply but I needed someone for myself. She had married Dad when she was still young and he was ten years older than her. She was a very good housekeeper and cook and I was lucky to have her and my two sisters looking after my every need. Even when the girls got married and started their own homes, Mum was still there for me. For the next few years I was too busy building up the business to get married but then I met Miriam. She was a girl from Arimathea, ten years younger than me, and we were very happy in the few years that we had together. When she fell pregnant we were both delighted but she died as Saul, my son, was born. Mum looked after him with help from a village girl whose daughter had not survived birth. I loved Saul deeply but I could not shake off the feeling that his birth had cost me my beloved Miriam. Mum used to challenge me about this but Saul and I were never as close as I had been with Dad. I regret this very much. The memories of Miriam are still fresh in my mind and I never had any desire to remarry.

Running the business was always interesting and gave me great satisfaction. Over the next thirty years it grew and developed enormously. I learnt many lessons and in particular that results are far better if the workers are treated as individuals. If they are just seen as machines to help the owner make money, they will have no loyalty or enthusiasm for their work. Saul joined me in the business and shared my views on how this should be done. We were closer in this period than when he was young. He married a lovely girl from the village and had three sons and two daughters.

Because of his position Dad had been a leading figure in the local community. His name had come to the notice of the authorities in Jerusalem. I think the local priest had told them how generous Dad had been to the local synagogue. Anyway, out of the blue, he had received an invitation to become a member of the Sanhedrin, the body which ran the Temple and liaised with the Roman invaders in running Judea. It was run by the High Priest and was made up mostly of priests. However there were a few others appointed. I suppose there were two reasons for this; firstly to convince the Romans that the Sanhedrin was a representative body and secondly because it meant that outsiders who were important to the Temple were not tempted to ignore it. Dad was in the latter category as he supplied materials that the Temple really needed such as copper. The negotiations about price were long and stressful as the High Priest always thought he was entitled to a special deal. I remember Dad complaining that he didn't even cover his costs on the business he did with the Temple. All prospective members of the Sanhedrin had to be confirmed as acceptable by the Romans before appointment but this caused no difficulty as Dad was a major supplier to the garrison. Anyway he was appointed and, when he got used to things, began to believe that it was a useful activity.

Not long after Dad died I was invited to take his place on the Council. I had my doubts as I had more than enough on my plate but I was persuaded to allow myself to be appointed. I was one of the youngest members. I was quite surprised at what went on. The chief interest of the members seemed to be protecting their position and they were none too scrupulous how they went about this. When I eventually plucked up courage to question what was going on I was firmly put in my place. They considered it quite in order to deceive the Romans by saying one thing and doing another. I found it difficult to reconcile this with the Ten Commandments which were the basis of our beliefs. There were one or two others who seemed to share my views and I became particularly friendly with Nicodemus, a Pharisee who was reputed to be the leading teacher of the faith in Jerusalem. He too was disturbed by the way business was conducted. Caiaphas, the High Priest, and Annas, his predecessor, ran the Council with a rod of iron and what they said went. Caiaphas was the ultimate protector of orthodoxy. So far as he was concerned nothing should ever change. Annas was more of a realist. He enjoyed the exercise of power and was prepared to go to any lengths to protect his authority. The rest of us were there to make up the numbers. If we got out of line we were soon told about it and members who didn't conform after a warning were likely to suffer nasty accidents. The worst part of it was that one couldn't resign. Caiaphas would just not accept resignations as he was frightened that ex members might spill the beans about what was going on.

Because I had been appointed so young in due course I became one of the senior members of the Council. I was fully trusted as I had given no reason for them to doubt me. In fact I was becoming more and more concerned about how things were going. Matters were decided on the basis of convenience rather than in accordance with the Law. Annas, in particular, seemed to be living in a state far above what might have been expected and he had an enforcement unit, headed by his sidekick, Malchus, which made sure that anyone who disagreed with him was quickly told the facts of life. There were several unexplained deaths and injuries among those who had disagreed with the party line. Caiaphas was not involved in these activities but was certainly ready to take advantage of the results. It was difficult for me and other members to protest against what was happening as we did not dare talk to our fellow members. For years I took the line of least resistance until finally something occurred which caused me to take action.

Almost every year someone appeared claiming to be the Messiah. Caiaphas took these people seriously and was insistent that they be shown up as pretenders as early as possible. Usually this could be achieved by threats from Annas and his bully boys although occasionally it was necessary for the person concerned to disappear. The claims of these pretenders were often so far fetched as to be totally unbelievable and they took no notice of what had been prophesied about the Messiah in the scriptures. I had no difficulty in agreeing with the 'discouragement' of such people. However one year a man named Jesus of Nazareth came on the scene. He was from Galilee but had, as foretold, been born in Bethlehem just outside Jerusalem. He first came to our notice when he met with another troublemaker, John the Baptist. Annas had had people watching John for some time and he was regarded as harmless. His message was that people should repent of their sins and, as a sign that they had done so, be baptised in the River Jordan. He was certainly very rude about the

High Priest and the Pharisees but he didn't go so far as to encourage rebellion against them. When he met Jesus he wanted to be baptised by him but the Galilean insisted that John should treat him as he did all the others who came. After the baptism many witnesses agreed that they had seen a figure like a dove coming down from heaven and heard a voice saying 'This is my son who I love; with him I am well pleased'.

We heard nothing more about Jesus for a few months and then persistent rumours started coming from Galilee telling of miracles performed by him, of large crowds following him around and of highly unusual teaching. Some of the witnesses confirmed that he had claimed to be the Messiah. Caiaphas was worried about what was going on but, while Jesus remained in Galilee, there was nothing he could do about it. However there were strong rumours that Jesus was going to visit Jerusalem for the Feast of the Tabernacles. He did eventually come and performed a number of miracles while in the city. When ever he appeared he attracted large crowds although whether this was to hear what he had to say or to see his miracles it was difficult to judge. Certainly what he was reported to have said was very different from anything else we had heard. He claimed that the Kingdom of God was a kingdom of love and that this law took the place of Moses' Law by which we were all supposed to live. He was scathing about the hypocrisy of those who kept the letter of the Law rather than its spirit.

Although Annas had his agents out trying to capture Jesus he was unable to do so because, whenever Jesus was about, he was surrounded by crowds and to attempt to take him would have set off large scale riots. Eventually he returned to Galilee. Caiaphas again said we should watch and wait although there was an increasing feeling among the Sanhedrin that, if we did nothing, more and more people would follow Jesus.

By this time I was on the Inner Council of the Sanhedrin. We were told in confidence that Nicodemus had gone to visit Jesus secretly while the teacher was in Jerusalem. He was no longer to be trusted. I decided that I must talk to Nicodemus but I wanted to do so in secret. Eventually we managed to get together and fortunately it became clear that our meeting had not been noticed. Nicodemus told me of his conversation. He had gone expecting to question the Galilean and to be able to satisfy himself that Jesus was not the Messiah. However, far from controlling the conversation, he had found himself listening and responding to him. He had come away unsure of what he believed about him but as he thought about it, he became more convinced of the possibility that this man was the Promised One. He was not for the time being going to declare himself a follower of Jesus but he would watch what happened. When he saw if events followed the ancient prophecies, he would make up his mind. From time to time I gave him a little money to pass on to Jesus.

The stories from Galilee continued to come and I followed them with growing excitement. This Jesus if nothing else was a man to be admired. His teaching was consistent and showed a concern for ordinary people which I could only admire. Some of the things he said, although against orthodox teaching, were obviously right. One example which struck me particularly was his story about the alms giving by the rich man and the widow woman. The small amount she gave was clearly a bigger sacrifice than the generosity of the rich man. I also liked the parable about the traveller set upon by thieves who was helped not by the priest or the Levi but by the Samaritan. I became increasingly interested in what he was saying and doing.

There were again rumours that Jesus would return to Jerusalem for the Passover and these were discussed by the Inner Council. Many members were concerned but Caiaphas argued that if there was any trouble during the feast, Jesus was the perfect scapegoat. However news came that altered everything. Jesus had stayed with a family in Bethany just outside Jerusalem. Shortly after he left, the man of the household had died. Jesus had come back and, although he didn't arrive until four days after the man's death, he had raised him from the dead. There were too many witnesses including Pharisees and Priests for this story to have been made up. It was agreed that Jesus must be taken and brought to trial. Annas was instructed to provide evidence. I wondered if I should try to warn Jesus but did not see how I could do this without risking my own safety.

Jesus duly arrived and was welcomed outside the city by supporters hailing him as the Messiah and lining his route with palm branches. He went to the Temple and turned over the tables used by the moneychangers when they turned ordinary currency into 'Temple' coin. He also freed the doves which were kept for visitors to buy for sacrifice. I found no problem with this as the moneychangers were notoriously corrupt. He had arrived about a week before the feast and came each day to the Outer Court of the Temple to preach. I went to hear him speak and was deeply impressed. At least he was saying something which had the ring of honesty about it.

I was still a member of the Inner Council and therefore was party to all the plans put in place to capture and condemn Jesus. It was no longer good enough just to have him killed as people would suspect that Caiaphas was behind the killing. If he was to die he would have to be executed. For this the Romans had to give permission as only the Procurator could pronounce the death sentence. I heard the plans to use false witnesses and was there when Annas told us that one of Jesus' closest followers had undertaken to betray Jesus. It was agreed that the death had to take place before the feast. We were told that the betrayal would take place the night before the start of the feast. By now this was the only time possible if the execution was to be over by the start of the celebration.

I spoke to Caiaphas when I found a moment when he was on his own and told him I wanted no part in what he was planning to do. I remember his response well as it was unusually passionate for him. "For years I have walked a tightrope to maintain peace in Jerusalem. I have watched every word, every action for this purpose. I have kept us safe, our children and our city. In one day I have destroyed Pilate's trust in me and made an enemy of him; Roman soldiers now patrol our streets and my people condemn what I have done. Do you think I would have done this if I thought Jesus was innocent? He wanted us to worship him and I couldn't let this happen." There was no doubting his sincerity.

The capture took place as planned and Jesus was brought before the Sanhedrin. He had already been roughed up by Malchus, the enforcer used by Annas in the hope that he would disappear quietly but without success. The false witnesses were produced and convinced nobody. Their stories contradicted each other and they were obviously lying. However two witnesses were found who both said independently that Jesus had claimed that he would destroy the Temple and rebuild it within three days. This was taken as blasphemy and Jesus was rushed off to the house of Pilate, the Roman Procurator. It was clear to me that an innocent and supremely good man was about to be unjustly condemned to death. The way that Jesus stood up to his accusers, never losing his dignity, was enormously impressive. As I listened I became ever more convinced that he was the Messiah. I again told Caiaphas that I wanted no part in what he was doing. This man was not just a rabble rouser but someone with a real message. His response was that he was not going to allow a peasant from Galilee to destroy his life's work.

I followed the crowd to Pilate's house and, while there, sought out Nicodemus. I knew enough about Pilate to know that, if sufficient pressure was applied, he would do as he was asked. The last thing he wanted was a riot. Nicodemus agreed with me that Jesus was at the least an important prophet. We didn't think that we could save his life but wanted to ensure that, in death, his body was treated with dignity. We would go to see Pilate and see if we could recover Jesus' body after his execution. Otherwise it would be left in the open to be eaten by the wild animals or to rot. I had a tomb prepared for my own death but I was more than happy to use this for Jesus.

I knew the cost that I would have to pay if I did as I was planning. Caiaphas and Annas would certainly never trust me again and my life would be in danger. The only punishment for treachery by a member of the Inner Council was death. All my friends would forsake me. I thought through the consequences. Saul was perfectly capable of running the business on his own. Mum had recently died and there was no one else for whom I was directly responsible. However the thought of leaving home at my age and living in exile was not pleasant. I would never be able to return to Arimathea. Money was no problem but I would change from being someone of importance with a business to run to being a nobody with nothing I really had to do. Throughout my life I had prided myself on keeping busy but I had no option but to do what I planned. Over the last few years I had become convinced by Jesus' teaching that he was the Messiah and I now had to make a stand. I was ashamed of not having done so earlier.

Getting to see Pilate was no easy task. I knew him slightly through the business and through the Sanhedrin but certainly not well enough to get instant access. His reputation was that he was a proud, touchy man who would go to any lengths to protect Rome's interests and who would use his power for his own benefit. He was notoriously difficult to deal with. Eventually he agreed to see Nicodemus and me. We were given a ten minute audience. Persuading him to do as we wanted was not difficult. Pilate was angry with the Sanhédrin for involving him in this matter and felt that he had been forced to take actions against his wishes. He gave us the body as much to spite them as to please us. I knew that I would have to pay a high price for this favour but money was the least of my problems. We came away from the palace with the document giving us permission to take the body and made our way to the execution ground. I asked one of my staff to have the tomb opened up and Nicodemus went and bought the scents and ointments we would need. I had no idea that we would need so much for one body. They weighed 35 kilograms.

When we arrived at Calvary it was dark although it was only mid afternoon. Rain was pouring down, there was a huge wind; continuous thunder roared round the hills. Jesus was already dead. Even the ground seemed to be trembling. We showed the centurion in charge of proceedings our permission to take the body and he was very cooperative. He had obviously been deeply affected by the events of the day. His men brought the body down from the cross and handed it to us. We wrapped it in a white linen sheet we had brought with us and carried it to the tomb. His body, apart from the nail marks and the spear wound, was a mass of cuts and bruises. We straightened it out, washed it as best we could and anointed it with the ointment and scents that Nicodemus had bought. In doing this we could see the full extent of the mistreatment Jesus had suffered; scarcely an inch was left untouched. We tore the linen cloth into strips, wrapped it round his body and placed the corpse in the tomb. I never expected to act as an undertaker or certify Jesus' death.

We were watched while we were doing this by men from the Chief Priest's council who wanted to make sure that the body was disposed of securely. The last thing they needed was for the corpse to disappear and rumours that Jesus had risen from the dead to start. Some of the comments they made to me don't bear repeating. It was they who insisted that a huge stone be rolled across the entrance to the grave. Further away but watching just as intently were some of the women who had followed Jesus around. I thought about asking them to help in anointing the body but decided not to as I thought they had suffered enough for one day.

It was late when I left the tomb and we couldn't finish our work because we had to be back in the city before the gates were shut for the night. We left the rest of the spices in the corner of the tomb. I couldn't resist thinking how odd it was that Jesus, who had spent his life with the poor and needy, should be entombed with the rich and important men of the city. I made my way back to my lodgings knowing that nothing would happen to me on the evening before Passover. Next morning I rose early and made my way back to Arimathea. I told Saul what had happened and he was very angry with me for what I had done. He agreed that, if I was to be safe, I had no option but to leave the country. I left later the same day as soon as the feast was over. I made my way to Syria where we had some mines and lived there for a few months. It was there that I heard the news that Jesus had risen from the dead and finally knew that he was the promised Messiah Some of Jesus' other followers came from Jerusalem to find me and I went with them to various cities where we had the privilege of telling others about Jesus. I had great satisfaction in doing this and have no regrets for the actions I took. I have been astonished at the things I have been able to do because of the power of Jesus working through me.

Cleopas

The dream was over. All that we had hoped for lay in ruins round our feet. As we walked back to Emmaus that day we thought back to when we had set out. The high hopes for a change from the corrupt rule of the High Priest and his cronies, the possibility that Jesus would create a kinder society where the needs of the poor and the sick were considered and many other pipedreams were all gone. As we trudged back we could hardly talk to each other such was our disappointment.

We remembered when we had first heard of Jesus. Abigail my wife is from Galilee. We had been in Capernaum visiting her home when there were rumours that a new teacher was coming to town. We didn't take too much notice as there were always stories going the rounds. We went to the synagogue on the Sabbath and this young man was there. There wasn't anything special about his appearance. He had piercing brown eyes and when he really looked at you; he was one of those people who you thought were seeing right into your very being. He had a presence that drew everybody's attention to him and was impossible to ignore. His method of teaching was totally different from what we expected. He used to tell stories that illustrated the point he was trying to make and he left it to his hearers to reach their own conclusions about what he was saying.

In the middle of one Sabbath service a man cried out at the top of his voice. Apparently he was well known and had been mentally ill for many years. "What do you want of us, Jesus of Nazareth? Have you come to destroy us? I know who you are – the Holy One of God." Jesus looked at him sternly. "Be quiet. Come out of him". The man collapsed on the floor and Jesus helped him up. When the man spoke, he was calm and logical. We saw him twice more during our stay and he never reverted to his previous state.

You can imagine the uproar that caused. Who was this man and by what power had he driven the demon out? With many others we began to follow Jesus, keen to listen to him and see what he would do. He went round the area healing and teaching. What he said was completely different from anything we had heard before. He didn't order us around like the Pharisees, constantly calling for greater sanctity in our daily lives and more gifts for the Temple. He preached kindness and love for our neighbours. This was what we were seeking – something that would make the world less harsh and unforgiving. The Pharisees hated him because he did not put strict adherence to the Law before humanity. He would heal people on the Sabbath (as he had done when we first noticed him) and do other things that were supposedly not permitted under the Law. Jesus said that the Law was made for man and was not intended to act as a straitjacket.

We had to return to our home in Emmaus to look after our shop but we still heard much about Jesus. He came to Jerusalem for a feast and we went and saw him again there. We wondered if our memories were fooling us but, when we saw him, they had not played us false. We became friendly with one of his inner circle, John, and he told us of some of the marvellous things Jesus was doing. We got to know many of Jesus' closest followers although we didn't meet the Teacher himself.

We heard he was returning to Jerusalem for the Passover. He had stopped on his way in Bethany, a village not that far from Emmaus. It was here that, on a previous visit, the brother of his friends had died and Jesus had raised him from the dead. Too many people testified to his death for the story to be false. Some of those there were from Jerusalem and the story of what had happened quickly got back to the High Priest who decided from that moment that Jesus must be executed whatever the cost. Jesus' friends tried to dissuade him from going on to Jerusalem but nothing would stop him. The time of his arrival in the city became known and a large crowd, including Abigail and I, went to meet him. He was mounted on a donkey and we cut palm branches and laid them in the road on his route. We led him towards the Temple praising God and singing

"Hosanna! Blessed is he who comes in the name of the Lord! Blessed is the King of Israel". I suppose this did not help him with the High Priest but it seemed the natural thing to sing the old Psalms in this way.

On the next day Jesus went to the Temple. Many of those who had come to Jerusalem for the feast were gathered there. As he entered he saw the rich putting their offerings into the Treasury. At the same time an old widow was putting her tiny contribution of two mites in. He commented that her offering was worth more than any of those from the wealthy because she gave all she had to live on while they gave only a minute part of their riches. He went further into the Temple where the moneychangers were sitting and approached their stalls. He turned over their tables and drove them out of the Temple. We had all suffered at the hands of these charlatans and, when Jesus told them they were turning the holy place into a den of robbers, we were delighted. Jesus went each day to teach in the Temple and he certainly did nothing to calm the priests. We wondered how long it would be before he took control of the Temple.

On the eve of the feast we heard that he had been taken prisoner by the priests. After a night of furious activity in the Chief Priest's house and then at the palaces of Pilate and Herod, he was condemned to immediate crucifixion and the sentence was carried out then and there. We did not go to the execution ground, we felt too let down for that. We stayed in our lodgings throughout the day completely bewildered. All our hopes were dashed and we milled about wondering what to do next. I remember the weather on that day

---

---

seemed to match our mood. It was pouring with rain, blowing a gale, thunder rumbled and lightning flashed across the sky. It was so dark that it might have been night and at one stage it felt as if there was an earthquake.

We celebrated the feast as normal but our hearts were not in it. On the day after the feast we decided to go straight home. We set out about mid morning on our seven mile journey. We could not stand the disappointment any longer. As we walked along we talked about the events of the week. We had thought Jesus to be a prophet sent by God and the anticlimax was dreadful. We heard footsteps behind us and a man with his head in shadow from the hood of his cloak caught us up.

"What are you discussing so seriously as you walk along?" he asked. "You seem very upset."

We stopped surprised that there was anyone who had not heard of the events of the weekend. "Are you not aware of what has been happening in Jerusalem over the last few days?"

"What things?"

"The things that happened to Jesus of Nazareth. He was a prophet who performed wonderful miracles. He was a superb teacher, highly thought of by God and all the people. But the High Priest and the religious leaders arrested him and handed him over to the Romans to be crucified. We thought he was the Messiah who had come to save Israel. This all happened the day before the feast. This morning there was another surprise. Some of the women who had followed him around on his travels went to his tomb to see if they could anoint his body. They came back and told us that the stone guarding the tomb had been moved and the body was missing. They had seen angels who said that Jesus was alive. Some of our companions ran to the tomb and found it just as the women had said, but they did not see Jesus. We talked these stories over and decided they were fantasies and so we set out home."

"How stupid you are" the man said "Why do you find it so hard to believe all that the prophets foretold? Was it not predicted that the Christ would have to suffer all these things before entering his time of glory?" And starting with Moses, he went right through the writings of the prophets explaining exactly what was said in the scriptures about the Messiah. As we approached our village, we urged the man to stay with us as it was getting late. He had given us the impression he was going further. He came into our house and Abigail prepared a light meal. When we were sitting, he took a piece of bread, gave thanks, broke it and began to give it to us. I saw his hands and immediately realised who he was and, as I did so, he disappeared from our sight.

We began talking and realised that he had affected us both in the same way. As he talked, we had understood the truth of what he was saying and, even before we knew who he was, had begun to believe that Jesus was the Son of God. Now we knew for certain. We sat and looked at each other dumbstruck by what we had seen. How could we have been so foolish as not to recognise him earlier? We were so sure he had been killed and we had to go over all he had said and try to understand what had happened. His words came back to us and we remembered the times when he had foretold his own death. None of us had really believed him.

We had to go back and tell the disciples what had happened. We finished our snack and set off to Jerusalem. The morning's walk had been a dreary trudge but on the way back we almost ran. Neither of us felt any tiredness. We had to be quick to reach the city before the gates were locked for the night. We went to the house where our friends were staying. It was getting dark and, however loud we knocked, no one would come to the door. We were outside for about twenty minutes before our persistence paid off. The door was opened a crack and someone we didn't know stared suspiciously through the crack. We said why we had come and, after he had looked round to see if there were others with us, he reluctantly let us in. We told them of our meeting with Jesus and they told us of Mary Magdalene's encounter with an angel and how she had met Jesus in the garden surrounding the tomb. As we were discussing these things Jesus himself appeared and stood among us. "Peace be with you," he said. "Why are you frightened? Why do you doubt who I am?" He showed us his hands and feet but still many of us had difficulty believing what we were seeing and hearing.

"Do you have anything to eat?" he asked. He was given a piece of broiled fish and he ate it as we watched, I suppose to show that he was real and not a dream. He started talking to us and explained from the scriptures, as he had done for us earlier, that the Messiah must suffer and die and rise again from the dead on the third day. "With my authority take this message to all nations. Begin in Jerusalem. There is forgiveness of sin for anyone who believes in me. You are witnesses of all that has happened."

The disciples went back to Galilee and Abigail and I went back to Emmaus. Some weeks later we received a message that they were returning to Jerusalem. We went to meet them and Jesus appeared to all of us. Next day he went with his apostles, the inner group of disciples, out onto the Bethany road and from there he ascended to heaven in a cloud. They came back to Jerusalem and we all waited for the gift that Jesus had promised. Mary, Jesus' mother, and his four brothers were all there. We were gathered together when there was a sudden sound like the blowing of a violent wind that filled the whole house. Tongues of flame seemed to appear and rest on each one of us. We began speaking in different languages that we had never spoken before. We were certain that, as he had promised, we were filled with his spirit enabling us to do the things that he had done while he was alive.

Abigail and I returned to Emmaus to sell our house and bring the proceeds to share with our friends. We lived together with them and these were the most exciting days of our lives. There was an excitement about the place, a real buzz, which I have never encountered before. We saw many miracles and hundreds come to believe in Jesus as the Son of God who had died for them. We are still there now working for our master.

The Man at the Beautiful Gate

The man at the Beautiful Gate was healed after the ascension of Jesus. However he must have seen and heard Jesus going in and out of the Temple. He had been begging by the Temple for nearly 40 years and it is inconceivable that he had not remembered him and been affected by what happened in Jerusalem in those momentous days. He would have been in his place at the Temple when Jesus was brought there by his mother and met Simeon and Anna but he would probably not have remembered that far back.

I have been crippled from birth and I first started begging when I was very young. My parents paid the money for me to get a pitch right outside the main Temple gate known as the Beautiful Gate. These positions were licensed. You have to pay a lump sum when you first obtain one and then an annual fee. Gifts from passers-by easily cover the cost. Everyone entering or leaving the Temple had to pass us. Actually we got more from people on the way out as the moneychangers had a habit of telling the people coming to sacrifice that the cost of purified animals was greater than it was and so they had temple currency left over. The sacrifices had to be bought from the official suppliers and could only be purchased with Temple currency which could not be spent anywhere else. Of course people felt charitable as they went into the Temple and, if we looked sufficiently needy, they could be persuaded to be very generous.

My brothers took me down to the Temple each morning and fetched me in the evening. Whatever the weather, hot or cold, wet or dry, I never missed a day from when I was about five years old. I rapidly became the family's chief breadwinner and, although takings dropped as I got older and less pathetic, I still made a very good living. I was now over forty years old. It was an endlessly fascinating occupation, as I never knew who was going to come past me. Watching the pilgrims as they passed gave one a real clue to the sort of people they were. Some came to do their duty as quickly and cheaply as possible while to others it was obviously a great privilege to be able to visit and make their sacrifice at the Temple, a once in a lifetime experience. Visitors could range from King Herod to crowds of school children. I learnt a lot about human nature. Generally the richer the visitor, the less likely it was that he would drop any coins into our plates. There were exceptions of course but the chief priests and the Pharisees very rarely gave anything. On the other hand some people were very friendly and enquired about how we were managing. There were always preachers coming to speak in the Temple courts and if we were lucky, we could hear them.

We were used to seeing visitors, usually from Galilee, who tried to pass themselves off as the Messiah so, when I heard that yet another, this time named Jesus, had turned up, it did not mean much to me. I noticed him first attending the Feast of Tabernacles. He and his few followers, standing out because of their Galilean robes, came about halfway through the feast. Jesus always looked as if he belonged there but his followers in their unusual dress seemed out of place. They were gazing round as if they had never expected to see the Temple.

That evening, as people left the Temple, I heard their comments about the new preacher. They were astonished that an uneducated carpenter from Nazareth could have such knowledge and understanding of the scriptures. He claimed to be God's messenger using his words. He did not want glory for himself but for the one who sent him. He was a wonderful speaker with a clear voice that could be heard from a distance.

From the beginning he made enemies. Members of the crowd accused him of being sent by the devil. They made no secret of their hatred and, in the end, he asked why they were trying to have him killed. He accused the priests of hypocrisy in the way they applied the Law and this upset the High Priest. Jesus told his listeners to pay more attention to the 'Inner Person' than to outward appearance and strict observance of the Law and caused a big pandemonium. The High Priest plotted to have him seized and sent Temple Guards to arrest him but, because of the crowds, they were unable to do so. Even the guards listened and seemed impressed by what he had to say. I remember him shouting "If anyone is thirsty, let him come to me for drink. Whoever believes in me, as the Scripture has said, streams of living water will flow from within him". I didn't really understand what he meant but it certainly upset the priests. We heard that they were desperate to get rid of him but, for whatever reason, were unable to do so. He left for Galilee immediately the feast was over.

He didn't come back until the Passover the following year. This didn't mean we didn't hear of him. Visitors were always talking of his teaching and his healing ministry in Galilee. We learned he was on his way to Jerusalem but had stopped off to visit friends in Bethany. While there some months before, he had raised a young man named Lazarus from the dead. Excitement grew. The priests were constantly rushing in and out for meetings. On the Sabbath before the feast we heard he had reached Jerusalem and had been welcomed as a king by a large crowd. On the next day he was with us. He walked quietly into the Temple greeting us as he passed. His followers still looked overawed and out of place as they trailed behind him.

I had been told of his power to heal and wondered if he would heal me. I called out as he went by but, although he smiled at me, he didn't stop. When he arrived in the Temple, no one could accuse him of being quiet. He went straight to the moneychangers, upset the tables, released the animals held in cages to be sold for sacrifice and drove the moneychangers from the Temple. The sound of the lambs bleating and the moneychangers screaming was wonderful. These cheats deserved all they got. Offerings from people leaving the Temple that day were very large but I was sad. I wondered why he healed others but not me. Each day folk who had been afflicted in some way came out of the Temple healed but, however much I called out, he never noticed me. What had I done that I was ignored? Why others and not me?   I thought my chance was gone and I became quite bitter about it.

He came to the Temple each day to teach but, on the eve of the feast, we heard that the priests had got their man and he was to be crucified later in the day. I was resigned to the fact that my chance of a normal life had gone. The Temple was unnaturally calm; all the usual noise and bustle was hushed. Most of the visitors had heard Jesus preach and been impressed by what he said. They did not understand why the priests were so much against him. The weather was horrible, cold and windy with rain teeming down and frequent outbursts of thunder and lightning. In spite of my wrappings I was wet to the skin and hardly anyone gave us any money. In the middle of the afternoon it was as dark as night. There was a tremendous ear-splitting bang and the ground seemed to move under where I was sitting. It was very frightening. We later heard that the huge curtain separating the 'Holy of Holies' from the rest of the Temple had torn from top to bottom and the rock on which the Temple was built had split wide open.

The feast itself was low key. Everyone went through the motions but their heart was not in it as they remembered what had happened the previous day. On the morning after the feast, amazing stories began to circulate. The body had been placed in a new tomb with an enormous stone across the entrance and three Temple guards had been posted to ensure that nobody interfered with the body. However it had disappeared. Someone had rolled the stone away and the corpse was gone. The priests said that Jesus' followers had stolen it but this seemed impossible. The people at the Temple were confused and again there were constant comings and goings among the priests and the members of the Council. A search was started but, as one would expect, it was unsuccessful. It took many days for things to settle down again and the rumours not only persisted but grew. Many were talking of having seen Jesus and of him being alive in Galilee. Excitement ran high in those days. We had wondered if Jesus was going to depose the High Priest and take control of the Temple or even lead a campaign to throw out the Romans. If he was alive again, these things might still happen. Few who used the Temple would be sorry to see the back of the High Priest and his supporters, as the way in which the Temple was run was notoriously corrupt.

Time passed and, about two months after the Passover, some of Jesus' followers began to visit the Temple again. They were the same but different. When they had come previously they had looked like fish out of water but now they had the same confidence and sense of purpose as Jesus used to have. They had always greeted us as they went past and I had always cried out for alms. Usually they just walked by but this time the two leaders stopped and came across to me. They looked straight at me.

The one they called Peter spoke. "I do not have any silver or gold, but I give you what I can. Look at me" I turned so that I was looking straight into his eyes wondering what was to come. "In the name of Jesus of Nazareth, walk." He took me by the right hand and gently pulled me to my feet. I could feel strength flowing into my legs. For the first time in my life I stood up. A large crowd had gathered and was watching. I began to walk and went with them into the Temple. I was shouting and jumping and praising God. Many recognised me for they had seen me sitting at the gate. As it was, they were filled with wonder and amazement at what had happened. People came running from all parts of the Temple and Peter spoke to them.

"Why are you surprised? Why are you staring at us as if, in our own strength or godliness, we made this man walk? The god of Abraham, Isaac and Jacob, the God of our fathers, has done this to glorify his servant Jesus. This is the same Jesus you handed over to be killed; you disowned him before the Governor, even though Pilate had decided to free him. You rejected this holy, righteous man and asked that a murderer be released to you instead. You killed the author of life, but God raised him to life again. We are witnesses of this. By faith in the name of Jesus, this man who you see and recognise, has been healed. It is Jesus' name and the faith that comes through him that has allowed this healing."

He went on to tell them that he knew they had acted in ignorance, as had their leaders. The prophets foretold all that would happen to Christ and the manner of his death. Now they must recognise their sins and repent of them so that they might be cleansed. There was more but I was too excited to remember it all. As Peter was finishing, the Temple guards came to arrest him and John. The Priests were greatly upset because Peter taught that Jesus had risen from the dead. They took them away and kept them in prison overnight. Next day they were brought before a full meeting of all the religious leaders. They asked Peter by what power he had been able to heal me and he again had the chance to tell them of the resurrection of Jesus and who he was. In the end there was nothing of which they could accuse them and they let Peter and John go after warning them not to speak or teach in the name of Jesus. That was like telling a fish not to swim and Peter told them so. They warned me also not to speak of what had happened but I was unable to keep quiet about it. Because so many people had seen me sitting by the gate, my recovery made a large impact.

The evening of the day I was healed I walked home. The reception I got when I arrived could hardly be said to be rapturous. My cure might have been good for me but it had taken away the family's main breadwinner. My brothers, instead of being delighted as I was, were furious and said a lot of things that, later, they might have regretted. When I left in the morning I took my few possessions and said I would not be living there any more. I had no idea what I would do but I wanted to be with Peter and John and find out more about Jesus. When they came out from their meeting with the Priests and leaders, I told them what had happened and they invited me to stay with them. They took me to a large house that seemed to be absolutely crowded out with people. Everything was shared, so the fact that there were people like me who contributed nothing was not noticed. Not only did I have no money, I had no skills. I had never had the opportunity to do things for myself. Fortunately people knew who I was and made allowances and I became useful if only in menial tasks very quickly. I helped with the cleaning and with preparing vegetables. I went to visit my brothers but they did not want to know me. They would not listen when I told them about Jesus and my new life. My greatest delight is speaking to people about what he did for me and telling them of the sacrifice he made for all of us. In this way we make sure that who he was and what he did is not forgotten.

Sources

Sources

The title of this book is taken from the hymn by William Cowper, "God moves in a mysterious way his wonders to perform"

In many of the stories details of miracles or parables have been included. The references to these are shown under those for the character even though they do not form part of his or her story but are there to illustrate a state of mind or to a factor affecting the person's attitudes. Where a story or quotation is used more than once, the reference is only included on the first mention unless it is essential to understanding the story.

Birth

The story of the birth of Jesus is only told in two of the four gospels. Even in these two accounts there are differences. Each writer is trying to emphasise the points that are important to him in drawing the overall picture that he wants his book to show. Matthew concentrates on how Jesus fulfils the Law and the Prophets while Luke is more interested in the history. To get as complete an account as possible, it is necessary to combine the two accounts and to work out a chronology. Matthew (Chapter 2, verse 13) says that as soon as the wise men had gone, Joseph had his dream and the young family made their escape to Egypt. This means that the visit of the Wise Men must have been after Jesus was formally presented in the Temple when he was 40 days old. It is extremely unlikely that the family would have returned to Nazareth in the period between his birth and the presentation as it would have been a health risk for a newborn baby and it was a long way. By the time that Mary was fit to make the journey there would hardly have been time to get to Nazareth and back. Therefore the likelihood is that Mary and Jesus stayed in Bethlehem.

Bethlehem was a very small village with perhaps 500 people living there. It is highly doubtful that there would have been an inn as has been assumed for many years. It is more likely that the room described as being full was a guestroom in the house of one of Joseph's relatives and the original text can certainly be read in this way. The house itself would have had an upper level in which the family lived and beneath it would have been the area where the cattle sheltered from the weather and where the mangers for the cattle's feed were located. This would have been the area where Jesus was born.

There is no evidence in the Bible of where Mary was born. There is a body of opinion that says that she was a servant in the Temple and this was where she met Joseph but there is no evidence to support this view. I like to think of her as a girl from a normal home. This opinion is possibly supported by her relationship with

Salome, the mother of the sons of Zebedee. In Mark chapter 16, verse 1 it says that Mary Magdalene, Mary the mother of James (Jesus' oldest brother) and Salome went to the tomb to anoint Jesus' body. In Matthew chapter 27, verses 55 and 56 the mother of the sons of Zebedee is placed as one of the women watching at the Cross. Luke (chapter 23 verse 49) says that the women watching the crucifixion were from Galilee. None of this represents proof but it is a possibility.

Mary

- **Joseph in the tribe of Judah** – Luke 1:26. Although this was relevant in showing that the old prophecies had been fulfilled, it was not likely to be important to Mary.
- **Mary betrothed to Joseph** – Luke 1:26 (Betrothal was a formal, legal agreement to marry rather than, as with a modern 'engagement', a promise to wed without real legal commitment).
- **Mary told about becoming the mother of Jesus** – Luke 1:26-38 and Matthew 1:18
- **The visit to Elizabeth** – Luke 1:39-56
- **Joseph's dream about the fatherhood of Jesus** – Matthew 1:19-25
- **The trip to Bethlehem and the birth of Jesus** – Luke 2:1-7
- **The Shepherds and the Angels** – Luke 2:8-20
- **Jesus is Circumcised** – Luke 2; 21

- Jesus presented at the Temple, Simeon and Anna – Luke 2:22-40
- The visit of the Wise Men – Matthew 2:1-12
- The escape to Egypt immediately after the visit of the wise men – Matthew 2:13-18
- The return to Nazareth avoiding Jerusalem– Matthew 2:19-23

Elizabeth

- Zechariah in the Temple – Luke 1:5-25
- Mary visits Elizabeth – Luke 1:39-45
- The birth of John the Baptist – Luke 1:57-66
- The death of John the Baptist – Matthew 14:3-12, Mark 6:14-29
- Zechariah's song – Luke 1:68-79

The Innkeeper

- There is no mention of the Innkeeper's wife in the Gospels. The birth of Jesus at the inn in Bethlehem is related in Luke 2:7

The Three Wise Men –

- The story – Matthew 2:1-12.
- 500 people see the risen Jesus at one time – 1 Corinthians 15:6

Life

All the Stories told in this section occur in the three years of Jesus' active ministry leading up to his crucifixion. Again the chronology is difficult to establish. Each of the gospel writers places them in an order that will maximise the dramatic impact of their stories. Their intent is to show Jesus, as they want him to be seen. The first major event described in all four gospels is the calling of the apostles. Even this is confusing. Each of the gospels includes the story. Matthew and Mark place the event as soon as Jesus returns from his temptation, Luke says it was a little while after Jesus had begun his preaching and teaching ministry and John says that Andrew and Simon were called on the day following Jesus' baptism with the others a day later. The most likely explanation may be that Jesus met Andrew and Simon before his Temptation but only called them and the others to follow him when he returned from it. John does not mention the Temptation.

The only events, which give some shape to the chronology, are Jesus' visits to Jerusalem. It is probable that the meeting with the Samaritan woman at the well took place during Jesus' return to Galilee following his baptism. The first visit to Jerusalem was to go to the Feast of the Tabernacles and includes the story of the healing of the blind man who was sent to wash in the Pool of Bethesda and the secret visit of Nicodemus. It is impossible to say how many visits Jesus made as the gospels disagree on this. Only John is definite that there was more than one visit. The narrative of the last visit contains all the events leading up to the crucifixion as well as the two happenings in Jericho on the way to Jerusalem (the meetings with Zacchaeus the tax collector and Bartimaeus, the blind man sitting by the roadside), the stop at Bethany when Mary washed Jesus' feet in her tears, the Triumphal entry and the eviction of the moneychangers. It goes on to the Last Supper and the events of the trial and crucifixion. The order of the events in Galilee and the surrounding neighbourhood is uncertain. The people welcoming Jesus to Jerusalem on his last visit were mainly visitors as, on the whole, the Judeans did not want the Status Quo disturbed.

Mary

- **Jesus visits the Temple at 12 years old** – Luke 2:41-52
- **John the Baptist baptising in the Jordan** – Matthew 3:1-12, Mark 1:1-8, Luke 3:1-18, John 1:19-28.

- **The Baptism of Jesus** – Matthew 3:13-17, Mark 1:9-11, Luke 3:21-22, John 1:29-34.
- **Jesus worked as a carpenter** – Mark 6:3
- **The wedding at Cana** – John 2:1-11
- **Calling of the disciples** – Mark 1:14-20
- **The leper who talked** – Mark 1:40-45
- **Jesus rejected in Nazareth** – Luke 4:14-30, Mark 6:1-6
- **Jesus' brothers and sisters** - Matthew 13:55-56
- **A prophet is not respected by his own family** – Matthew 13:57
- **The quotation used by Jesus preaching in Nazareth** – Isaiah 61:2
- **Philip also from Bethsaida** – John 12:21
- **Mary believes Jesus to be out of his mind** – Mark 3:21
- **Jesus' brothers do not believe in him** – John 7:5
- **Mary visits Jesus to bring him home but is ignored** - Mark 3:31-35, Matthew 12:46-50
- **The visit to the Feast of the Tabernacles** – John 7:1-10

Mary's Mother:-

- There are no direct references to Mary's mother in the gospels

John the Baptist

- **Birth and circumcision** – Luke 1:57-66, Luke 1:24-25

- **His work as a Baptist** – Matthew 3:1-12, Mark 1:1-8, Luke 3:1-18, John 3:23-36
- **Baptises Christ** – Matthew 3:13-17, Mark 1:9-11, Luke 3:21-22
- **Insults Herod** – Luke 3:19-20
- **Imprisoned** – Matthew 4:12, Mark 1:14, Luke 3:20
- **Sends friends to Jesus** – Matthew 11:2, Luke 7:18
- **Herod's birthday party** – Matthew 14:1-9, Mark 6:14-26
- **Execution** – Matthew 14:12, Mark 6:27-29

Andrew

- **The ministry of John the Baptist** - Mark 1:1-8
- **The baptism of Jesus** – Mark 1 9-11
- **Andrew follows Jesus** – John 1:37
- **The fetching of Simon** – John 1:40-42
- **Jesus returns to Galilee and picks the Twelve** – John 1:35-52, Matthew 4:18-32
- **The disciples baptise people on behalf of Jesus** – John 4:1-3
- **The wedding at Cana** – John 2:1-11
- **Jesus teaches and heals in Galilee** – Mark 6:53-56
- **The healing of the official's son** – John 4:46-54
- **The pool of Bethesda** – John 5:1-15
- **All who came to Jesus healed** – Mark 1:32-34

- 'Come unto me all you who labour.....' – Matthew 11:28-30
- The man lowered through the roof – Luke 5:18-26
- The man with the withered hand – Matthew 12:10-13, Mark 3:1-5, Luke 6:6-10
- Jesus uses a boat to escape from the crowds – Mark 3;9
- The blind man from Bethsaida – Mark 8:22-26
- The widow of Nain – Luke 7:11-15
- The feeding of the five thousand – John 6:1-15, Matthew 14:15-21
- The people want to crown Jesus king – John 6:14
- Followers desert Jesus – John 6:60-66
- Simon acknowledges Christ to be the Son of God – Matthew 16:13-20, Mark 8:27-30, Luke 9:18-27
- Jesus walks on water – Mark 6:45-52, Matthew 14:27-33
- Jesus calms the storm – Mark 4:37-41, Matthew 8:23-27, Luke 8:22-25
- The log and the sawdust – Matthew 7:3-5, Luke 6:41-42
- The Pharisees following Jesus to spy on him – Mark 2:23-27
- The Pharisees called 'white washed tombs' – Matthew 23:27
- Jesus' teaching about the poor and needy – Luke 6:20-26
- Bethsaida criticised for lack of faith – Matthew 11:21

- **The Mother of James and John asks for special privileges for her sons** – Matthew 20:20-28, Mark 10:35-40
- **Discussion about who will be the greatest** – Luke 9:46-48
- **Faith like little children** – Luke 18:15-17, Mark 9:35-37
- **All the apostles except Judas from Galilee** – Acts 1:11
- **Judas Iscariot a thief** – John 12:6
- **Bringing a party of Greeks to Jesus** – John 12:22
- **Jesus forecasts his death and resurrection** – Matthew 20:17-19, Mark 9:30-32, Matthew 26;2, John 12:23-27
- **God speaks from heaven** – John 12:28-29
- **The disciples sent out in pairs** – Matthew 10:1-42, Luke 9:1-6
- **Simon the Pharisee and the woman washing Jesus' hair** – Luke 7:36-50
- **Transfiguration** – Mark 9:2-13, Matthew 17:1-13, Luke 9:28-36
- **The healing of the demon possessed boy** – Mark 9:14-29
- **Simon tells Jesus off for saying he will be killed** – Matthew 16:20-23, Mark 8:32
- **The Gadarene swine** - Luke 8:26-39, Mark 5:1-20, Matthew 8:28-34
- **The Canaanite woman** – Matthew 15:21-28, Mark 7:24-30 (In Matthew the woman is described as Canaanite and in Mark as Greek born in Syrian Phoenicia).

- **The feeding of the four thousand** – Matthew 15:29-39, Mark 8:1-10

Martha

- **Too busy to listen to Jesus** – Luke 10:39-42
- The raising of Lazarus – John 11:1-44
- **Mary, her sister anoints Jesus' feet** – John 12:1-3 (also mentioned in Mark 14:3-5 and Matthew 26:6-13 where, at the home of Simon the Leper, Mary poured ointment over Jesus' head (Matthew and Mark) or feet (John). This seems a completely separate incident from that in Luke 7:36-38 when Jesus was a guest at the house of Simon the Pharisee.
- **Jesus stays in Bethany when visiting Jerusalem** – Matthew 21:17
- **The priests decide that Lazarus as well as Jesus must be killed** – John 12:10

Mary Magdalene

- **Demons cast out of her** – Mark 16:9, Luke 8:2
- **Come unto me all who labour and are heavy laden** – Matthew 11:28-30
- **Take up your cross and follow me** – Matthew 10:38 and 16;24
- **Good Samaritan** – Luke 10:30-37
- **Feeding of the five thousand** – Matthew 14:15-21
- **The Gentile woman's daughter** – Matthew 15:21-28

- **The ten lepers** – Luke 17:11-19
- **The raising of Lazarus** – John 11:1-44
- **Mary anoints Jesus' feet** – John 12:1-3, Mark 14:3-5
- **Zacchaeus** – Luke 19:1-10
- **Bartimaeus** –Mark 10:46-52, Luke 18:35-43. The story is also told in Matthew 20:29-34 but in this account there are two blind men.

The Centurion in Galilee

- **Healing of his servant** - Matthew 8:5-13, Luke 7:1-10
- **Death of John the Baptist** – Matthew 14:1-12, Mark 6:17-28

Simon's Mother-in-Law

- **Husband named John** – John 21:15
- **The miraculous catch of fish** – Luke 5:1-11
- **Healed by Jesus** - Matthew 8:14-15
- **Simon and John at the tomb on the day after Passover** – John 20:1-10

Nicodemus

- **The death of John the Baptist** – Matthew 14:6-12, Mark 6:17-28
- **Visits Jesus secretly by night** - John 3:1-21
- **He defends Jesus at the Sanhedrin** – John 7:50

- Takes Jesus' body to the tomb with Joseph of Arimathea – John 19:39
- Provides spices for the burial - John 19:39

The Samaritan Woman

- Story – John 4:1-32
- Philip flees to Samaria – Acts 8:4-8

The Leper

- Healing of the 10 lepers – Luke 17:11-19
- The leper in Galilee – Luke 5:12-13, Matthew 8:2-4

The Woman with a Haemorrhage – Luke 8:43-48, Matthew 9:20-22, Mark 5:25-34 (The story is interwoven with that of the raising of Jairus's daughter)

The Woman taken in Adultery – John 8:1-11

The Man born Blind – John 9:1-41

The Rich Young Man:- Mark 10:17-22, Luke 18:18-29, Matthew 19:16-22

Zacchaeus – Luke 19:1-10 followed by the parable of the ten minas – verses 11-27

Death and Resurrection

The story of the crucifixion forms a large part of each of the four gospels yet, even here, the writers are selective in the material they use. For example none of the gospels includes all the words Jesus said from the cross. There are two totally different accounts of the death of Judas Iscariot which can not be reconciled. This makes it quite difficult to put all the events into chronological order and to identify who was present at each stage of the drama. All the stories in this section are based on the same understanding and so are consistent. The interpretation used appears to fit in with all the gospel accounts.

The post resurrection narrative after Easter Day is even more confusing.

❑ **Matthew**, in a brief afterthought, says the remaining 11 apostles went to Galilee and finishes with the Great Commission (All authority on heaven and earth has been given to you. Therefore go and make disciples of all nations - Matthew 28:19).

❑ **Mark** mentions briefly the meeting with 2 disciples on the road to Emmaus, Jesus' first meeting with the disciples after he rose from the dead and the Great Commission. He then says Jesus was taken up to heaven giving no details at all.

❑ **Luke,** in his gospel tells in full the story of the 2 disciples on the Road to Emmaus. He then describes the appearance of Jesus to the disciples after the two had returned from Emmaus to Jerusalem and gives a very brief account of the Ascension. He gives a fuller account in his second book, the Acts of the Apostles.

❑ **John** describes the meeting with the disciples on the first night after the resurrection without mentioning the two from Emmaus; he gives a full account of his appearance to Thomas (John 20:19-31). As a postscript in chapter 21, he writes about the return to Galilee, the miraculous catch of fish and the reinstatement of Peter before again finishing his story. He makes no mention of the Ascension.

Mary

- **Mary present at the crucifixion** – John 19:25
- **The Notice on the Cross** – John 19:19
- **Refuses offer of wine mixed with myrrh to dull the pain** – Matthew 27:34

- **Jesus says "Father forgive them for they know not what they are doing"**- Luke 23:34
- **Mockery of the crowd** - Luke 23:32-36, Matthew 27:39-40, Mark 15:29-30
- **The two thieves** – Luke 23:39-43
- **Mary put under John's protection** – John 19:26-27
- **His brothers do not believe in Jesus** – John 7:5
- **Jesus says "My God, My God, why have you forsaken me?"** – Matthew 27:46
- **Jesus says "Into your hands I commend my spirit"** – Luke 23:46
- **Jesus says "I am thirsty"** – John19: 28
- **Jesus says "It is finished"** – John 19:30
- **Mary goes to the tomb** –Mark 16:1, Matthew 28:1, Luke 24:1, John 20:1 (In Luke and Mark's gospels she is referred to ass the mother of James. This has been assumed to be Mary's second oldest son)
- **Two angels appear to Mary and Salome** – Luke 24:4-7
- **Mary present with her 4 younger sons after the Ascension** – Acts 1:14
- **The appointment of Matthias** – Acts 1:21-26

Andrew

- **The triumphal entry** – John 12:12-16
- **The Moneychangers driven out of the Temple** – John 2:13-22, Mark 11:15-18
- **The washing of the disciples' feet** – John 13:1-17

- **The Last Supper** – Luke 22:7-23, John 13:1-30, Mark 14:12-26, Matthew 26:17-30
- **Jesus identifies Judas as his betrayer** – John 14:26
- **Simon says that he will always be loyal to Jesus** – Matthew 26:33
- **The other disciples echo Simon** – Matthew 26:35
- **The Garden of Gethsemane** – Matthew 26:36-46
- **Judas betrays Jesus and he is captured** – John 18:1-9, Matthew 26:47-50
- **Simon strikes off the guard's ear** - John 18:10-11, Mark 14:43-51
- **Mark follows Jesus** – Mark 14:51-52
- **Simon and John follow Jesus and Simon denies him three times** – John 18:15-18 and 25-27, Luke 22:54-62, Mark 14:66-72
- **The apostles after the resurrection** – John 20:19-31
- **The miraculous catch of fish** – John 21:1-14
- **The Ascension** – Acts 1:9-11
- **The coming of the Holy Spirit** – Acts 2:1-13

Malchus

- **Judas Iscariot offers to betray Jesus** – Mark 14:10-11, Matthew 26:14-16
- **Jesus arrested in the garden of Gethsemane** – Luke 22:47-53, John 18:1-11
- **Malchus' ear cut off and he is healed by Jesus** – John 18:10, Luke 22:50-51

- **Mentioned by name** – John 18:10. Also mentioned but not by name in Luke 22:50-52
- **Jesus taken to Annas** – John 18:12-14
- **The use of false witnesses** – Mark 14:55-59, Matthew 26:59-62
- **The release of Barabbas** – John 18:39-40, Mark 15:6-11
- **Jesus before Annas** – John 18:19-24
- **The servant slaps Jesus face** – John 18:22
- **The suicide of Judas Iscariot** – Matthew 27:3-10 (A very different version is told in Acts 1:18-19)
- **A relative tells him that Simon denied Jesus** – John 18:26
- **Pilate refuses to use Romans to guard the tomb** – Matthew 27:62-66
- **'Disappearance' of the three guards at the tomb** – Matthew 28:11-15

Judas Iscariot

- **Disciples baptising by the Jordan** – John 4:1-2
- **A thief** – John 12:6
- **Betrays Jesus** – Matthew 26:14-16
- **Calls Jesus 'Rabbi' rather than 'Master like the other disciples** – Matthew 26:25
- **His remorse and attempt to return the 30 pieces of silver** – Matthew 27:3
- **Commits suicide** – Matthew 27:5 (there is a different version in Acts 1:18-19)

Barabbas

- **Released in place of Jesus** – Matthew 27:15-21, Mark 15:6-11, Luke 23:18, John 18:39-40

Mary Magdalene

- **The first to see the resurrected Jesus** – John 20:1 and 11-13
- **Jesus appears to the disciples** – John 20:19-31
- **The day of the resurrection** – John 20:1-18 (There are other differing accounts in Matthew 28:1-10, Mark 16:1-8 and 9-14{2 separate accounts} and Luke 24:1-12. All of these are similar but, particularly in Matthew and Mark, have substantial differences.
- **The coming of the Holy Spirit** –Acts 2:1-13

Caiaphas

- **False Messiahs** – Acts 5:34-39
- **The healing at the pool of Bethesda** – John 5:1-15
- **Caiaphas as High Priest** – Matthew 26:3
- **Son-in-Law of Annas** – John 18:13
- **Jesus rejected at Nazareth** – Luke 4:16-30
- **Discussions with the Sanhedrin** – John 11:47-53
- **Quoted as saying that it is better that one man dies for the people than that the whole nation die** – John 11:49-50

- **Worried by Roman reaction to Jesus' claims** – John 11:48-53, John 18:14
- **Jesus to be captured dead or alive** – Matthew 26:2
- **Jesus calls the Jewish leaders hypocrites** – Matthew 23
- **Jesus asked under whose authority he acted** – Matthew 21:23-27
- **Jesus before Caiaphas and the Sanhedrin** – Luke 22:66-71
- **Splitting of the Temple curtain** – Matthew 27:51
- **Jesus' body taken by Joseph of Arimathea** – Luke 23:50-56
- **Hears that Jesus body has disappeared** – Matthew 28:11-15
- **Present when Peter and John are taken before Sanhedrin** – Acts 4:6
- **Large number of priests turn to follow Jesus** – Acts 6:7

Pontius Pilate

- **The priests unable to enter Pilate's palace** – John 18:28
- **Jesus sent to Herod for judgment** – Luke 23:6-11
- **Pilate and Herod become friends** – Luke 23:12
- **Jesus returned to Pilate** – Luke 23:15
- **Pilate told by Jesus that his authority is from God** – John 19:11

- **The warning of Pilate's wife** – Matthew 27:19
- **Jesus' trial before Pilate** – Matthew 27:11-26, Mark 15:1-15, Luke 23:1-25, John 18:28 to 19:16
- **Washes His hands to disclaim responsibility** – Matthew 27:24
- **Orders that Jesus be flogged** – John 19:1, Matthew 27:26
- **Refuses to allow Romans to guard the tomb** – Matthew 27:62-66 (The guards on duty at the time of the discovery that the body was gone were Temple Guards)

The Centurion at the Cross-

- **The triumphal entry** – John 12:12-16, Luke 19:28-44
- **The moneychangers at the Temple** – Luke 19:45-46
- **The soldiers mock Jesus** – Matthew 27:27-31 (The story of the soldiers mocking Jesus is in all four gospels. Mark tells roughly the same story as Matthew except that the robe is purple. Luke says that the mockery by the soldiers took place before Jesus appeared before Pilate. John's version is the same as Mark's but takes place immediately before Pilate pronounces judgment).
- **The women follow Jesus to his crucifixion** – Luke 23 27-31
- **The soldiers cast lots for Jesus' robe** – John 19:24

- **Those long dead emerge from their tombs** – Matthew 27:52-53:
- **Acknowledges Jesus as the Son of God** – Mark 15:39, Matthew 27:54

Simon from Cyrene

- **Ordered to carry the cross** – Mark 15:21, Luke 23:26
- **The father of Rufus and Alexander** – Mark 15:21 *(It is unlikely that this Rufus is the same as that mentioned in Romans 16:13)*
- **Take up your cross and follow me** – Matthew 16:24
- **Cyrenian language spoken at Pentecost** – Acts 2:10
- **Cyrenians active in early church** – Acts 11:20 (Antioch) and 13:1

Joseph of Arimathea

- **Burial of Jesus** – Matthew 27:57-61, Mark 15:42-47, Luke 23:50-56, John 19:38-42
- **Nicodemus, Israel's teacher** – John 3:10
- **The Widow's Mite** – Mark 12: 42-44
- **The Good Samaritan** – Luke 10:25-35
- **35 kg of scents and ointment** – John 19:39

Cleopas

- **On the road to Emmaus** – Luke 24:13-35

- **Healing of the man possessed** – Mark 1:23-26, Luke 4:33-35
- **The widow's mite** – Luke 21:1-4

The Man at the Beautiful Gate

- **People healed in the Temple in the week before the crucifixion** – Matthew 21:14
- **Healed by Peter and John** – Acts 3:1-10
- **Peter and John speak to the onlookers** – Acts 3:11-26
- **Peter and John before the Sanhedrin** – Acts 4:1-22
- **Age of the man healed** – Acts 4:22